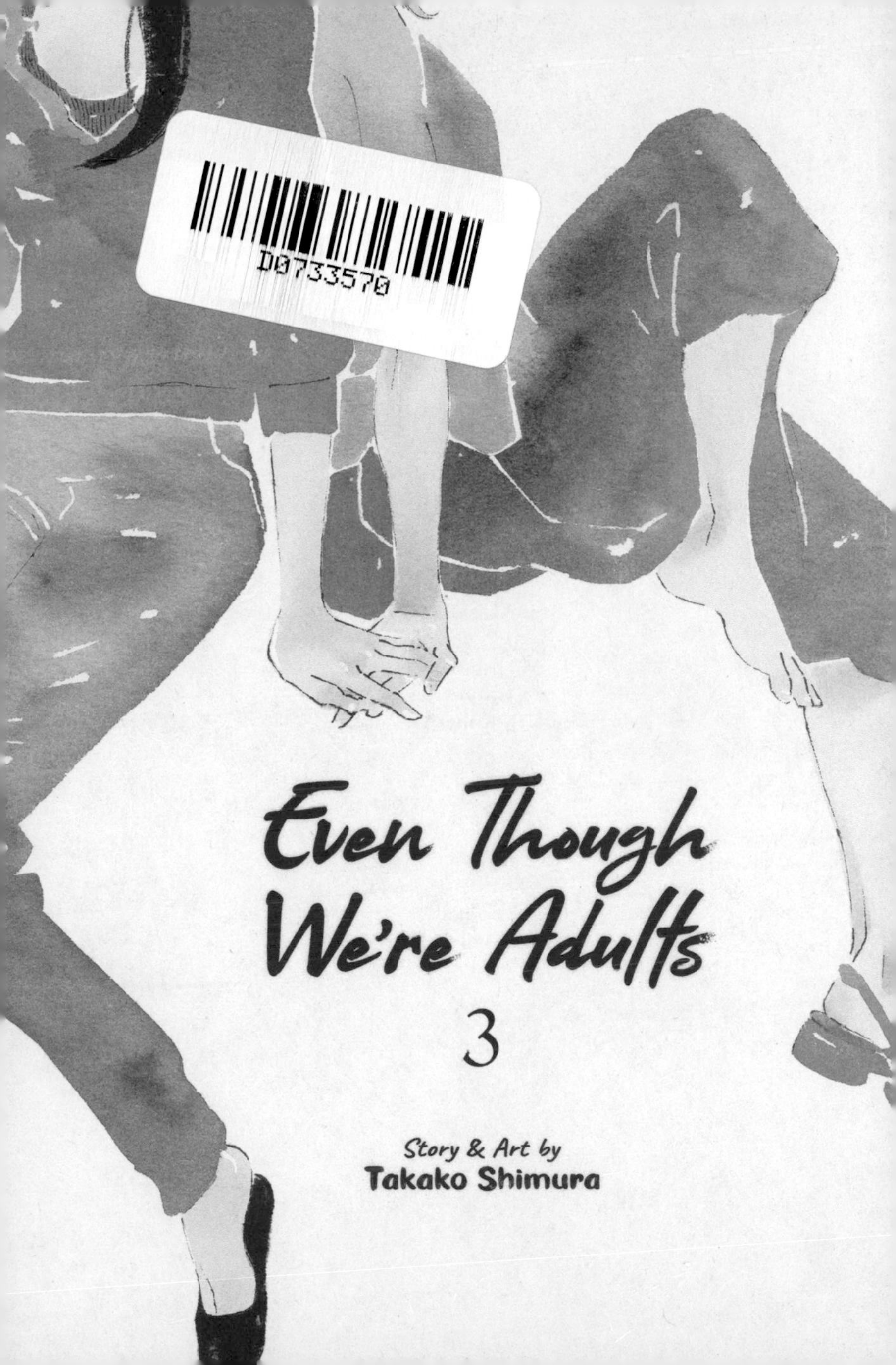

Even Though We're Adults

3

Story & Art by
Takako Shimura

CONTENTS

Chapter 11
Bonjour Tristesse

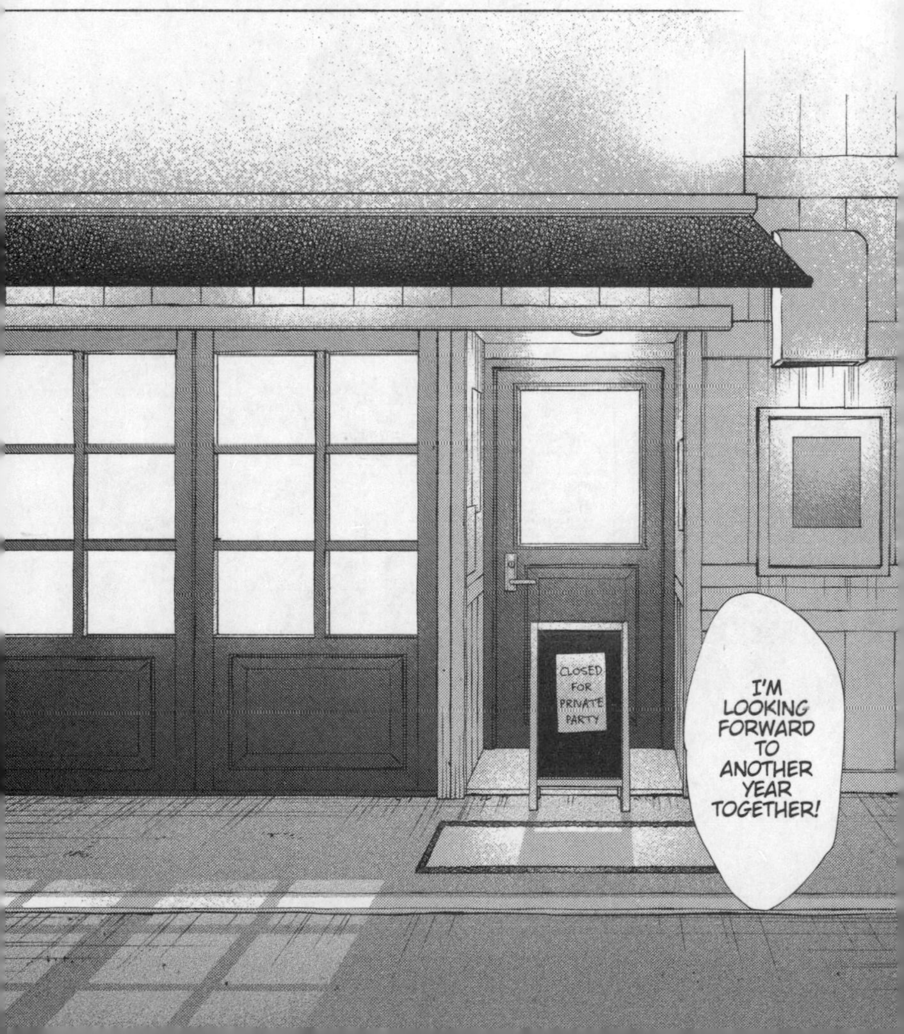
CLOSED FOR PRIVATE PARTY
I'M LOOKING FORWARD TO ANOTHER YEAR TOGETHER!

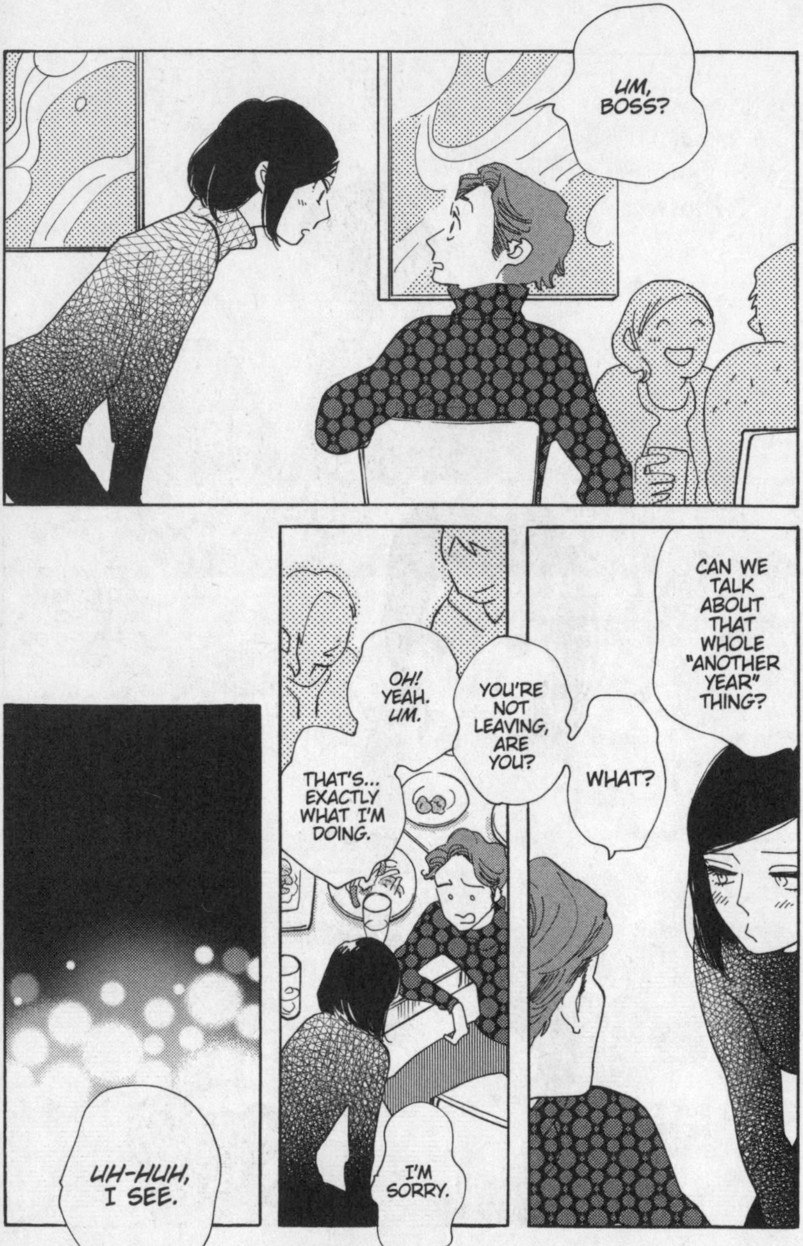
UM, BOSS?
CAN WE TALK ABOUT THAT WHOLE "ANOTHER YEAR" THING?
WHAT?
YOU'RE NOT LEAVING, ARE YOU?
OH! YEAH. UM.
THAT'S... EXACTLY WHAT I'M DOING.
I'M SORRY.
UH-HUH, I SEE.

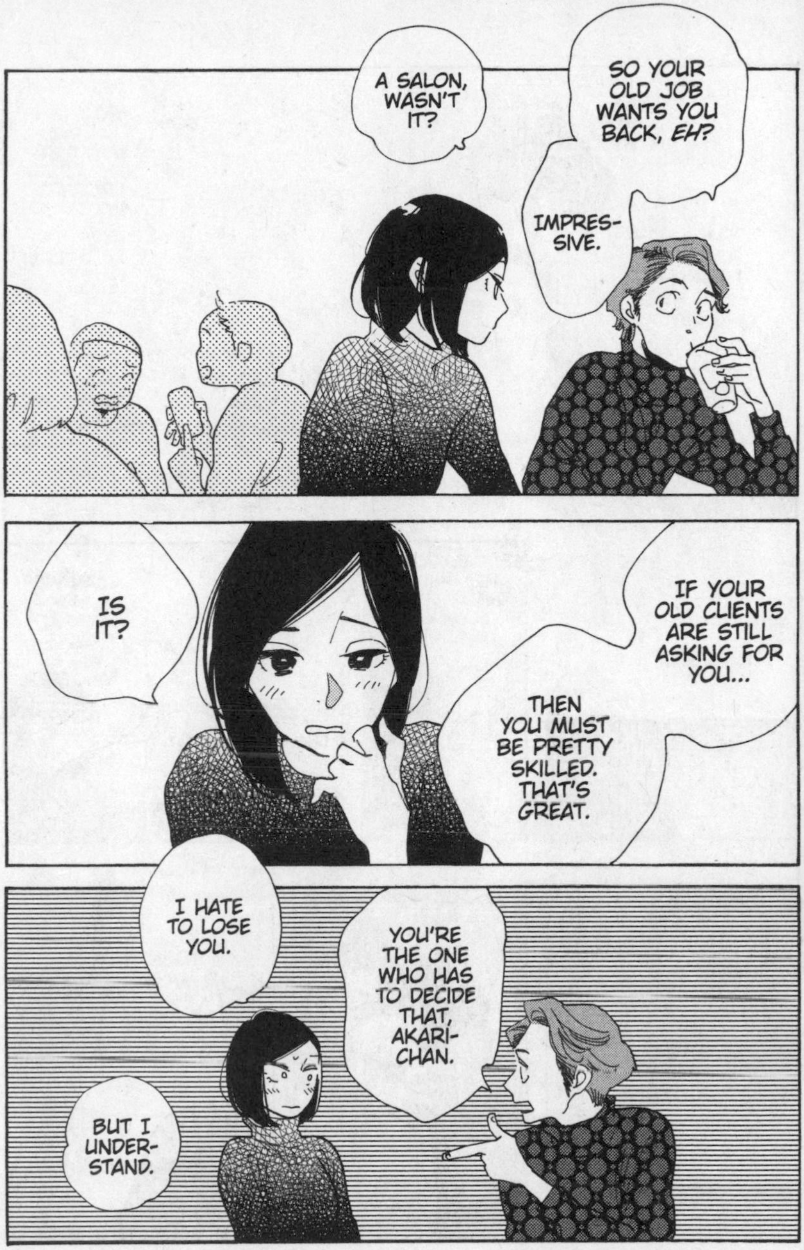
SO YOUR OLD JOB WANTS YOU BACK, *EH?*
A SALON, WASN'T IT?
IMPRES-SIVE.
IF YOUR OLD CLIENTS ARE STILL ASKING FOR YOU...
THEN YOU MUST BE PRETTY SKILLED. THAT'S GREAT.
IS IT?
YOU'RE THE ONE WHO HAS TO DECIDE THAT, AKARI-CHAN.
I HATE TO LOSE YOU.
BUT I UNDER-STAND.

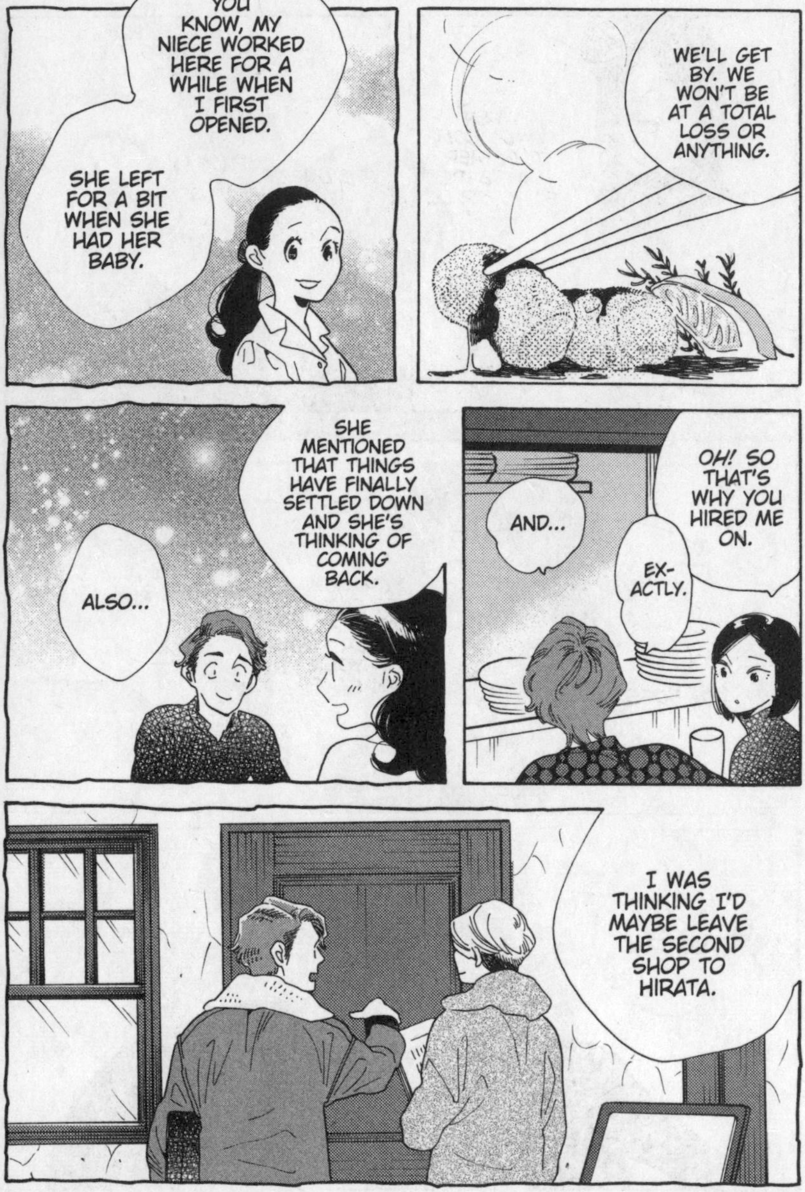
WE'LL GET BY. WE WON'T BE AT A TOTAL LOSS OR ANYTHING.
YOU KNOW, MY NIECE WORKED HERE FOR A WHILE WHEN I FIRST OPENED.
SHE LEFT FOR A BIT WHEN SHE HAD HER BABY.
OH! SO THAT'S WHY YOU HIRED ME ON.
EX-ACTLY.
AND...
SHE MENTIONED THAT THINGS HAVE FINALLY SETTLED DOWN AND SHE'S THINKING OF COMING BACK.
ALSO...
I WAS THINKING I'D MAYBE LEAVE THE SECOND SHOP TO HIRATA.

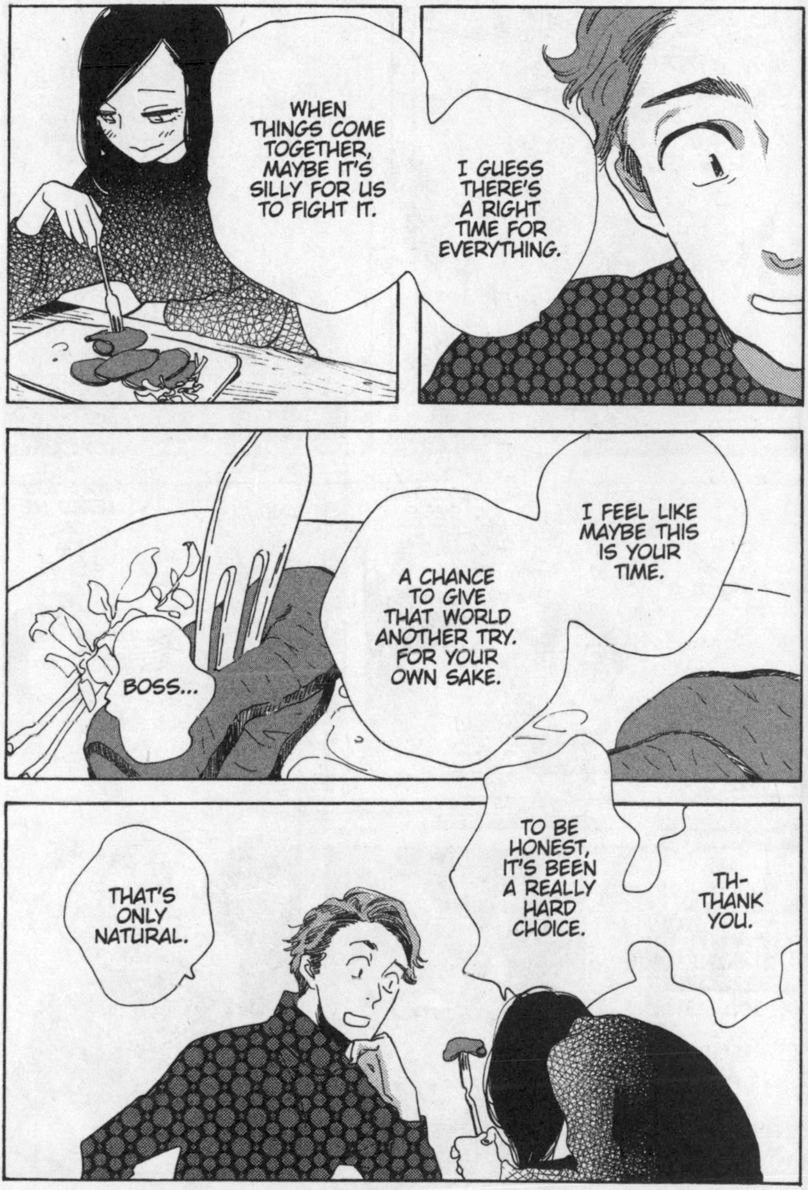
I GUESS THERE'S A RIGHT TIME FOR EVERYTHING.
WHEN THINGS COME TOGETHER, MAYBE IT'S SILLY FOR US TO FIGHT IT.
I FEEL LIKE MAYBE THIS IS YOUR TIME.
A CHANCE TO GIVE THAT WORLD ANOTHER TRY. FOR YOUR OWN SAKE.
BOSS...
TH- THANK YOU.
TO BE HONEST, IT'S BEEN A REALLY HARD CHOICE.
THAT'S ONLY NATURAL.

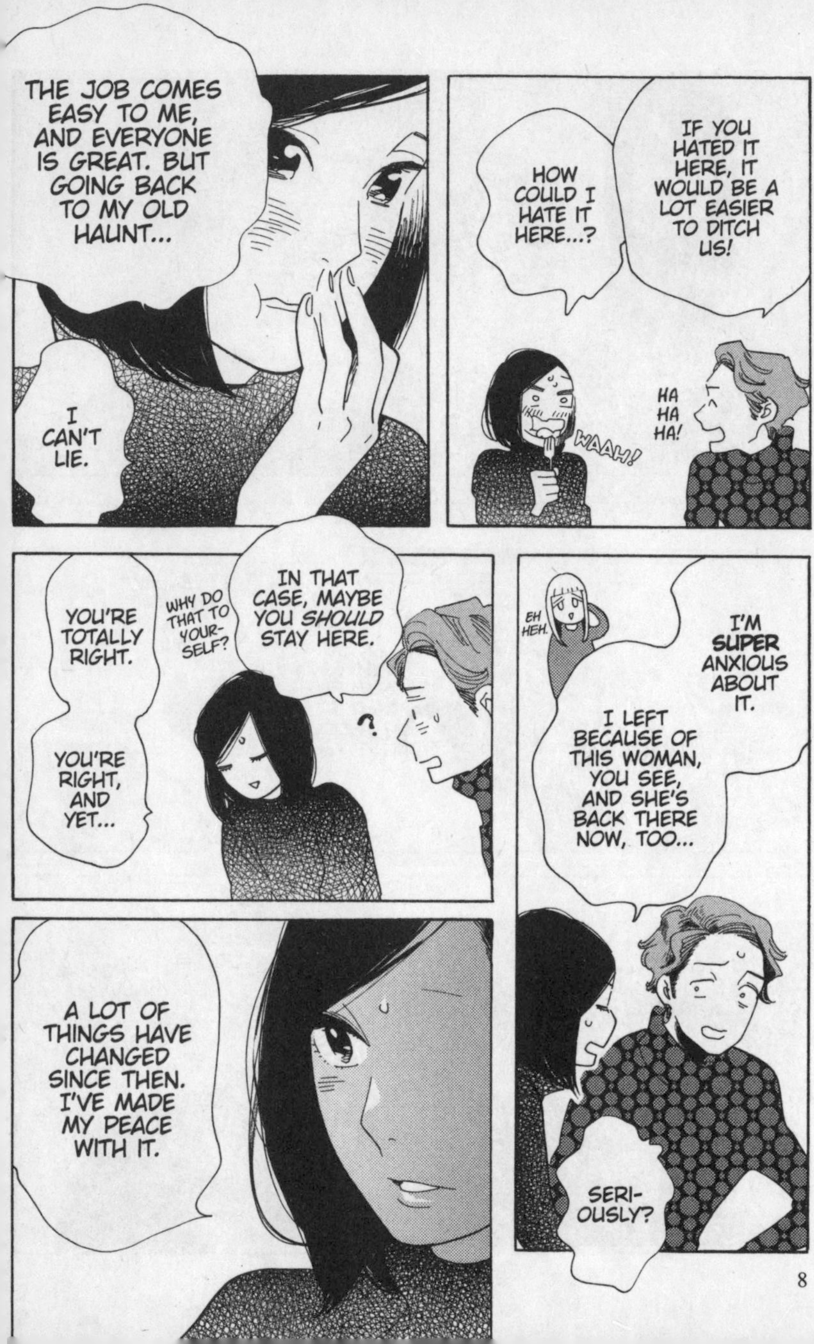
IF YOU HATED IT HERE, IT WOULD BE A LOT EASIER TO DITCH US!
HOW COULD I HATE IT HERE...?
HA HA HA!
WAAH!
THE JOB COMES EASY TO ME, AND EVERYONE IS GREAT. BUT GOING BACK TO MY OLD HAUNT...
I CAN'T LIE.
I'M SUPER ANXIOUS ABOUT IT.
EH HEH.
I LEFT BECAUSE OF THIS WOMAN, YOU SEE, AND SHE'S BACK THERE NOW, TOO...
SERI-OUSLY?
IN THAT CASE, MAYBE YOU SHOULD STAY HERE.
WHY DO THAT TO YOUR-SELF?
YOU'RE TOTALLY RIGHT.
YOU'RE RIGHT, AND YET...
A LOT OF THINGS HAVE CHANGED SINCE THEN. I'VE MADE MY PEACE WITH IT.

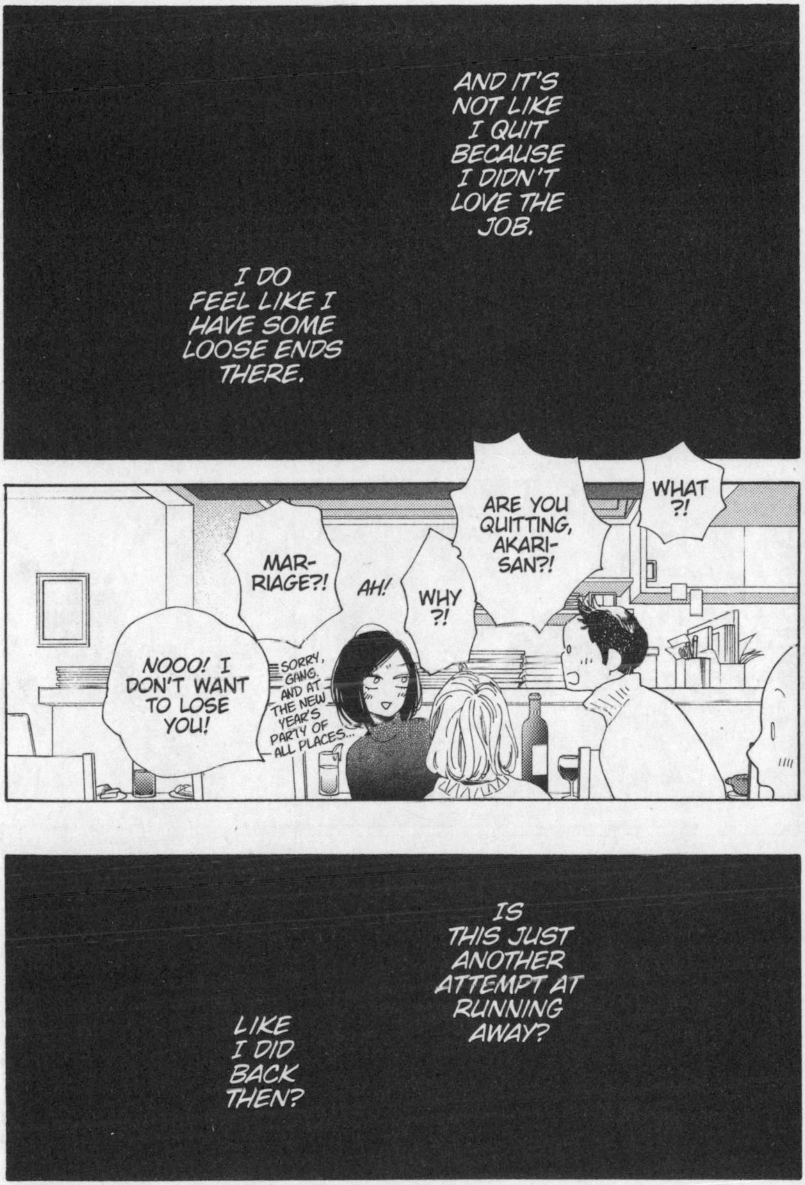
AND IT'S NOT LIKE I QUIT BECAUSE I DIDN'T LOVE THE JOB.
I DO FEEL LIKE I HAVE SOME LOOSE ENDS THERE.
WHAT ?!
ARE YOU QUITTING, AKARI-SAN?!
WHY ?!
AH!
MAR-RIAGE?!
SORRY, GANG. AND AT THE NEW YEAR'S PARTY OF ALL PLACES...
NOOO! I DON'T WANT TO LOSE YOU!
IS THIS JUST ANOTHER ATTEMPT AT RUNNING AWAY?
LIKE I DID BACK THEN?

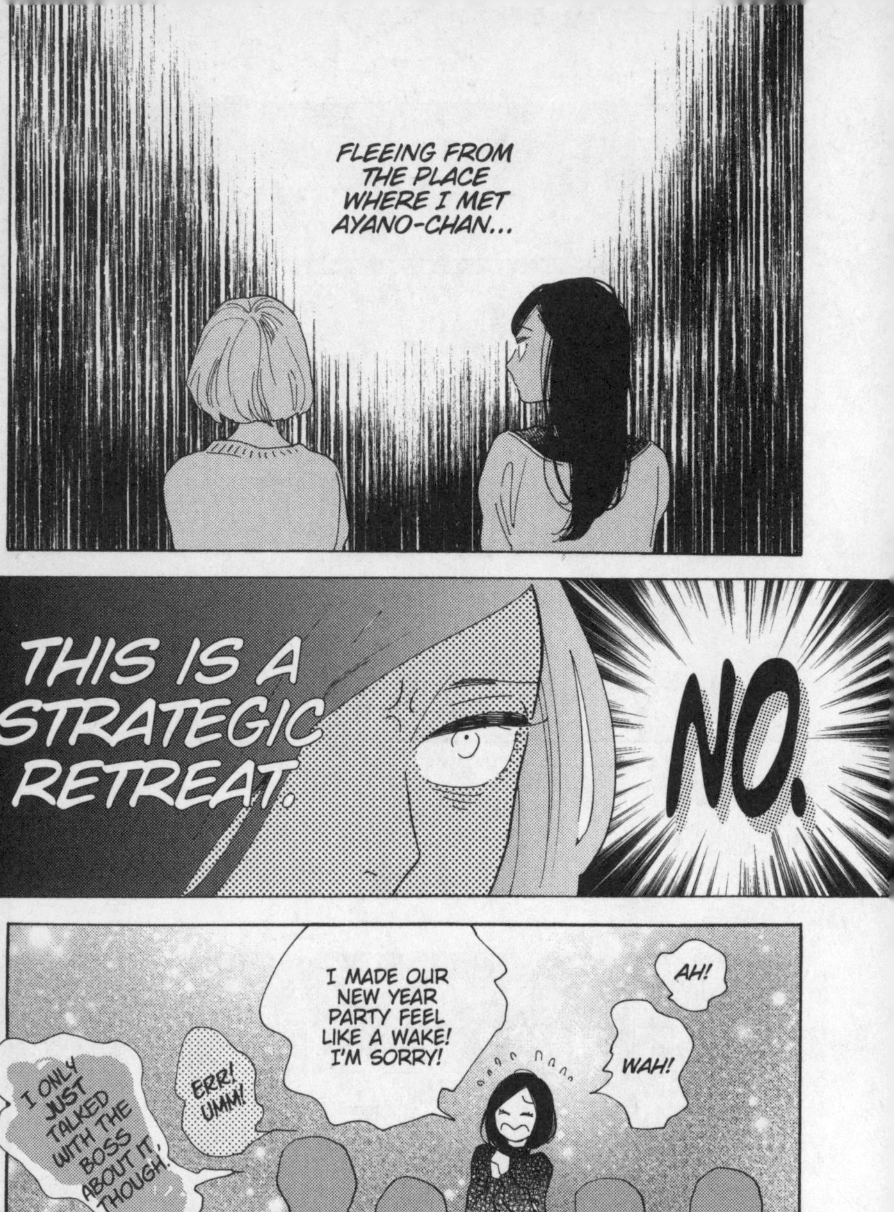
FLEEING FROM THE PLACE WHERE I MET AYANO-CHAN...
NO.
THIS IS A STRATEGIC RETREAT.
AH!
WAH!
I MADE OUR NEW YEAR PARTY FEEL LIKE A WAKE! I'M SORRY!
ERR! UMM!
I ONLY JUST TALKED WITH THE BOSS ABOUT IT, THOUGH.

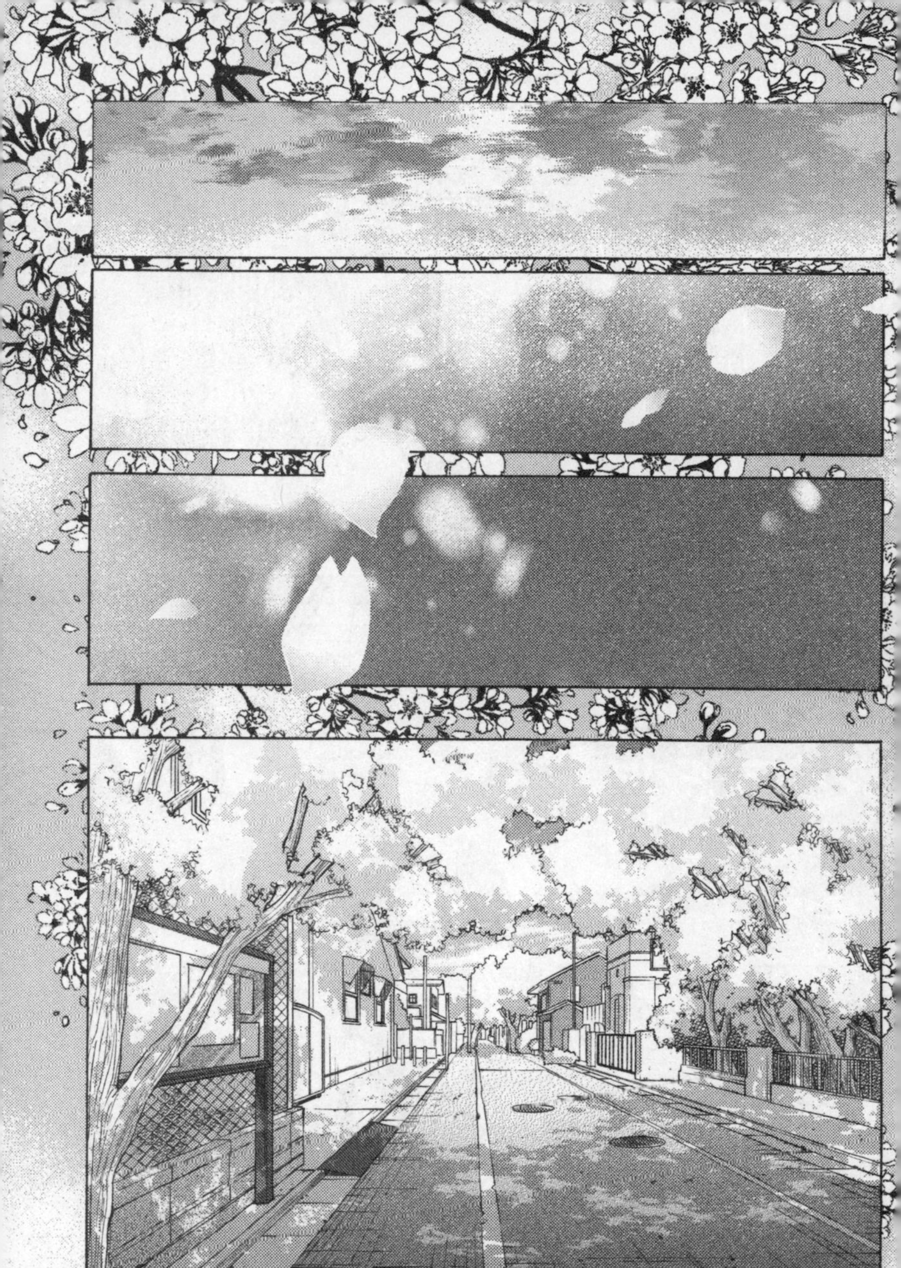

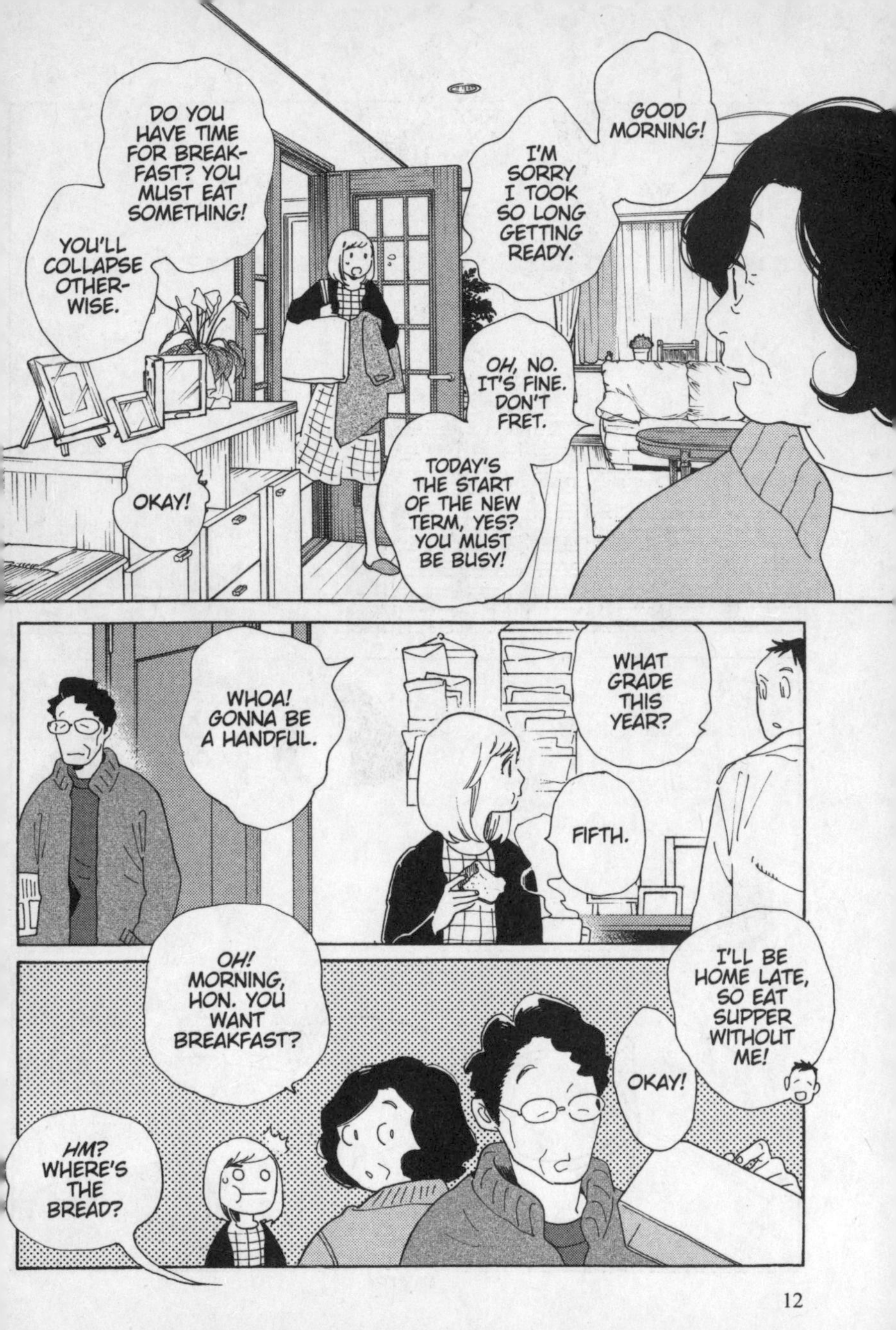
GOOD MORNING!
I'M SORRY I TOOK SO LONG GETTING READY.
OH, NO. IT'S FINE. DON'T FRET.
TODAY'S THE START OF THE NEW TERM, YES? YOU MUST BE BUSY!
DO YOU HAVE TIME FOR BREAK-FAST? YOU MUST EAT SOMETHING!
YOU'LL COLLAPSE OTHER-WISE.
OKAY!
WHAT GRADE THIS YEAR?
FIFTH.
WHOA! GONNA BE A HANDFUL.
I'LL BE HOME LATE, SO EAT SUPPER WITHOUT ME!
OKAY!
OH! MORNING, HON. YOU WANT BREAKFAST?
HM? WHERE'S THE BREAD?

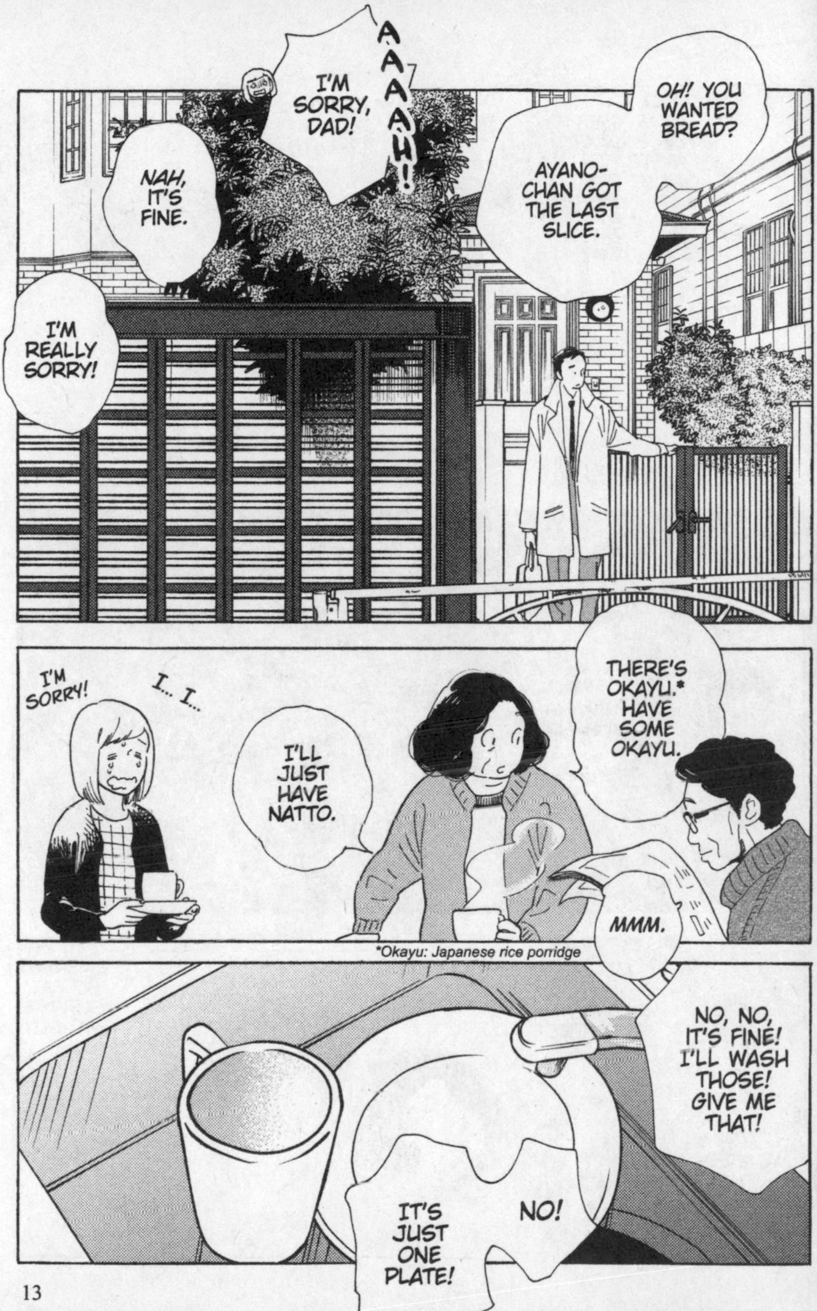
OH! YOU WANTED BREAD?
AYANO-CHAN GOT THE LAST SLICE.
AAAAH!
I'M SORRY, DAD!
NAH, IT'S FINE.
I'M REALLY SORRY!
THERE'S OKAYU.* HAVE SOME OKAYU.
MMM.
I'LL JUST HAVE NATTO.
I... I...
I'M SORRY!
NO, NO, IT'S FINE! I'LL WASH THOSE! GIVE ME THAT!
NO!
IT'S JUST ONE PLATE!

*Okayu: Japanese rice porridge

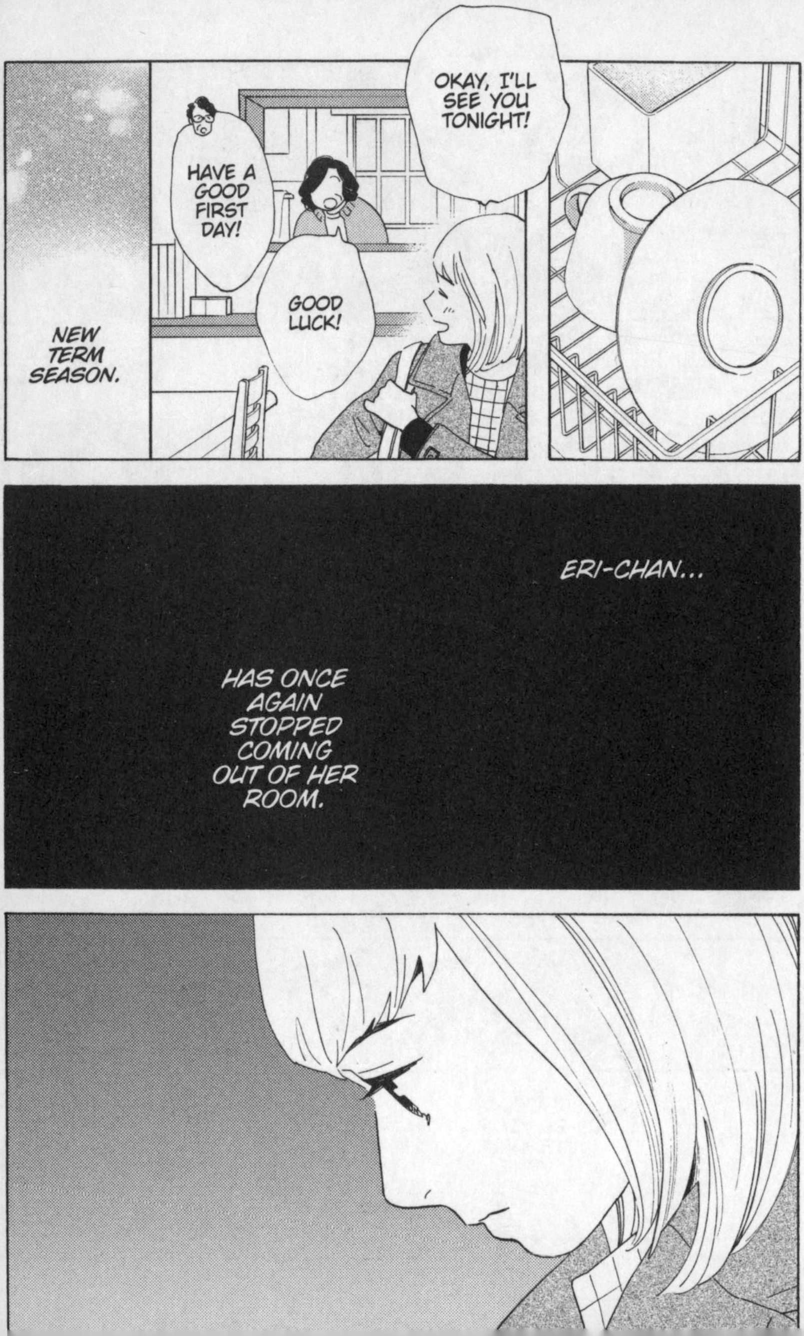
OKAY, I'LL SEE YOU TONIGHT!
HAVE A GOOD FIRST DAY!
GOOD LUCK!
NEW TERM SEASON.
ERI-CHAN...
HAS ONCE AGAIN STOPPED COMING OUT OF HER ROOM.

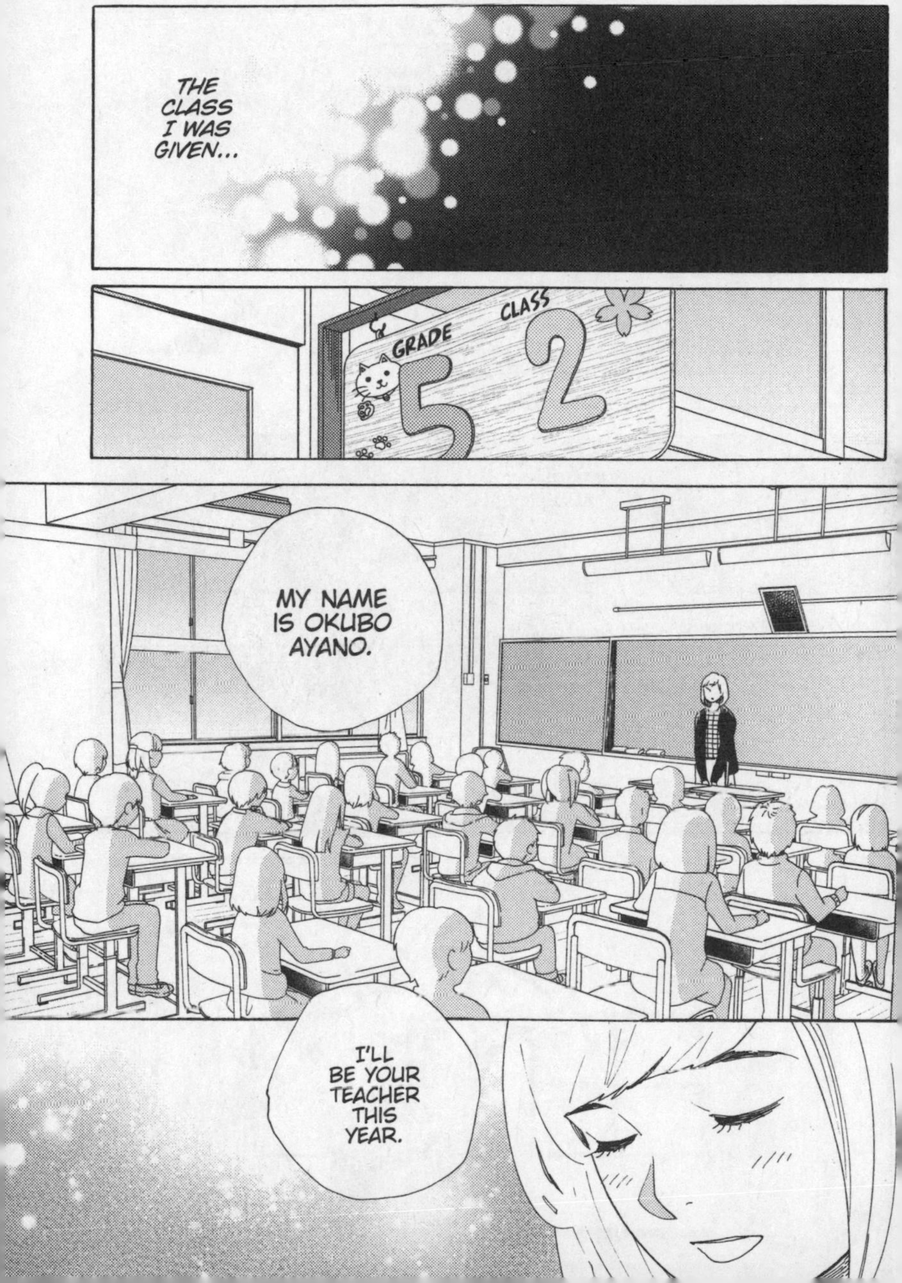
THE CLASS I WAS GIVEN...
GRADE 5
CLASS 2
MY NAME IS OKUBO AYANO.
I'LL BE YOUR TEACHER THIS YEAR.

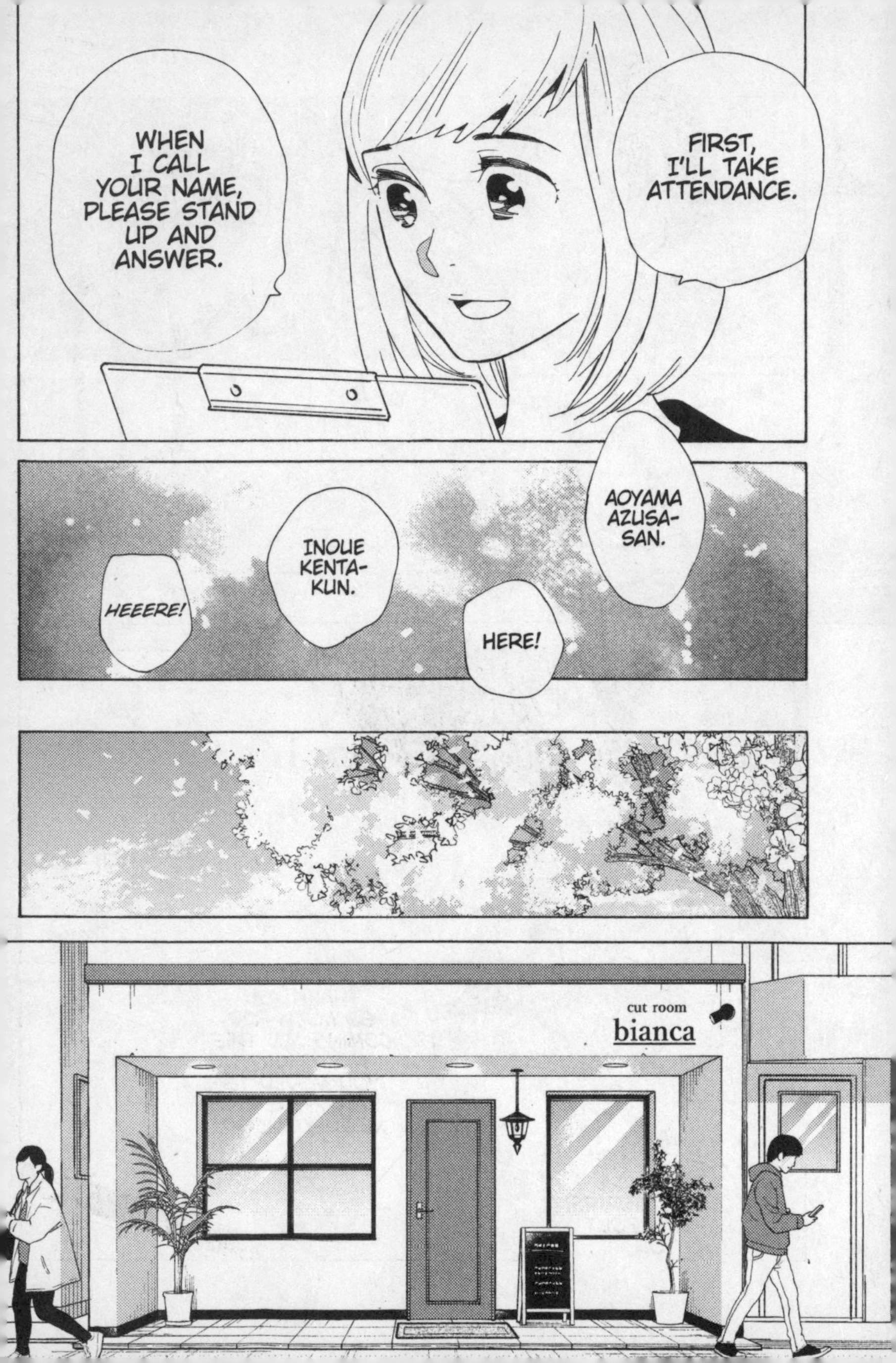
FIRST, I'LL TAKE ATTENDANCE.
WHEN I CALL YOUR NAME, PLEASE STAND UP AND ANSWER.
AOYAMA AZUSA-SAN.
HERE!
INOUE KENTA-KUN.
HEEERE!
cut room
bianca

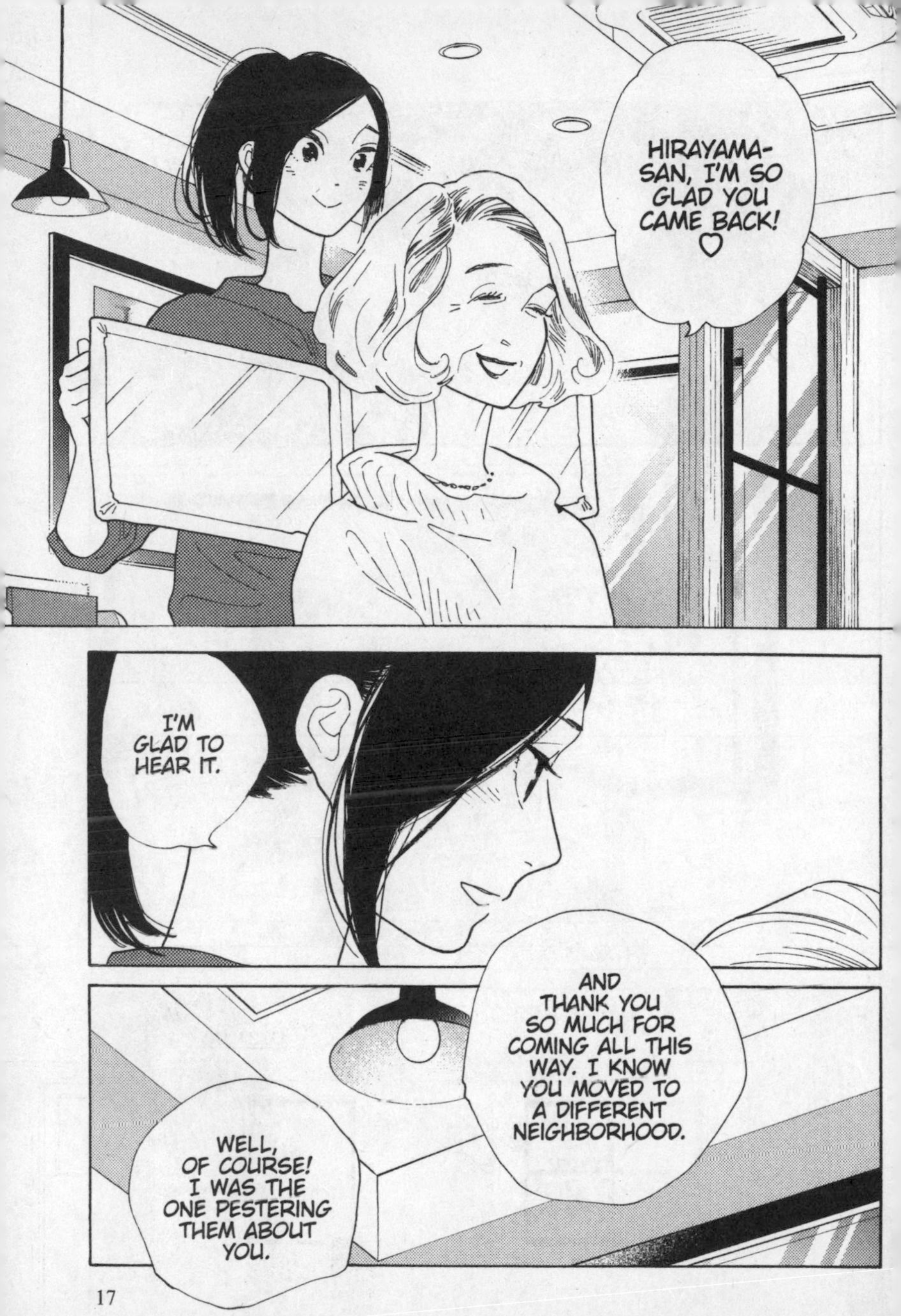
HIRAYAMA-SAN, I'M SO GLAD YOU CAME BACK! ♡
I'M GLAD TO HEAR IT.
AND THANK YOU SO MUCH FOR COMING ALL THIS WAY. I KNOW YOU MOVED TO A DIFFERENT NEIGHBORHOOD.
WELL, OF COURSE! I WAS THE ONE PESTERING THEM ABOUT YOU.

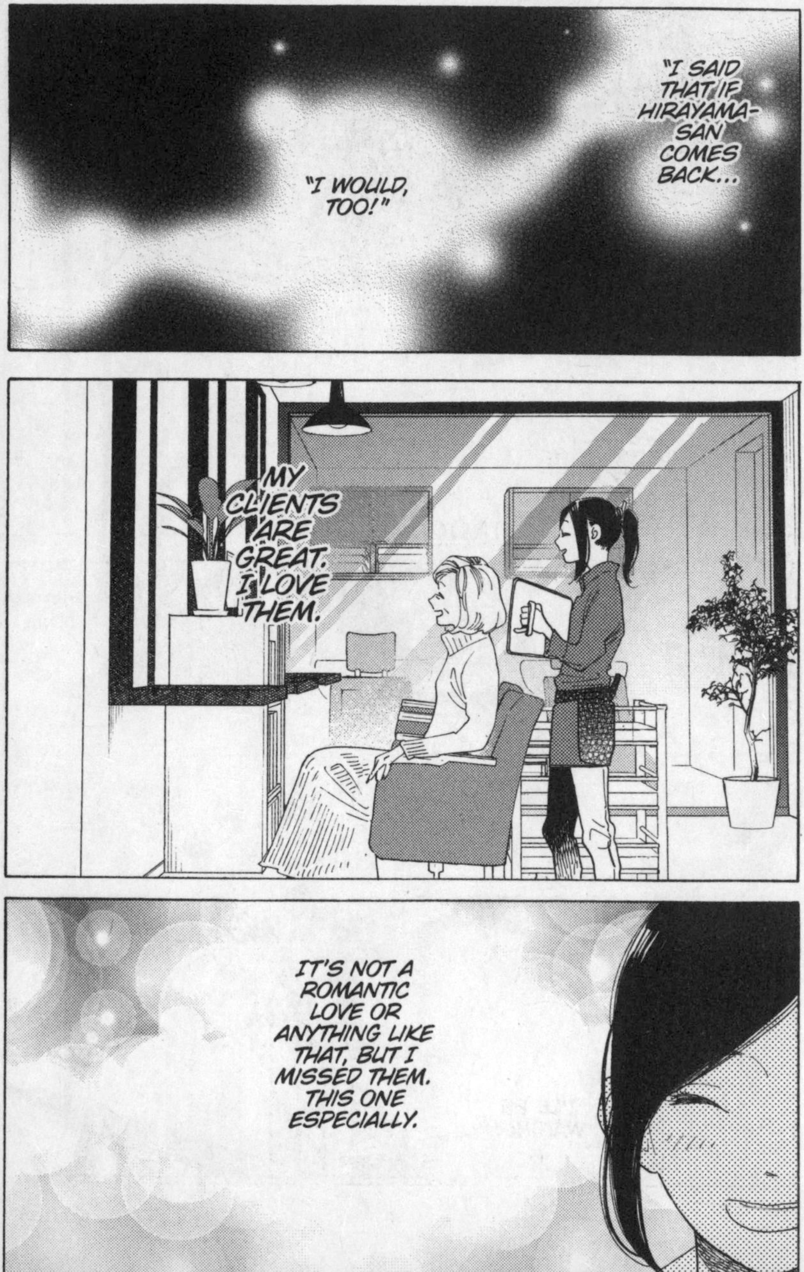
"I SAID THAT IF HIRAYAMA-SAN COMES BACK...
"I WOULD, TOO!"
MY CLIENTS ARE GREAT. I LOVE THEM.
IT'S NOT A ROMANTIC LOVE OR ANYTHING LIKE THAT, BUT I MISSED THEM. THIS ONE ESPECIALLY.

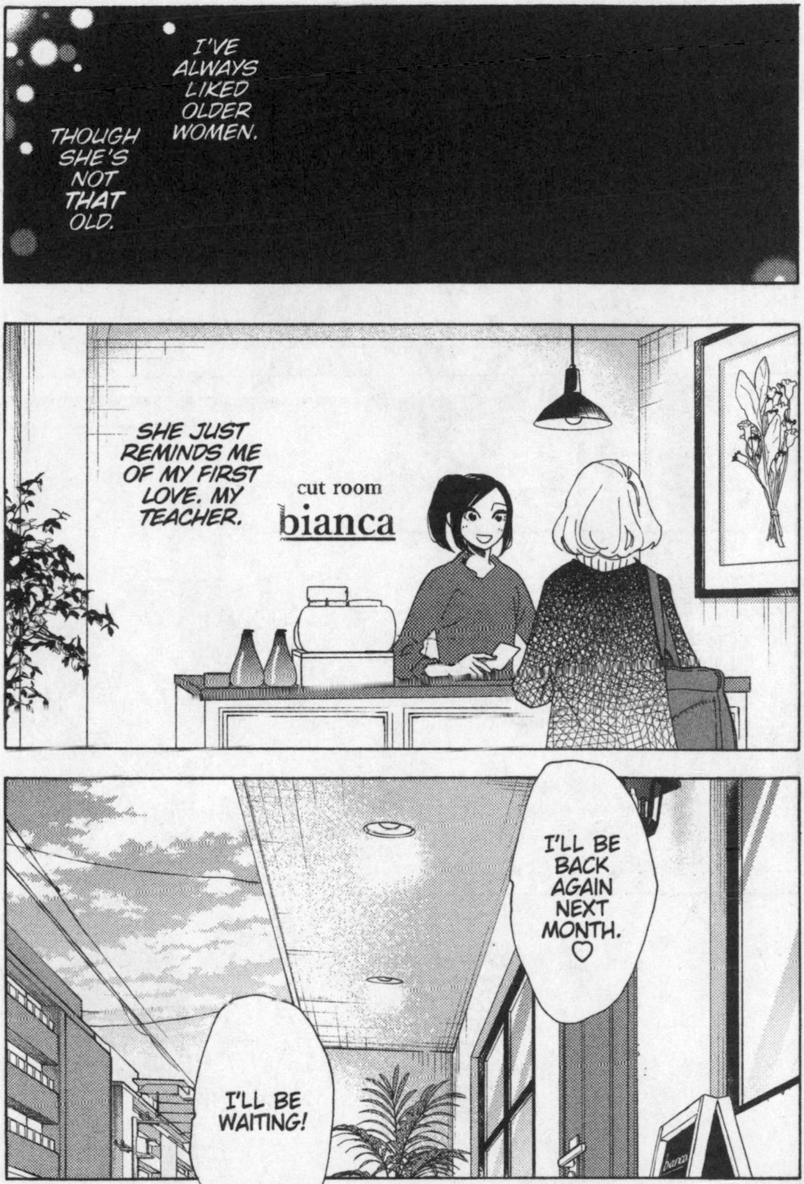
I'VE ALWAYS LIKED OLDER WOMEN.
THOUGH SHE'S NOT THAT OLD.
cut room bianca
SHE JUST REMINDS ME OF MY FIRST LOVE. MY TEACHER.
I'LL BE BACK AGAIN NEXT MONTH. ♡
I'LL BE WAITING!

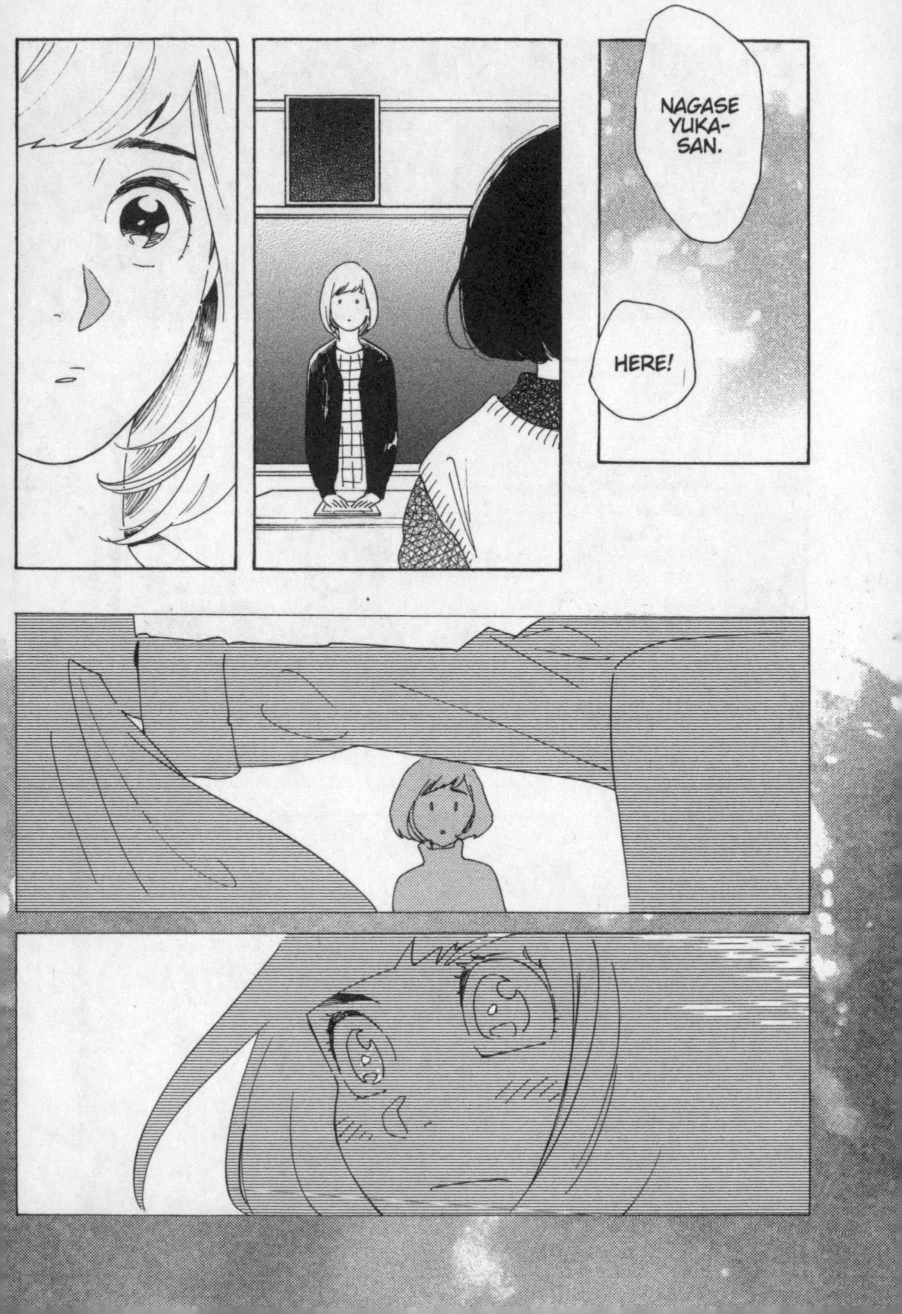
NAGASE YUKA-SAN.
HERE!

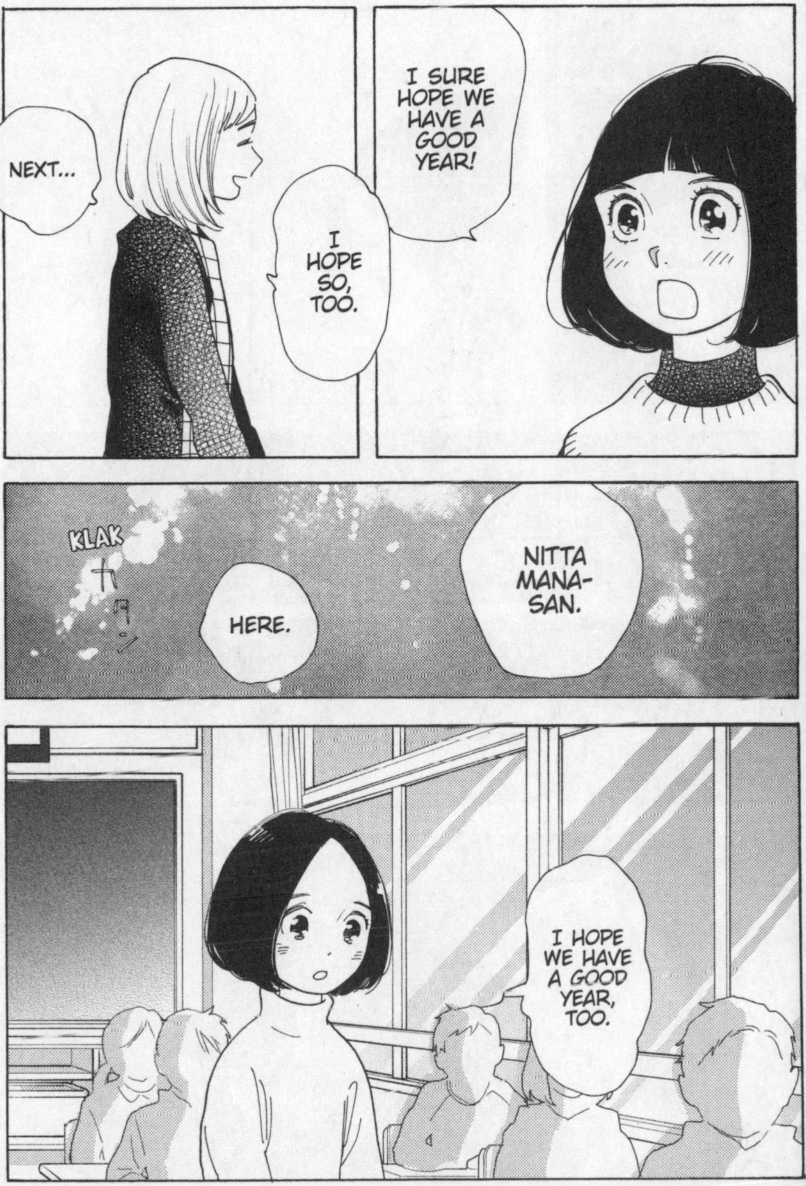

I SURE HOPE WE HAVE A GOOD YEAR!
I HOPE SO, TOO.
NEXT...
NITTA MANA-SAN.
HERE.
KLAK
I HOPE WE HAVE A GOOD YEAR, TOO.

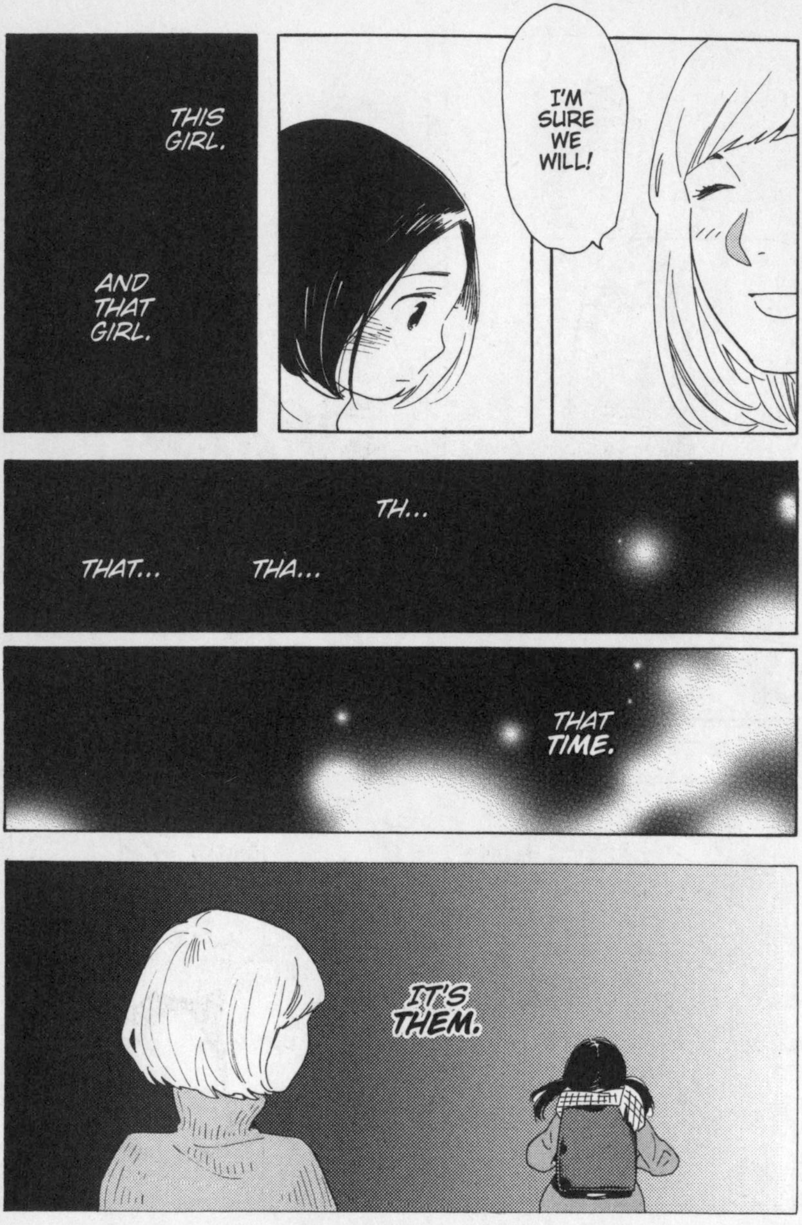
I'M SURE WE WILL!
THIS GIRL.
AND THAT GIRL.
TH...
THA...
THAT...
THAT TIME.
IT'S THEM.

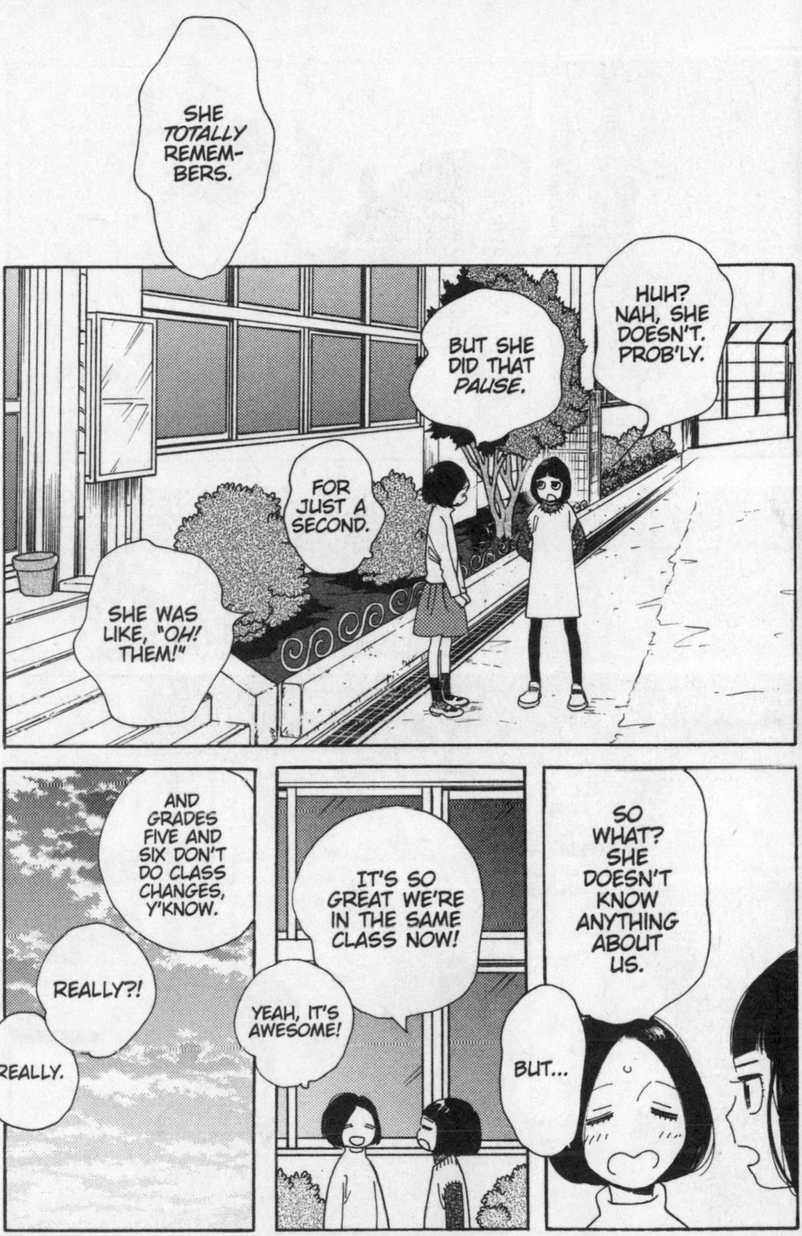
SHE *TOTALLY* REMEMBERS.
HUH? NAH, SHE DOESN'T. PROB'LY.
BUT SHE DID THAT *PAUSE.*
FOR JUST A SECOND.
SHE WAS LIKE, "OH! THEM!"
SO WHAT? SHE DOESN'T KNOW ANYTHING ABOUT US.
BUT...
IT'S SO GREAT WE'RE IN THE SAME CLASS NOW!
YEAH, IT'S AWESOME!
AND GRADES FIVE AND SIX DON'T DO CLASS CHANGES, Y'KNOW.
REALLY?!
REALLY.

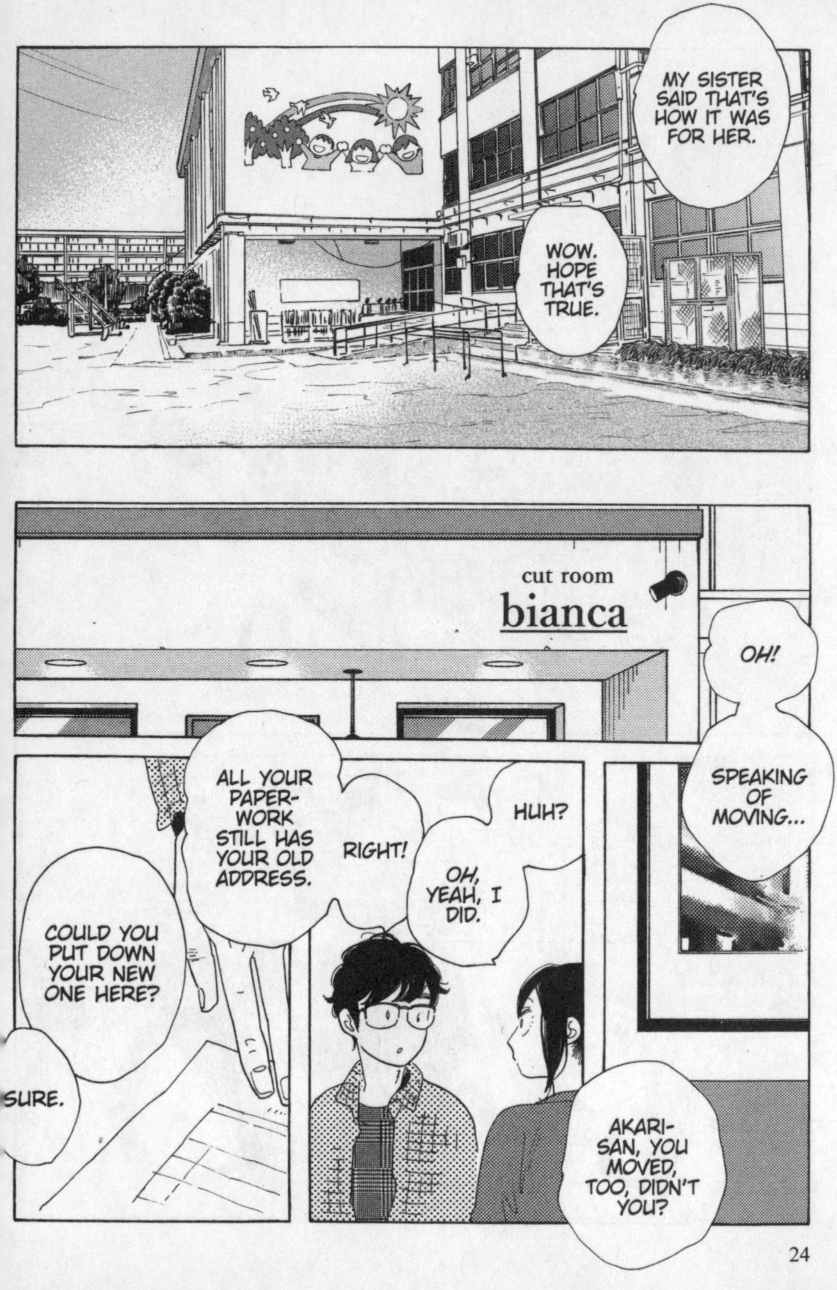
MY SISTER SAID THAT'S HOW IT WAS FOR HER.
WOW. HOPE THAT'S TRUE.
cut room
bianca
OH!
SPEAKING OF MOVING...
AKARI-SAN, YOU MOVED, TOO, DIDN'T YOU?
HUH?
OH, YEAH, I DID.
RIGHT!
ALL YOUR PAPER-WORK STILL HAS YOUR OLD ADDRESS.
COULD YOU PUT DOWN YOUR NEW ONE HERE?
SURE.

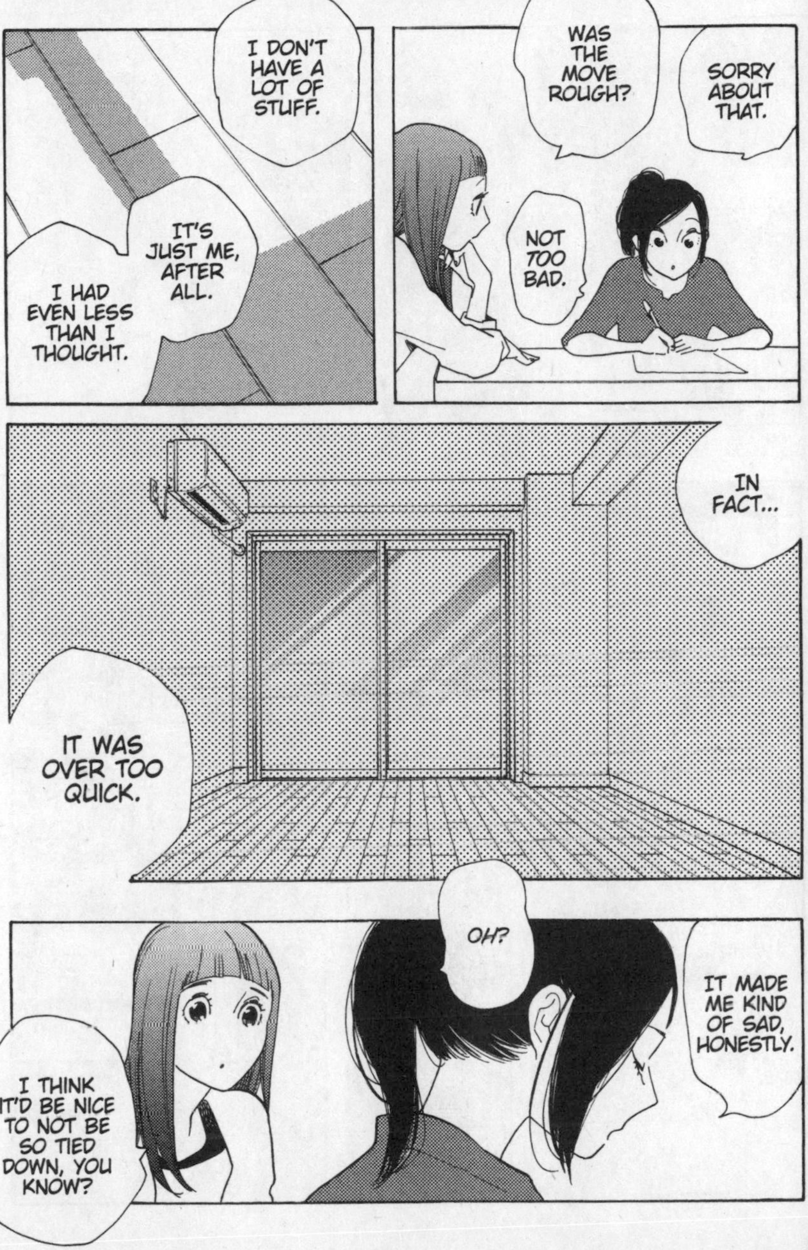
SORRY ABOUT THAT.
WAS THE MOVE ROUGH?
NOT TOO BAD.
I DON'T HAVE A LOT OF STUFF.
IT'S JUST ME, AFTER ALL.
I HAD EVEN LESS THAN I THOUGHT.
IN FACT...
IT WAS OVER TOO QUICK.
IT MADE ME KIND OF SAD, HONESTLY.
OH?
I THINK IT'D BE NICE TO NOT BE SO TIED DOWN, YOU KNOW?

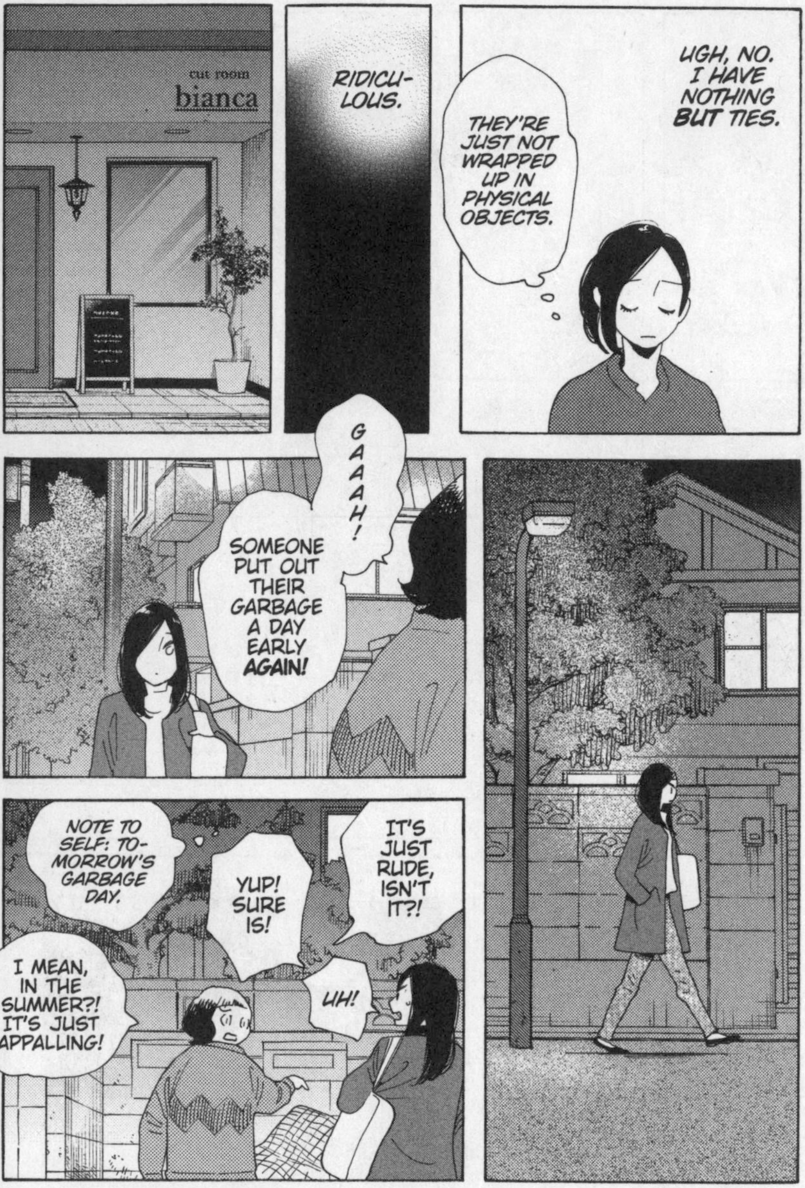
UGH, NO. I HAVE NOTHING BUT TIES.
THEY'RE JUST NOT WRAPPED UP IN PHYSICAL OBJECTS.
RIDICU-LOUS.
cut room
bianca
GAAAAH!
SOMEONE PUT OUT THEIR GARBAGE A DAY EARLY AGAIN!
IT'S JUST RUDE, ISN'T IT?!
YUP! SURE IS!
NOTE TO SELF: TO-MORROW'S GARBAGE DAY.
UH!
I MEAN, IN THE SUMMER?! IT'S JUST APPALLING!

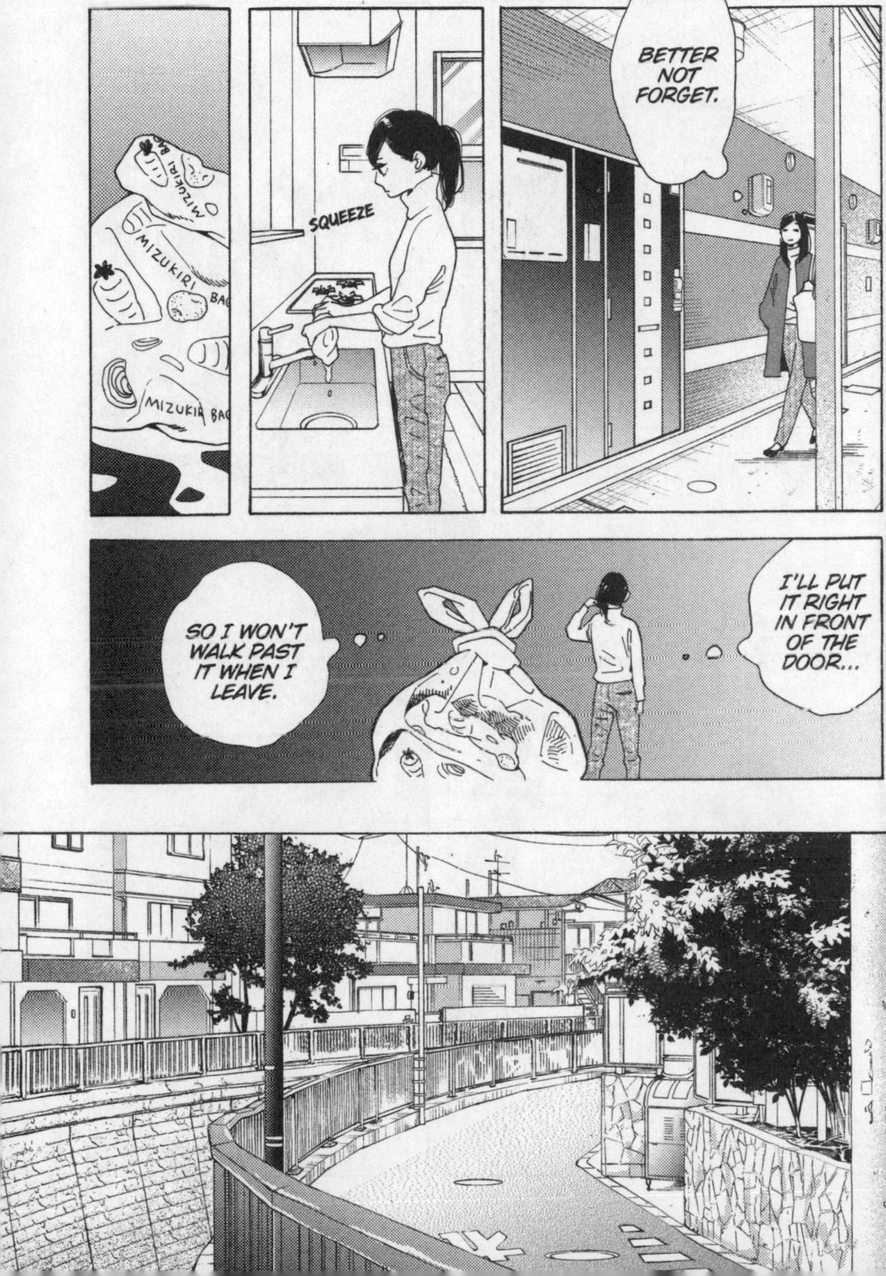
BETTER NOT FORGET.
SQUEEZE
MIZUKIRI BAG
I'LL PUT IT RIGHT IN FRONT OF THE DOOR...
SO I WON'T WALK PAST IT WHEN I LEAVE.

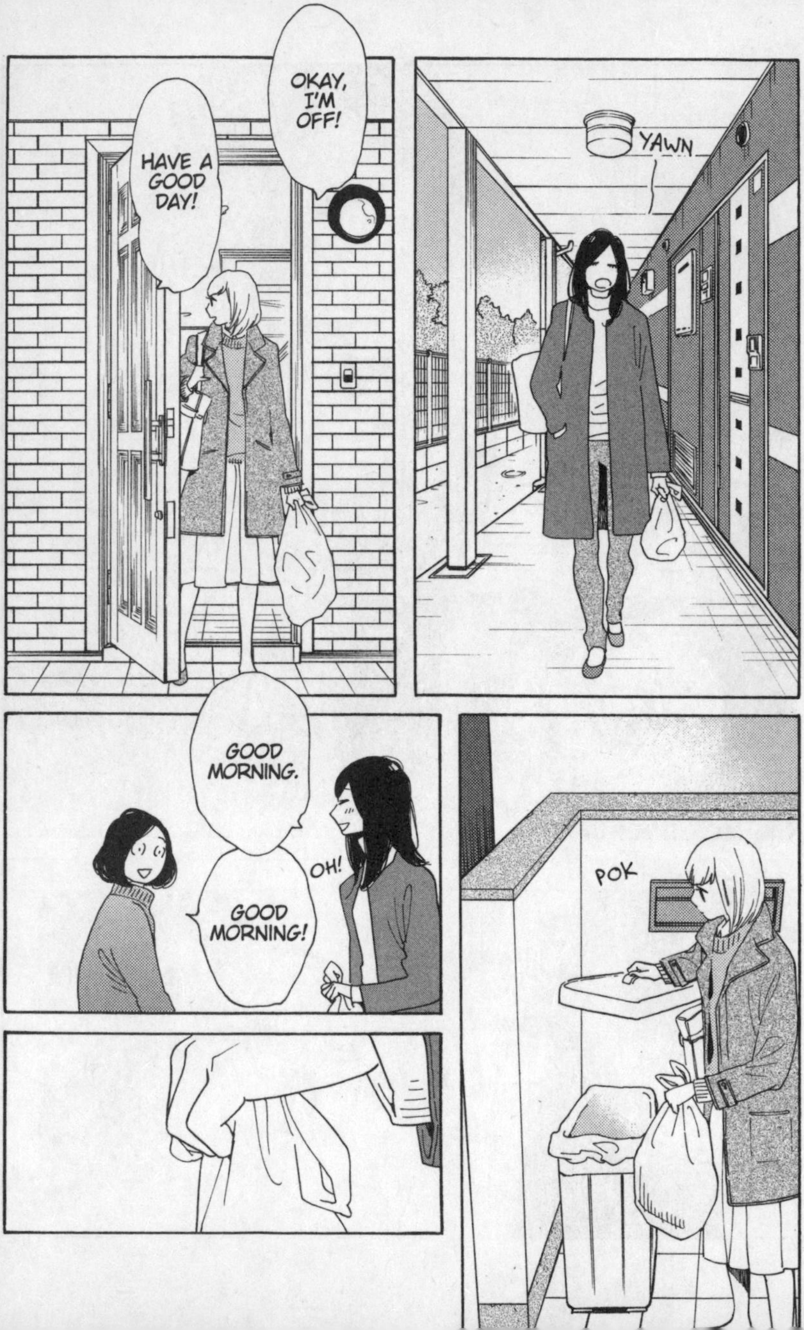
YAWN
OKAY, I'M OFF!
HAVE A GOOD DAY!
POK
GOOD MORNING.
OH!
GOOD MORNING!

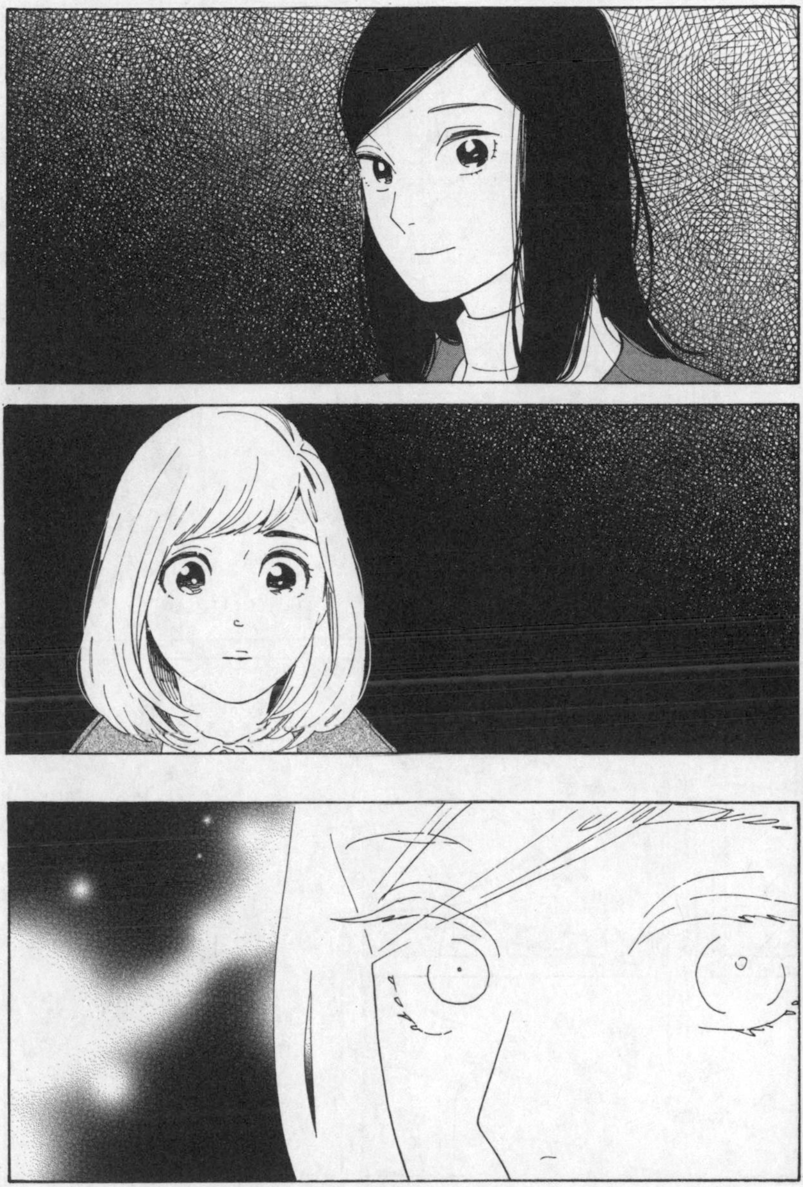

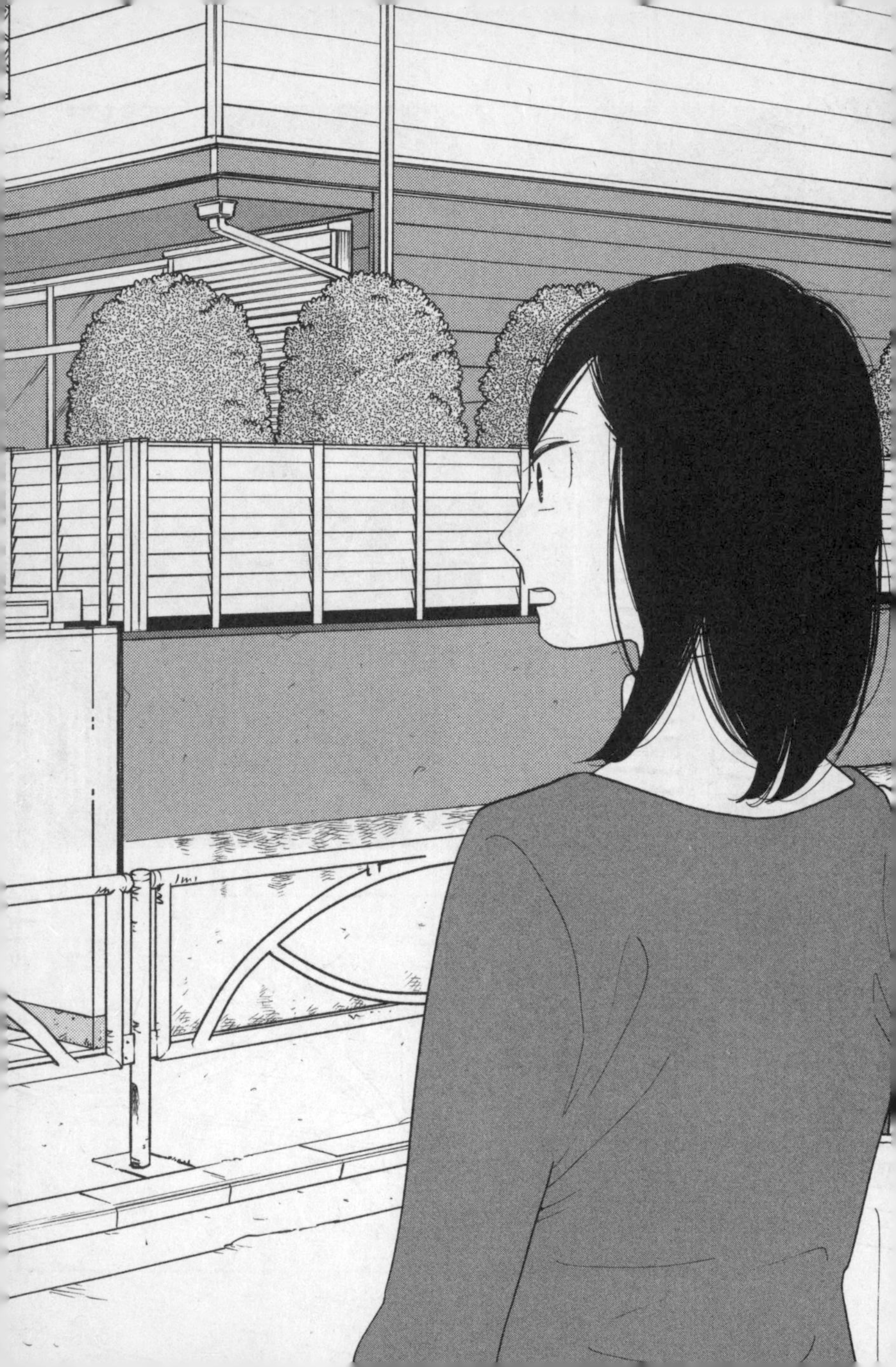

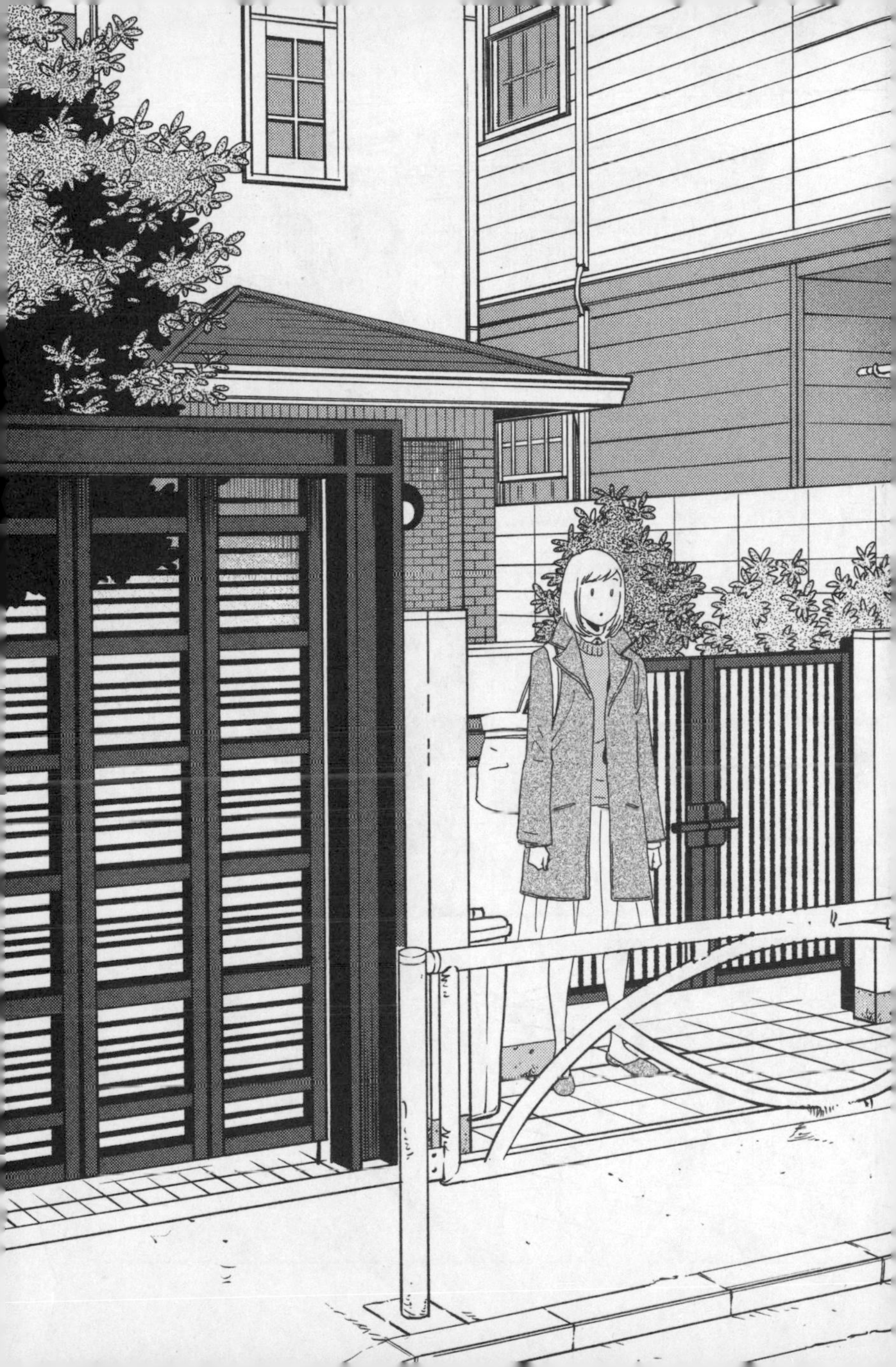

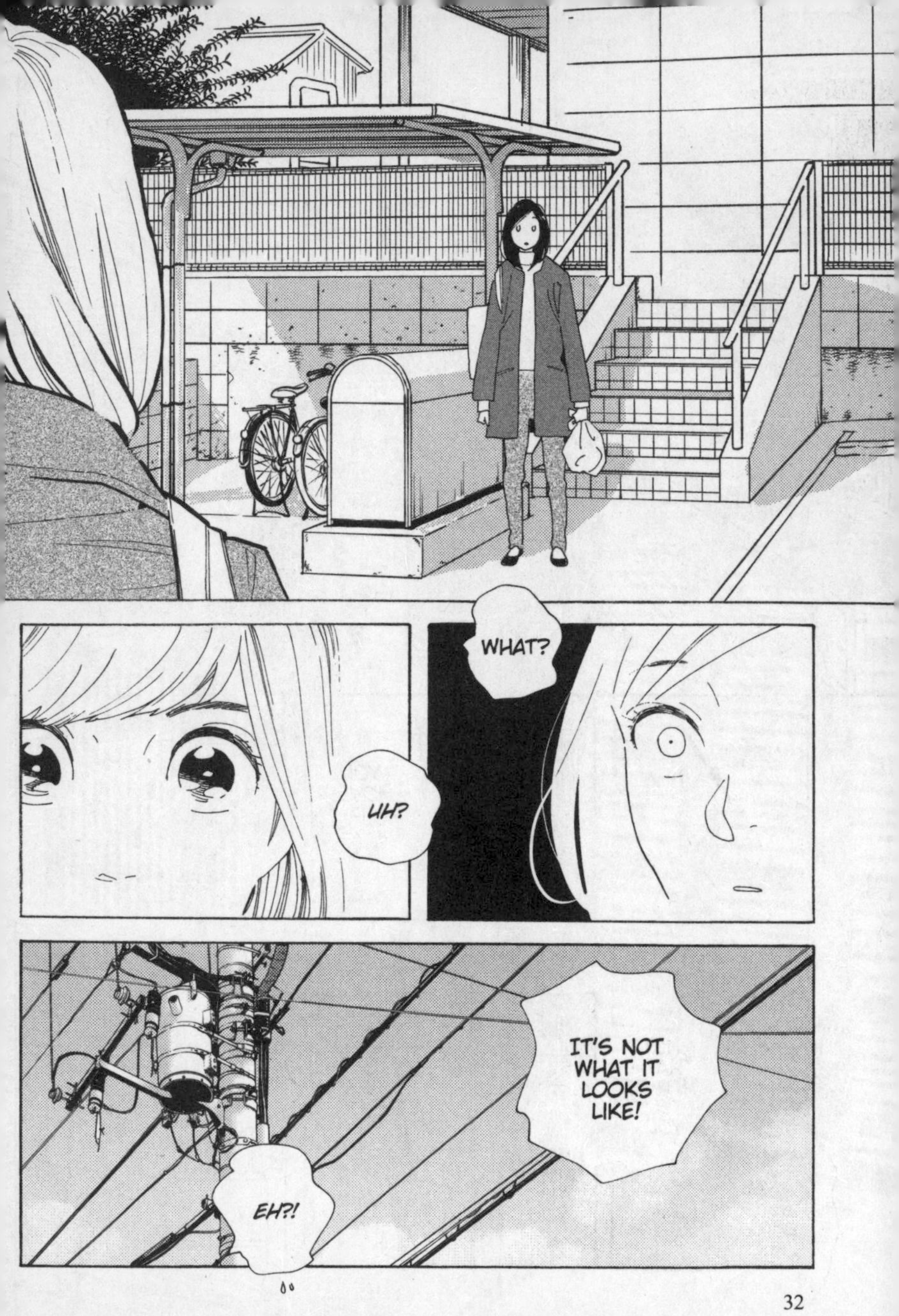
WHAT?
UH?
IT'S NOT WHAT IT LOOKS LIKE!
EH?!

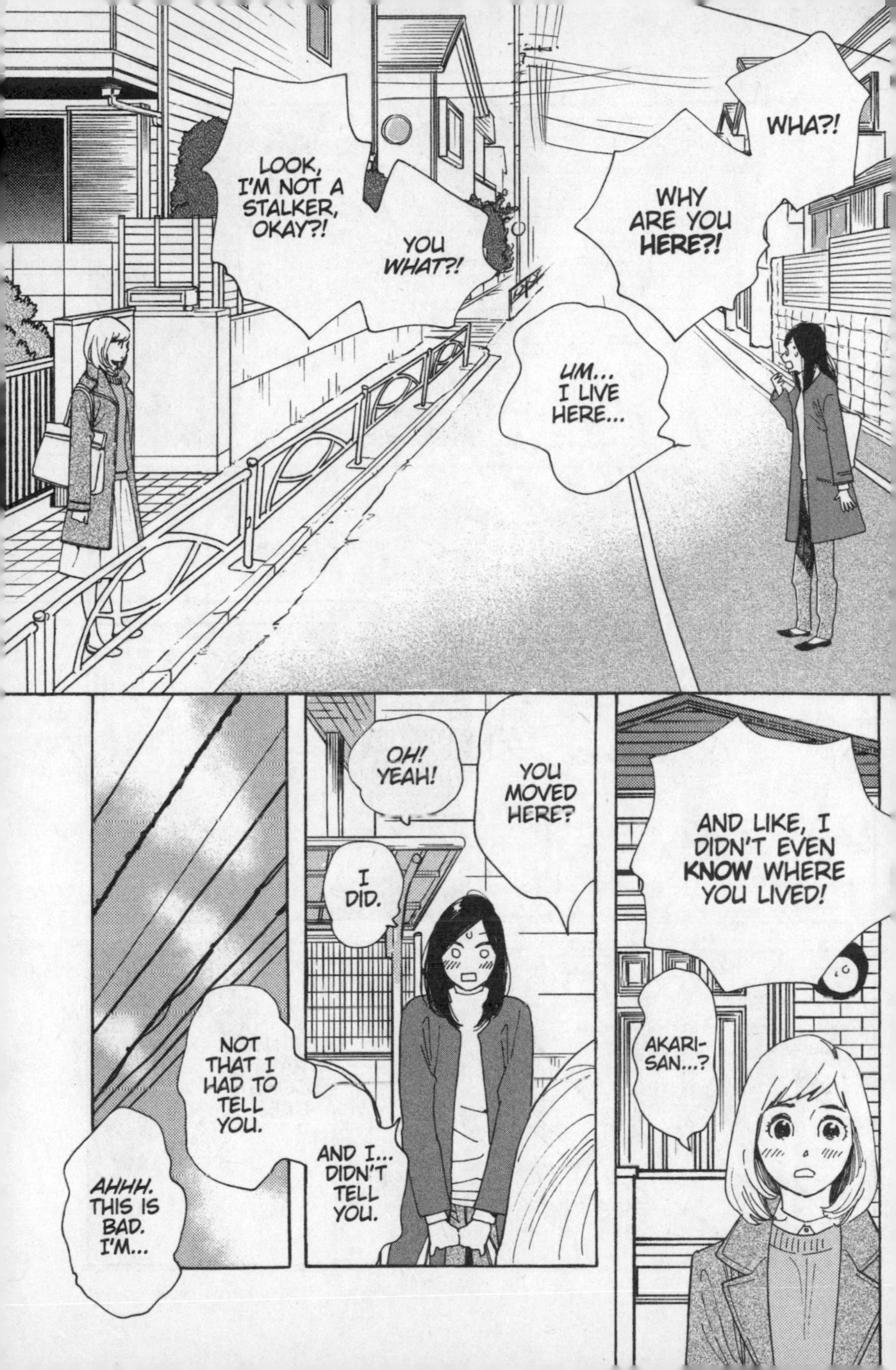
WHA?!
WHY ARE YOU HERE?!
UM... I LIVE HERE...
YOU WHAT?!
LOOK, I'M NOT A STALKER, OKAY?!
AND LIKE, I DIDN'T EVEN KNOW WHERE YOU LIVED!
AKARI-SAN...?
YOU MOVED HERE?
OH! YEAH!
I DID.
NOT THAT I HAD TO TELL YOU.
AND I... DIDN'T TELL YOU.
AHHH. THIS IS BAD. I'M...

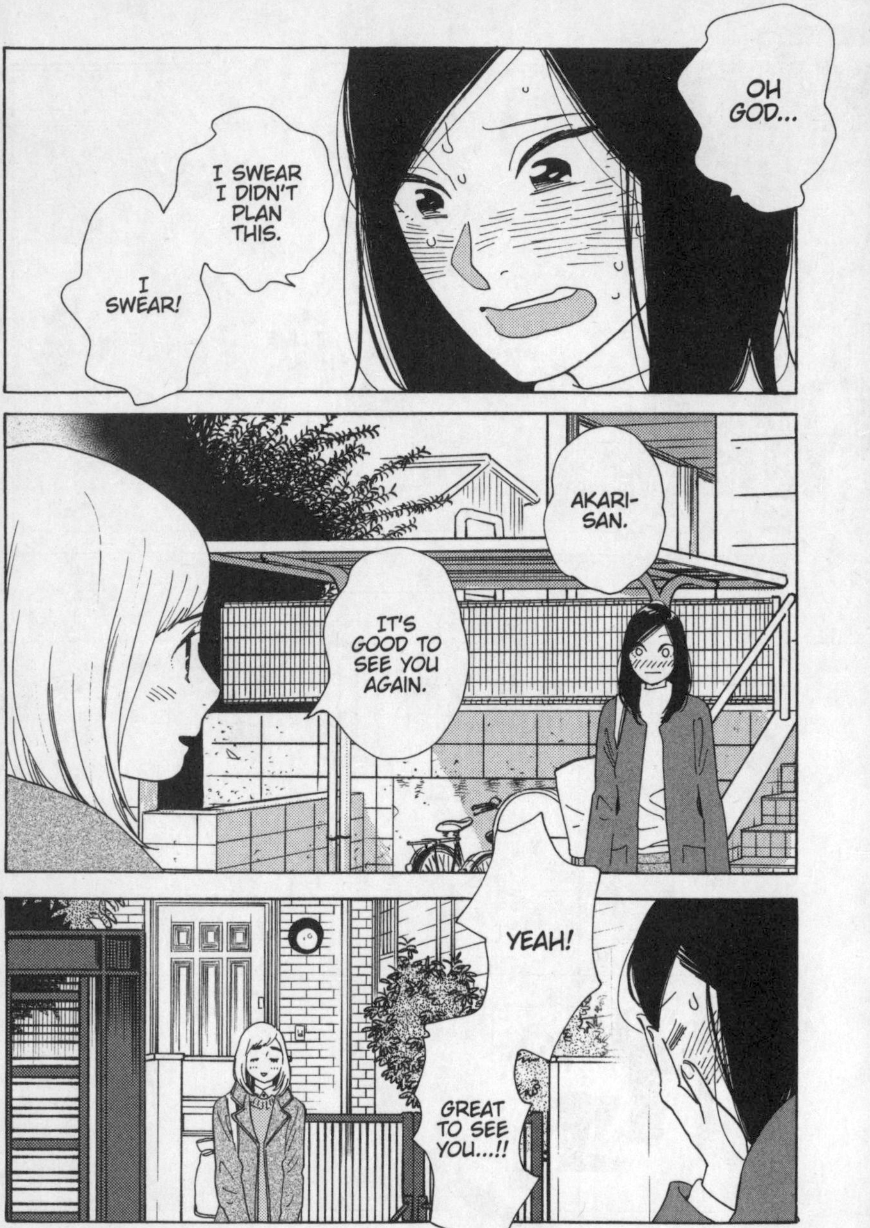
OH GOD...
I SWEAR I DIDN'T PLAN THIS.
I SWEAR!
AKARI-SAN.
IT'S GOOD TO SEE YOU AGAIN.
YEAH!
GREAT TO SEE YOU...!!

Chapter 12

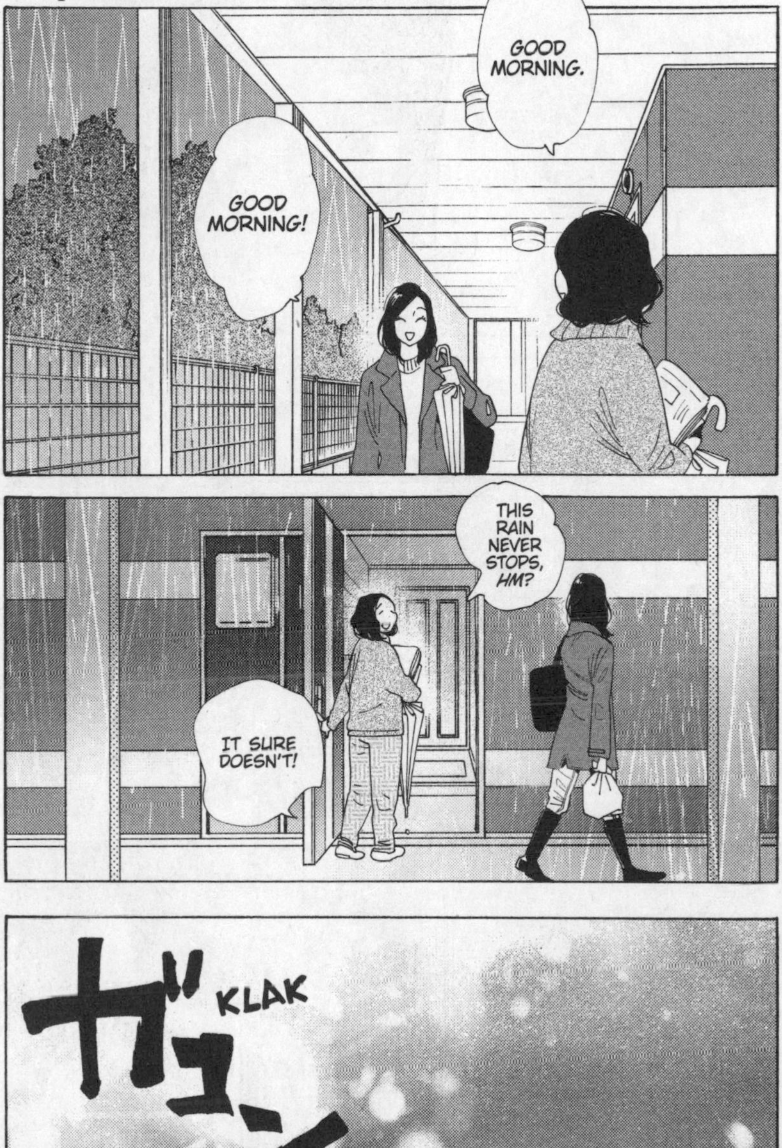
GOOD MORNING.
GOOD MORNING!
THIS RAIN NEVER STOPS, HM?
IT SURE DOESN'T!
KLAK

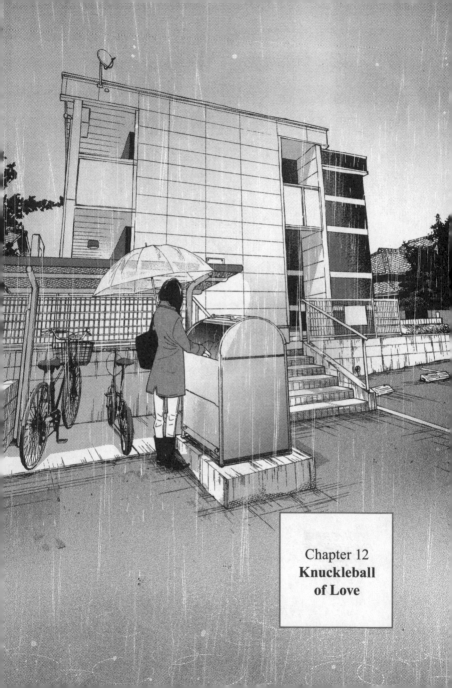

Chapter 12
**Knuckleball
of Love**

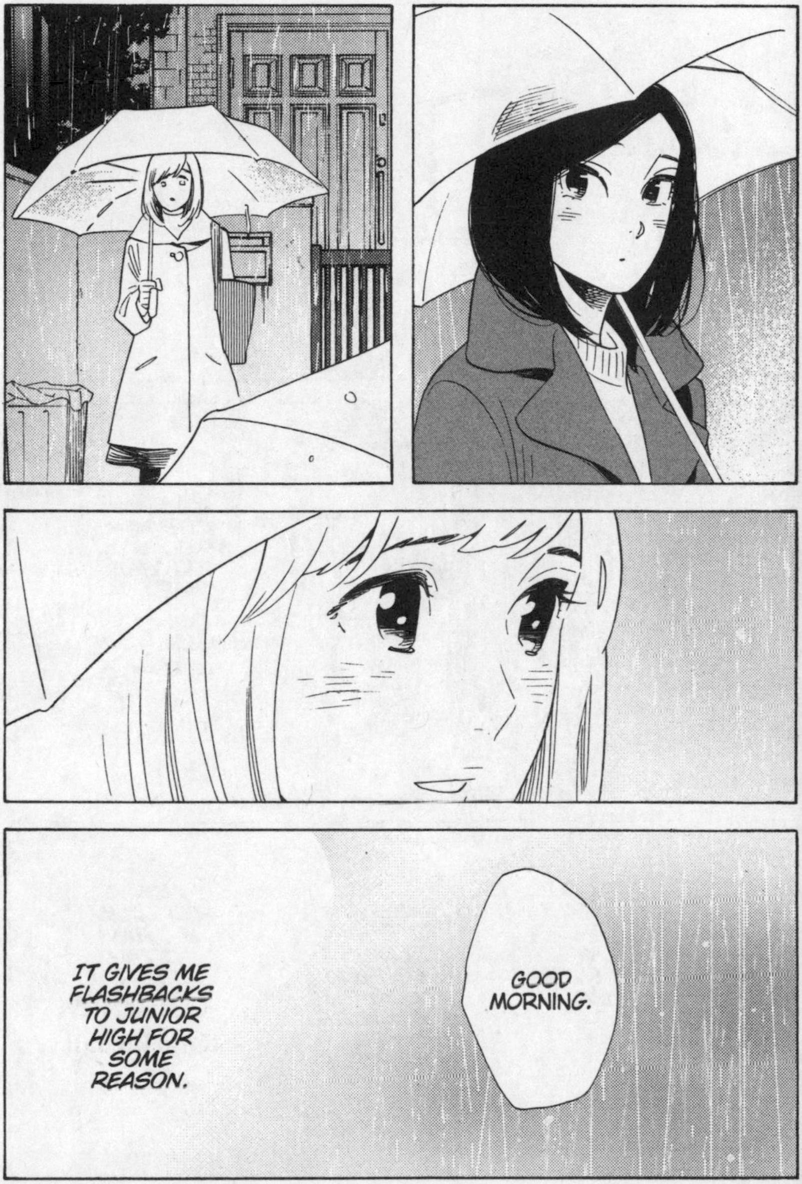
GOOD MORNING.
IT GIVES ME FLASHBACKS TO JUNIOR HIGH FOR SOME REASON.

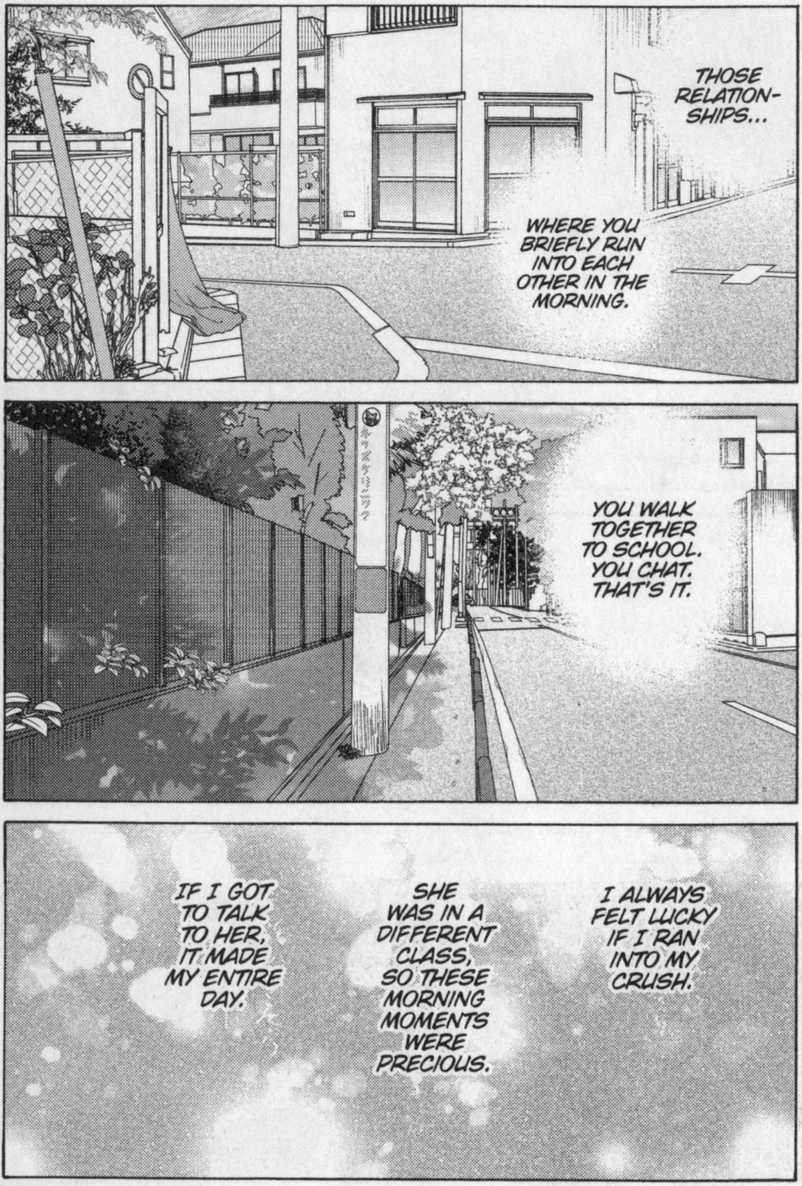
THOSE RELATION-SHIPS...
WHERE YOU BRIEFLY RUN INTO EACH OTHER IN THE MORNING.
YOU WALK TOGETHER TO SCHOOL. YOU CHAT. THAT'S IT.
I ALWAYS FELT LUCKY IF I RAN INTO MY CRUSH.
SHE WAS IN A DIFFERENT CLASS, SO THESE MORNING MOMENTS WERE PRECIOUS.
IF I GOT TO TALK TO HER, IT MADE MY ENTIRE DAY.

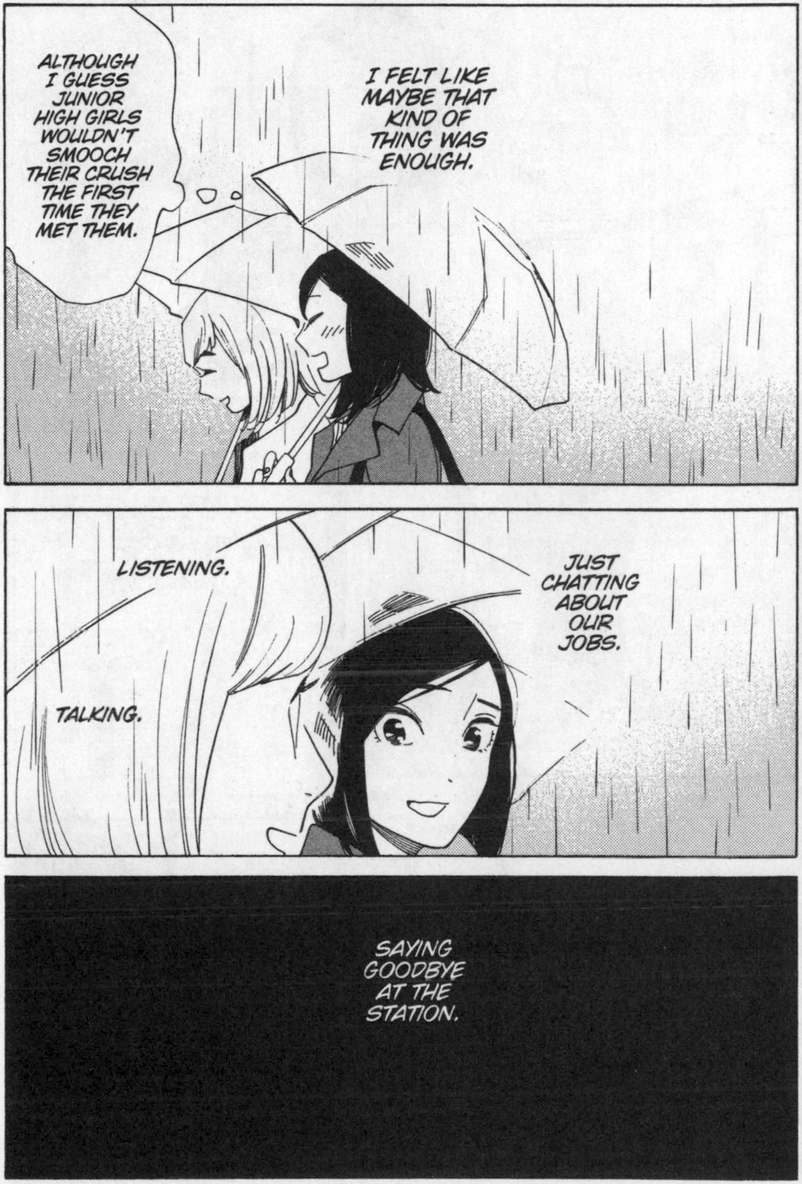
I FELT LIKE MAYBE THAT KIND OF THING WAS ENOUGH.
ALTHOUGH I GUESS JUNIOR HIGH GIRLS WOULDN'T SMOOCH THEIR CRUSH THE FIRST TIME THEY MET THEM.
JUST CHATTING ABOUT OUR JOBS.
LISTENING.
TALKING.
SAYING GOODBYE AT THE STATION.

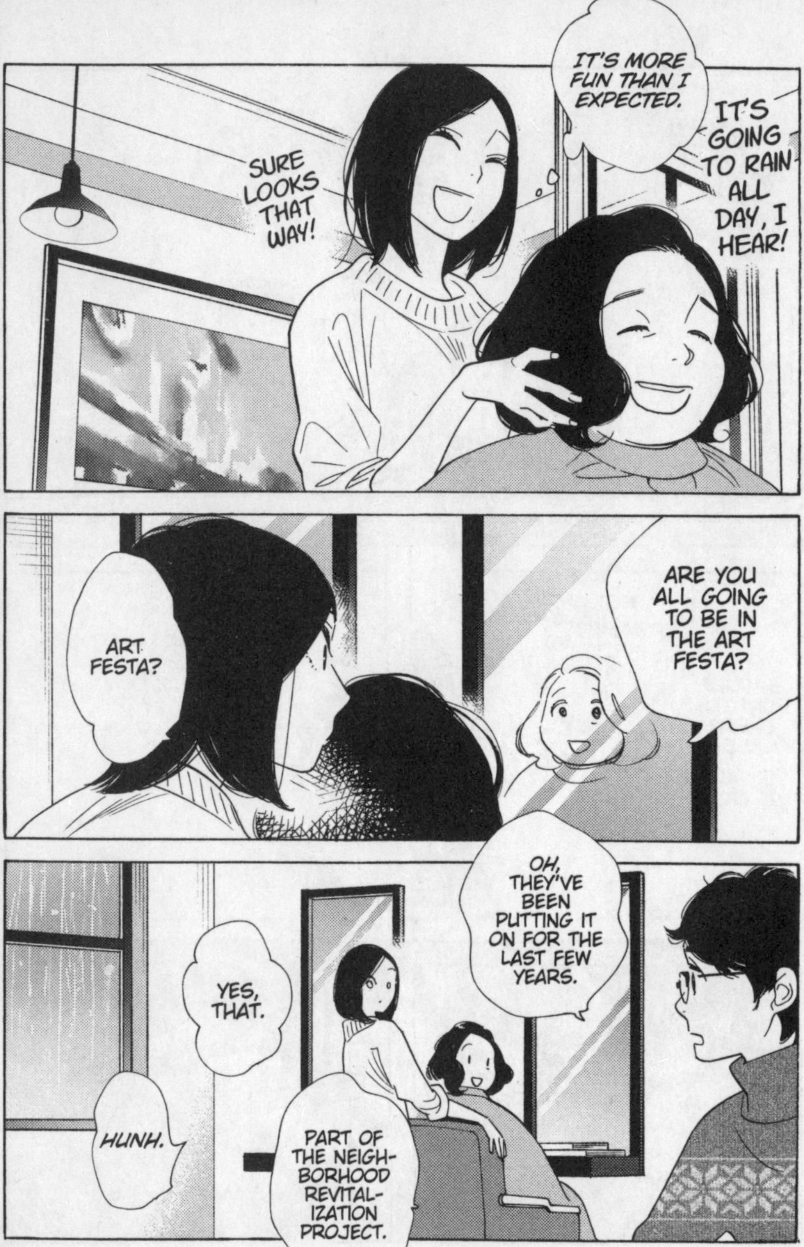
IT'S GOING TO RAIN ALL DAY, I HEAR!
IT'S MORE FUN THAN I EXPECTED.
SURE LOOKS THAT WAY!
ARE YOU ALL GOING TO BE IN THE ART FESTA?
ART FESTA?
OH, THEY'VE BEEN PUTTING IT ON FOR THE LAST FEW YEARS.
PART OF THE NEIGHBORHOOD REVITALIZATION PROJECT.
YES, THAT.
HUNH.

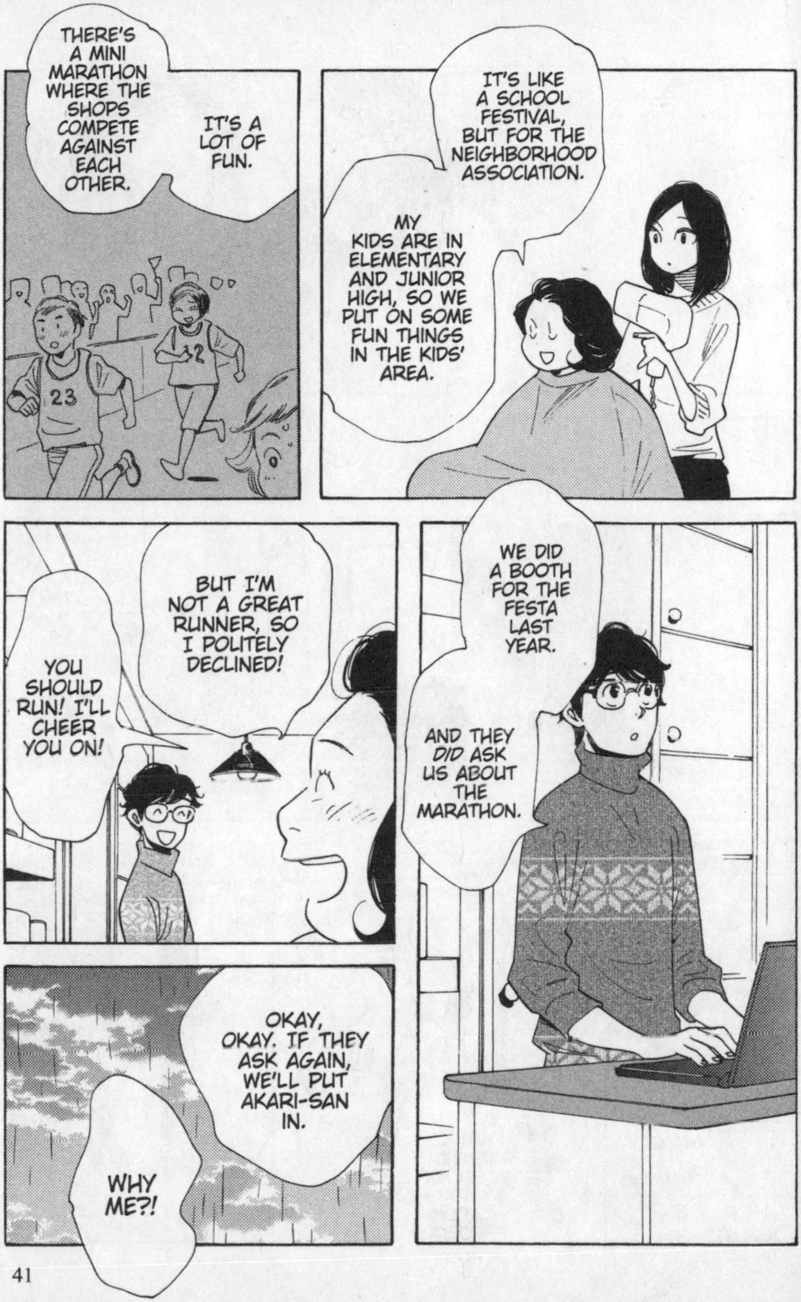
IT'S LIKE A SCHOOL FESTIVAL, BUT FOR THE NEIGHBORHOOD ASSOCIATION.
MY KIDS ARE IN ELEMENTARY AND JUNIOR HIGH, SO WE PUT ON SOME FUN THINGS IN THE KIDS' AREA.
THERE'S A MINI MARATHON WHERE THE SHOPS COMPETE AGAINST EACH OTHER.
IT'S A LOT OF FUN.
WE DID A BOOTH FOR THE FESTA LAST YEAR.
AND THEY *DID* ASK US ABOUT THE MARATHON.
BUT I'M NOT A GREAT RUNNER, SO I POLITELY DECLINED!
YOU SHOULD RUN! I'LL CHEER YOU ON!
OKAY, OKAY. IF THEY ASK AGAIN, WE'LL PUT AKARI-SAN IN.
WHY ME?!

cut room
bianca

42

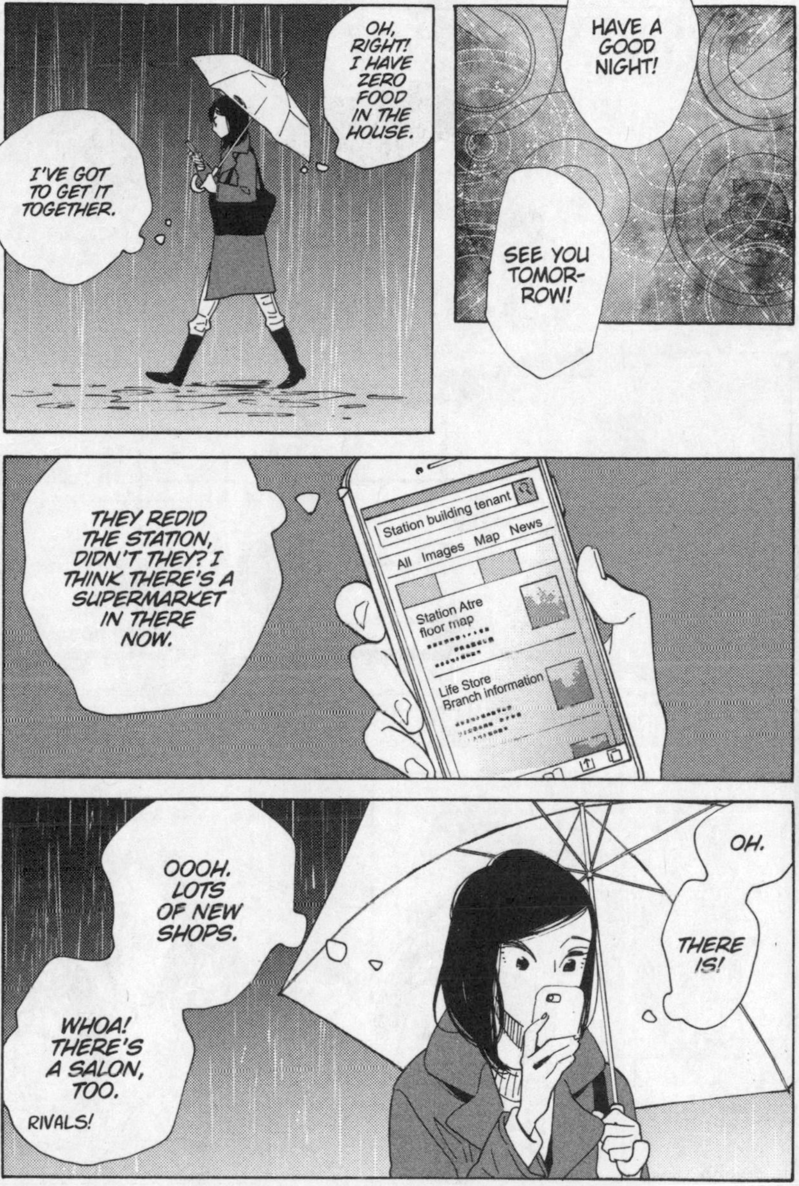
HAVE A GOOD NIGHT!
SEE YOU TOMORROW!
OH, RIGHT! I HAVE ZERO FOOD IN THE HOUSE.
I'VE GOT TO GET IT TOGETHER.
Station building tenant
All Images Map News
Station Atre floor map
Life Store Branch information
THEY REDID THE STATION, DIDN'T THEY? I THINK THERE'S A SUPERMARKET IN THERE NOW.
OH.
THERE IS!
OOOH. LOTS OF NEW SHOPS.
WHOA! THERE'S A SALON, TOO.
RIVALS!

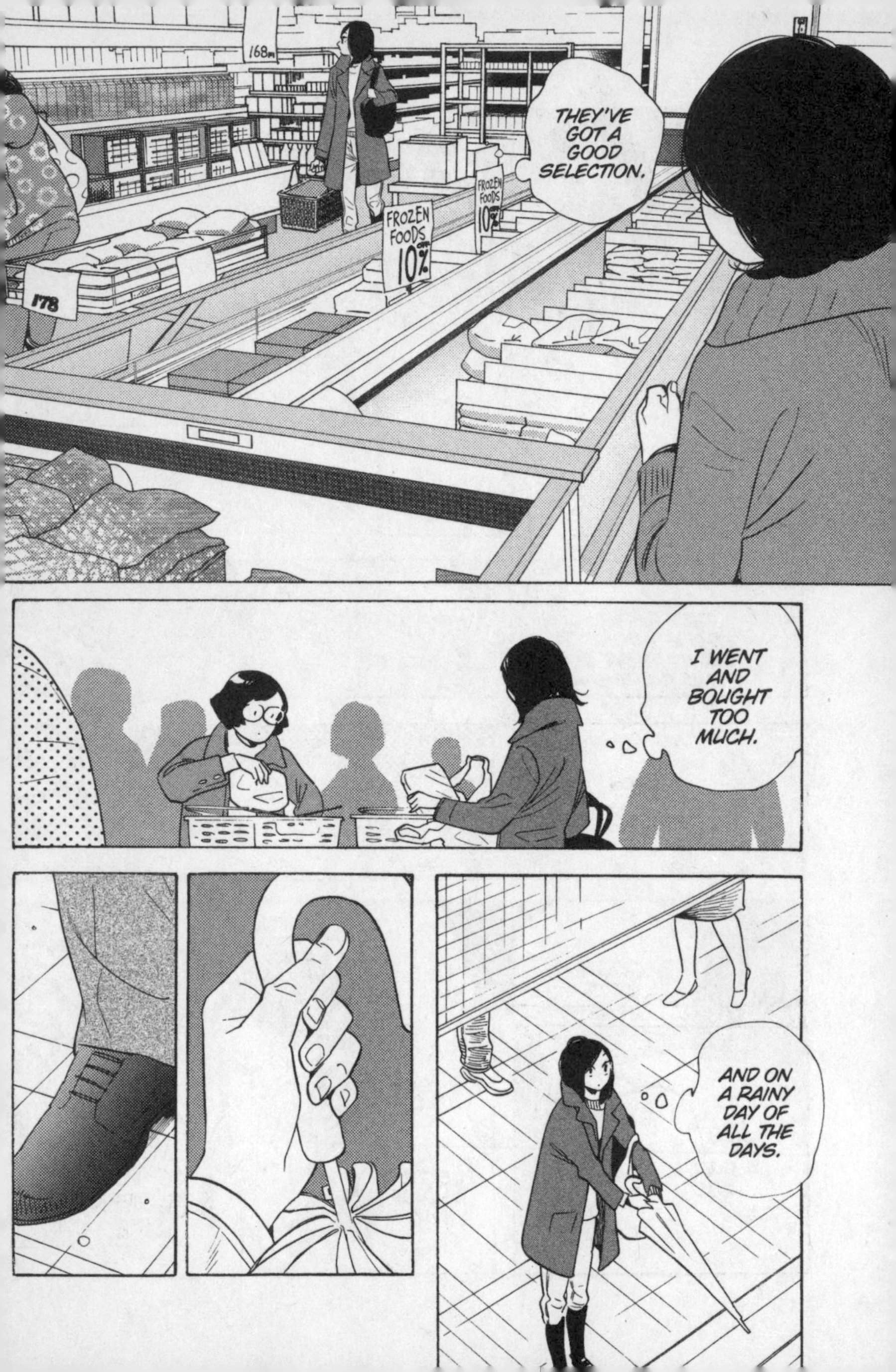
168円
THEY'VE GOT A GOOD SELECTION.
FROZEN FOODS 10% OFF
FROZEN FOODS 10%
178
I WENT AND BOUGHT TOO MUCH.
AND ON A RAINY DAY OF ALL THE DAYS.

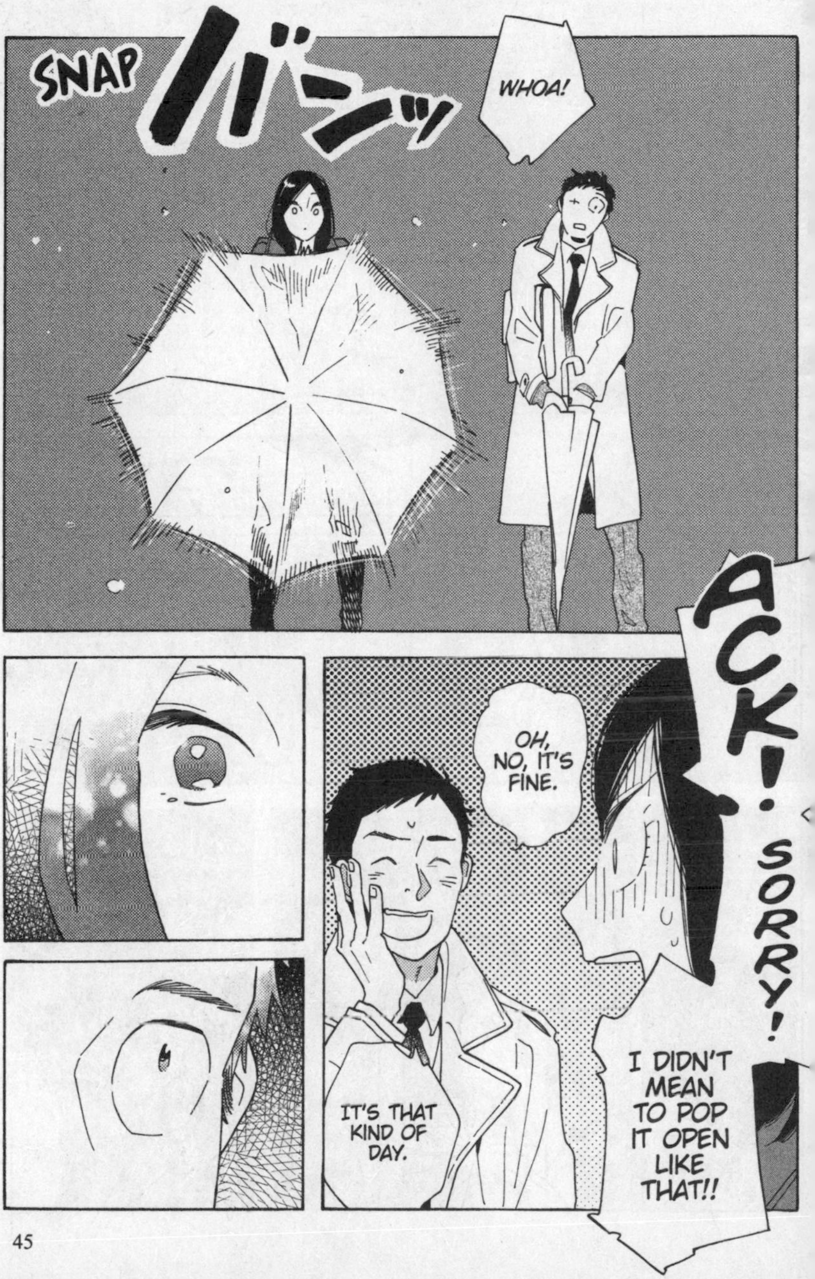
WHOA!
SNAP
バンッ
ACK! SORRY!
I DIDN'T MEAN TO POP IT OPEN LIKE THAT!!
OH, NO, IT'S FINE.
IT'S THAT KIND OF DAY.

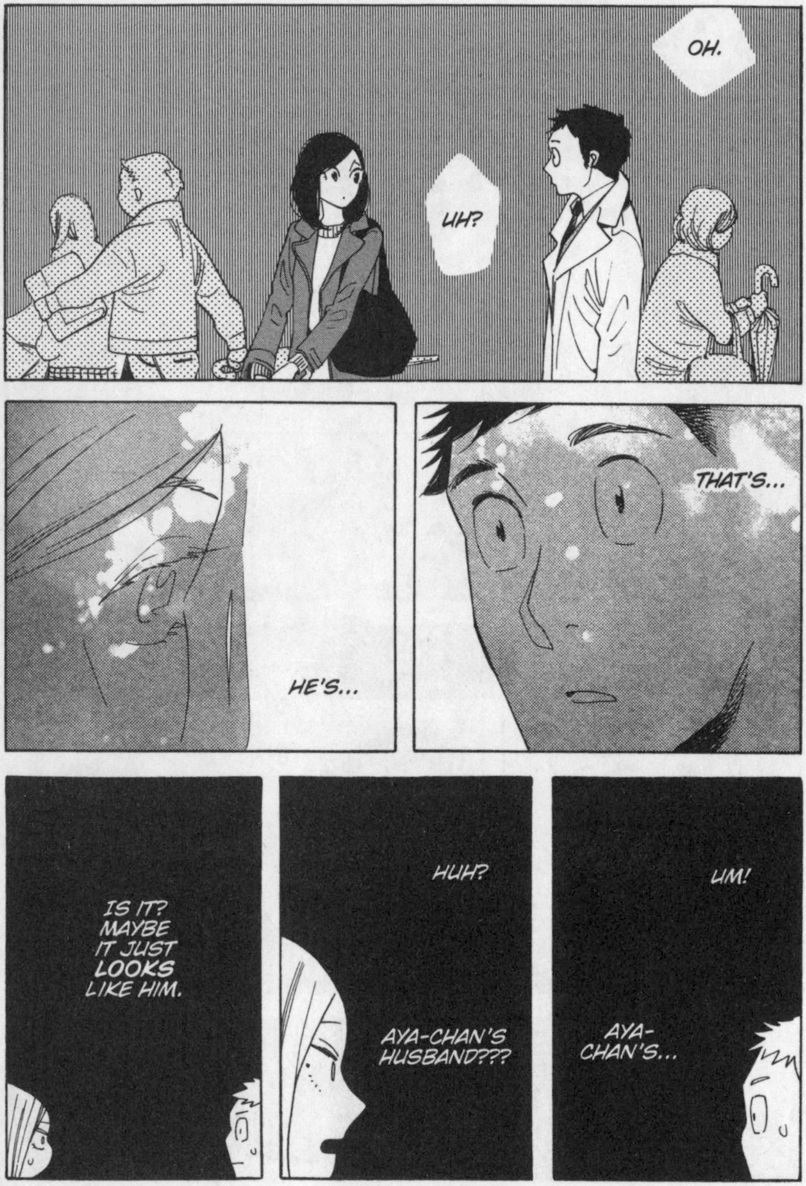
OH.
UH?
THAT'S...
HE'S...
UM!
AYA-CHAN'S...
HUH?
AYA-CHAN'S HUSBAND???
IS IT? MAYBE IT JUST **LOOKS** LIKE HIM.

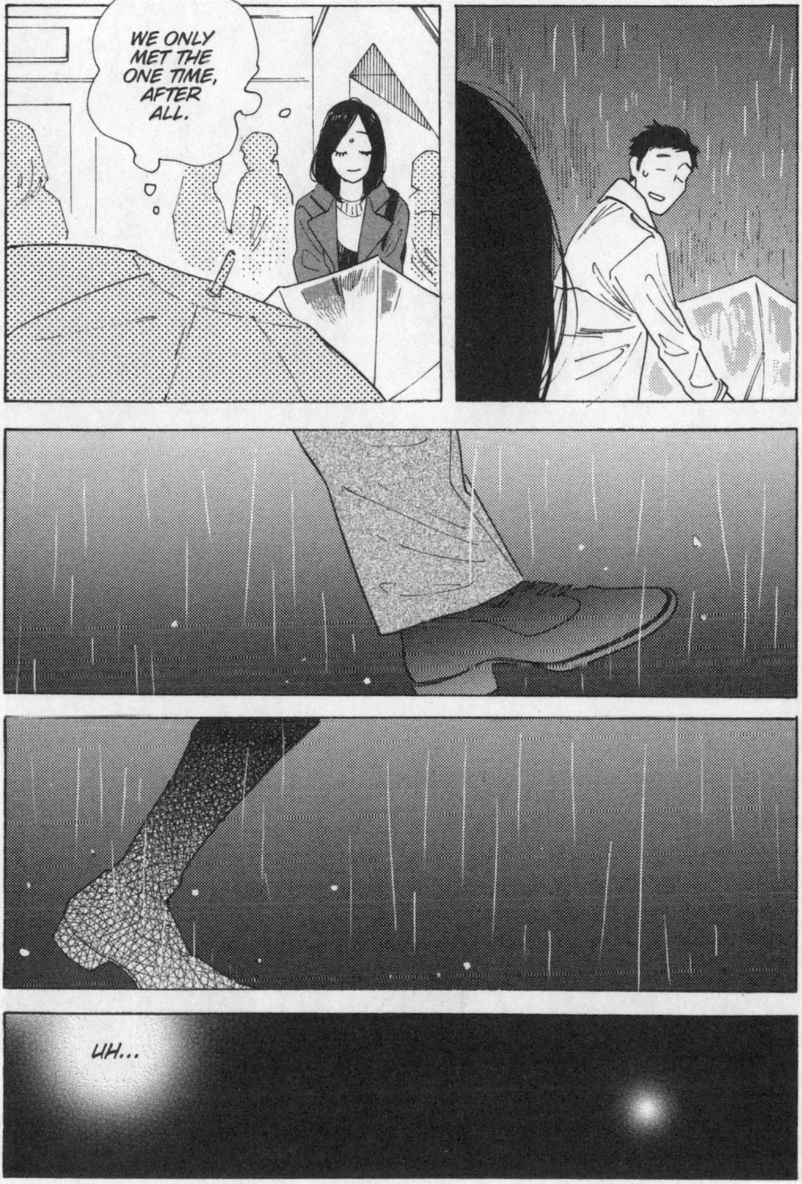
WE ONLY MET THE ONE TIME, AFTER ALL.
UH...

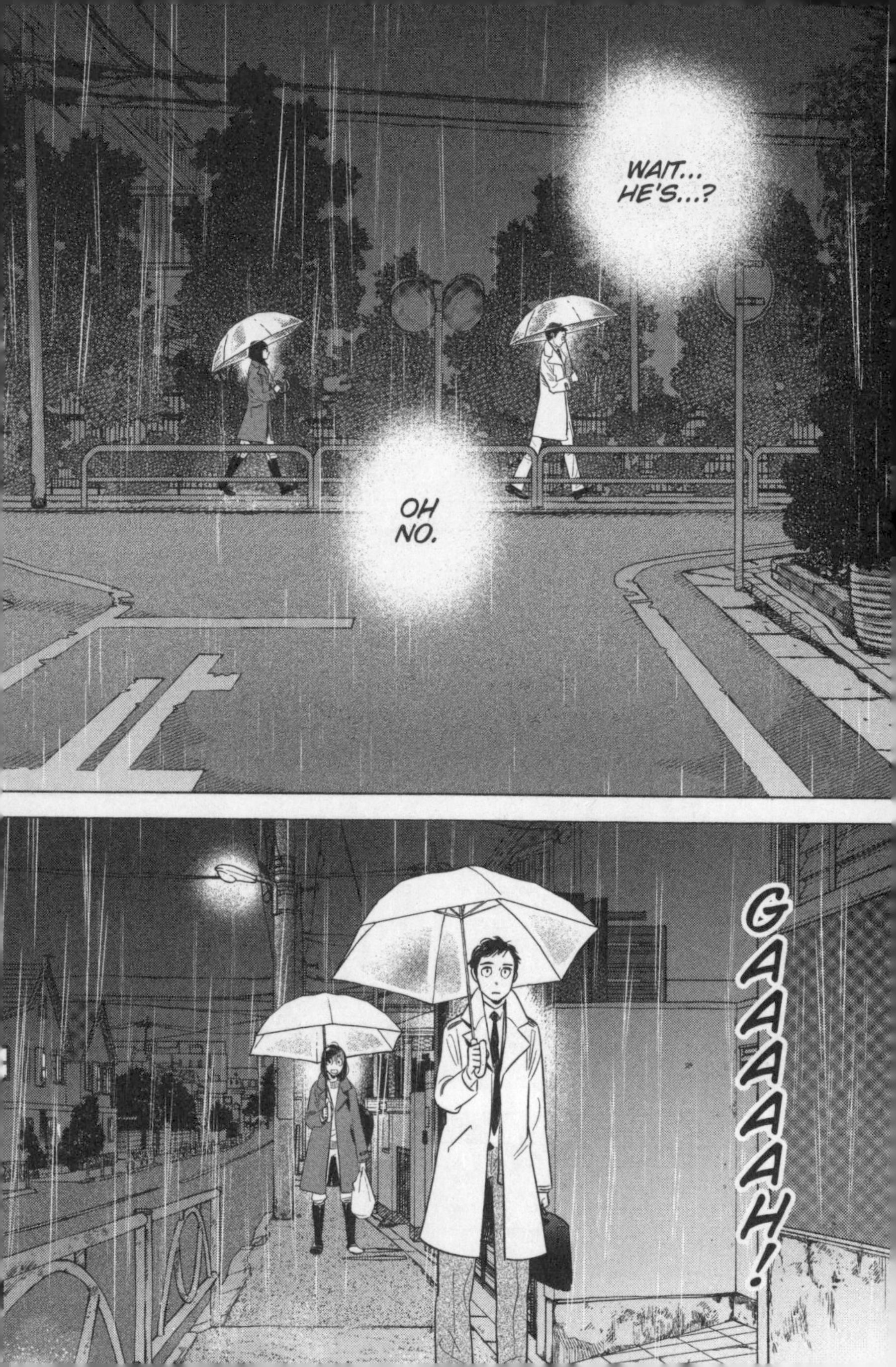
WAIT... HE'S...?
OH NO.
GAAAAAH!

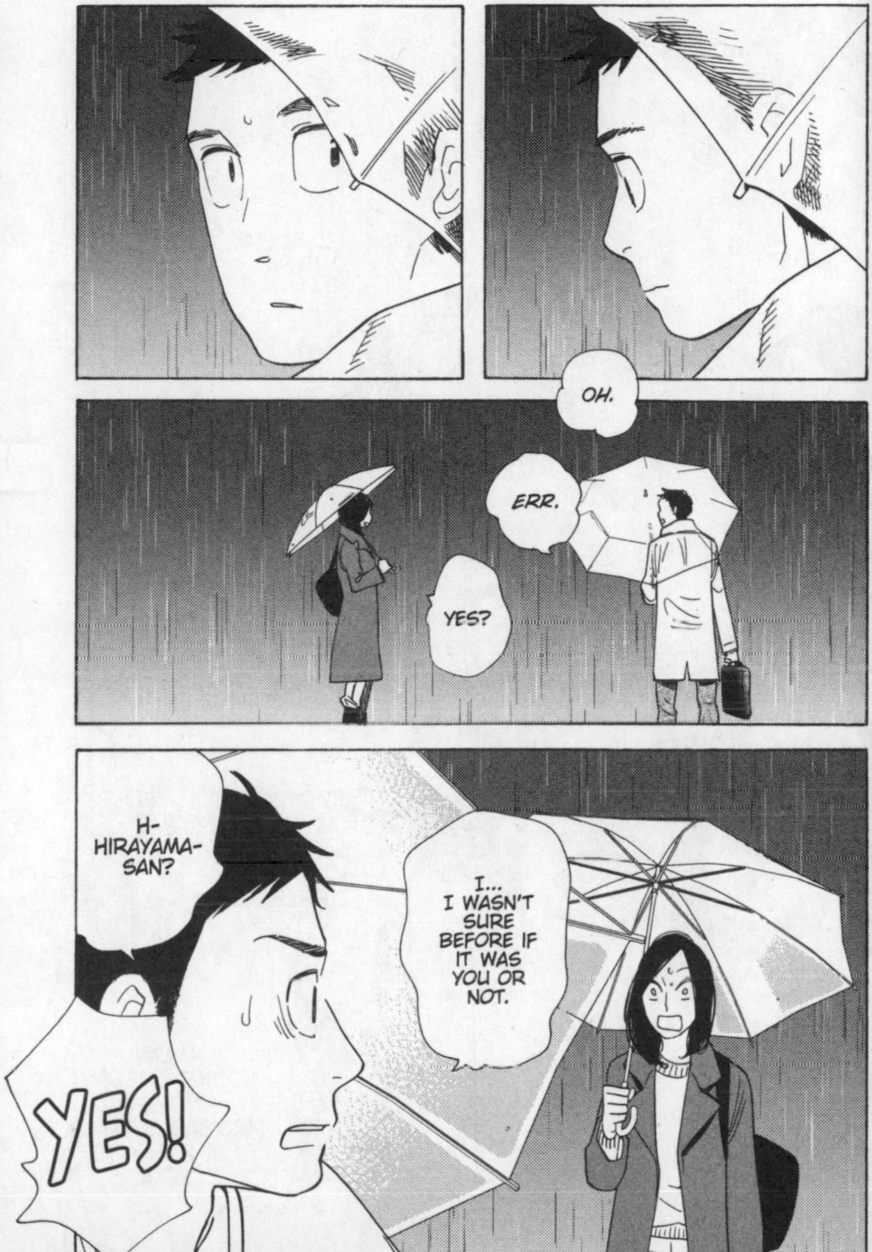
OH.
ERR.
YES?
I... I WASN'T SURE BEFORE IF IT WAS YOU OR NOT.
H-HIRAYAMA-SAN?
YES!

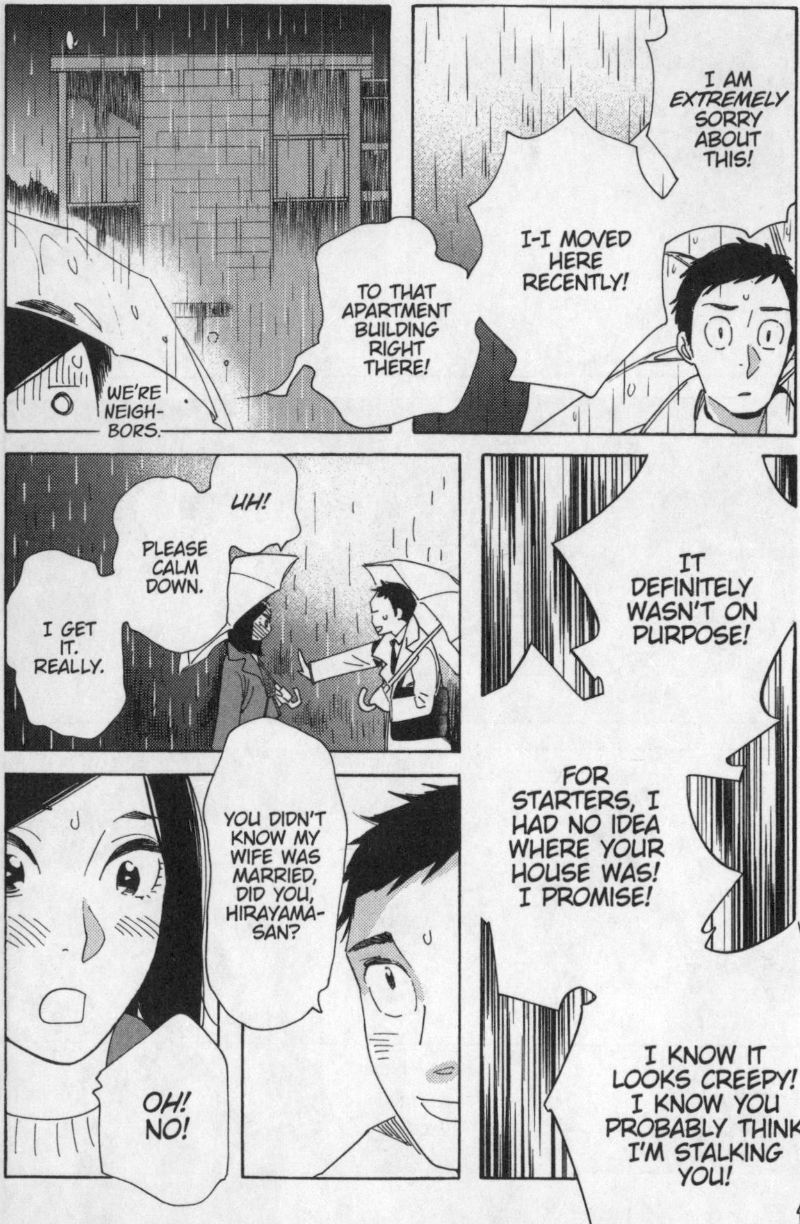
I AM EXTREMELY SORRY ABOUT THIS!
I-I MOVED HERE RECENTLY!
TO THAT APARTMENT BUILDING RIGHT THERE!
WE'RE NEIGH-BORS.
IT DEFINITELY WASN'T ON PURPOSE!
UH!
PLEASE CALM DOWN.
I GET IT. REALLY.
FOR STARTERS, I HAD NO IDEA WHERE YOUR HOUSE WAS! I PROMISE!
I KNOW IT LOOKS CREEPY! I KNOW YOU PROBABLY THINK I'M STALKING YOU!
YOU DIDN'T KNOW MY WIFE WAS MARRIED, DID YOU, HIRAYAMA-SAN?
OH! NO!

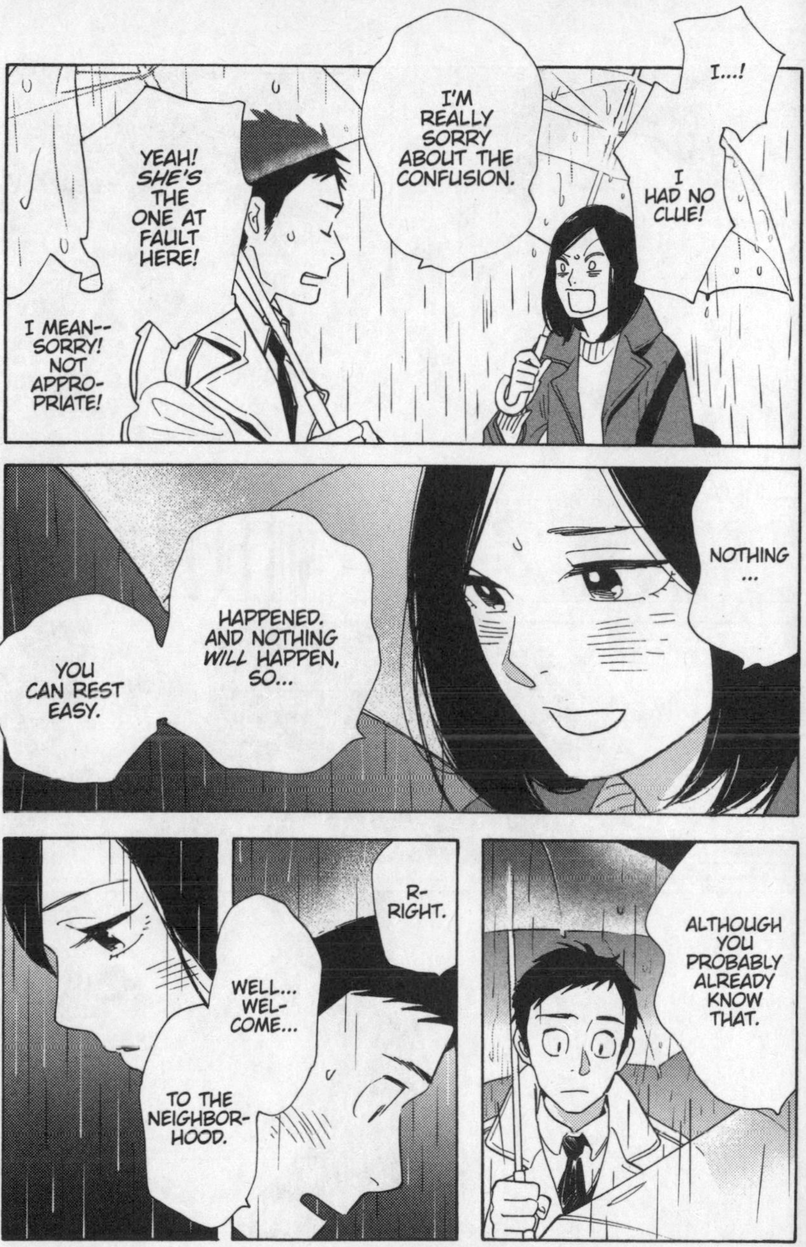
I...!
I HAD NO CLUE!
I'M REALLY SORRY ABOUT THE CONFUSION.
YEAH! *SHE'S* THE ONE AT FAULT HERE!
I MEAN-- SORRY! NOT APPROPRIATE!
NOTHING ...
HAPPENED. AND NOTHING *WILL* HAPPEN, SO...
YOU CAN REST EASY.
ALTHOUGH YOU PROBABLY ALREADY KNOW THAT.
R- RIGHT.
WELL... WEL- COME...
TO THE NEIGHBOR- HOOD.

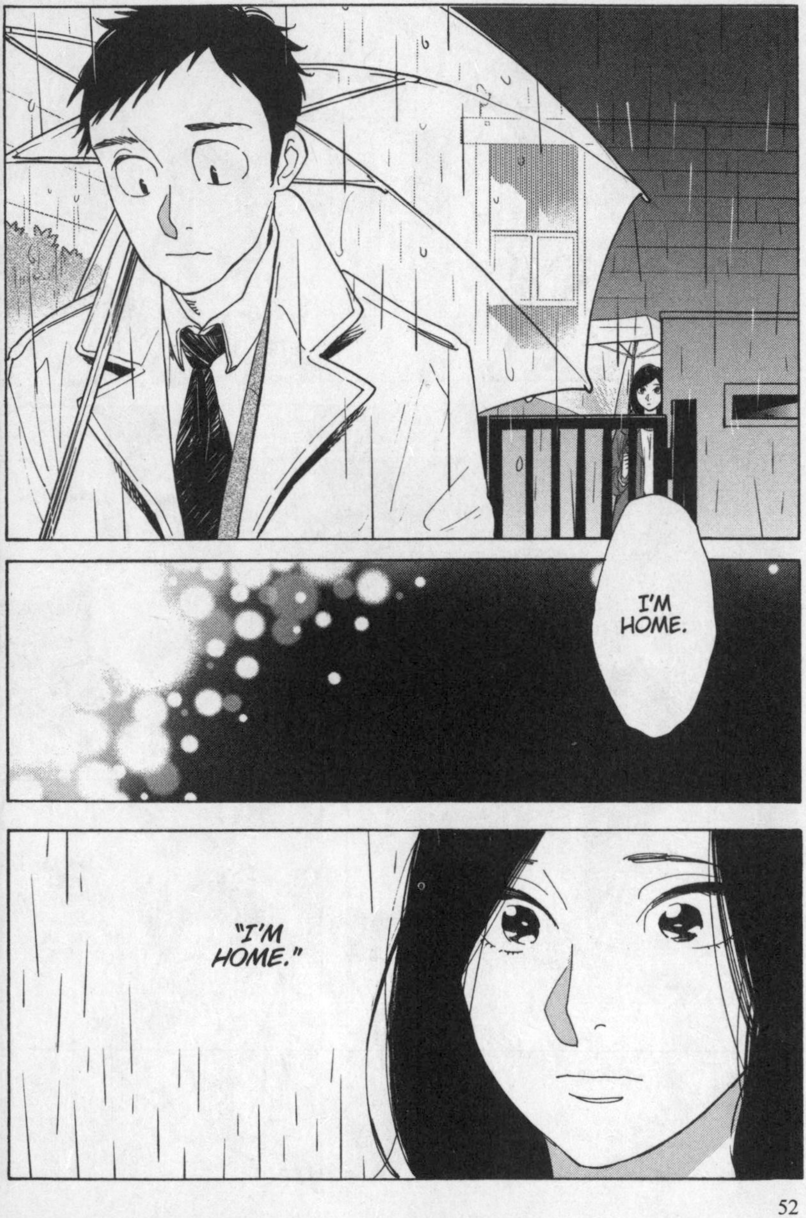
I'M HOME.
"I'M HOME."

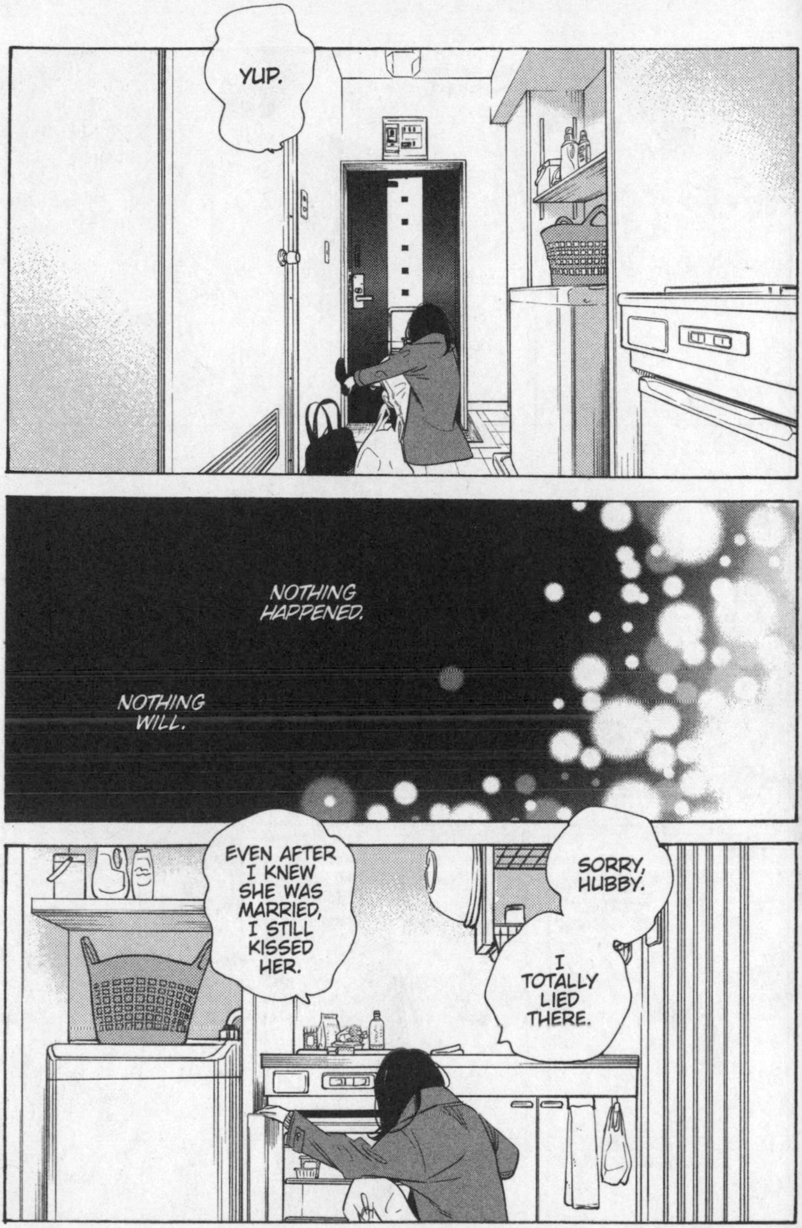
YUP.
NOTHING HAPPENED.
NOTHING WILL.
SORRY, HUBBY.
I TOTALLY LIED THERE.
EVEN AFTER I KNEW SHE WAS MARRIED, I STILL KISSED HER.

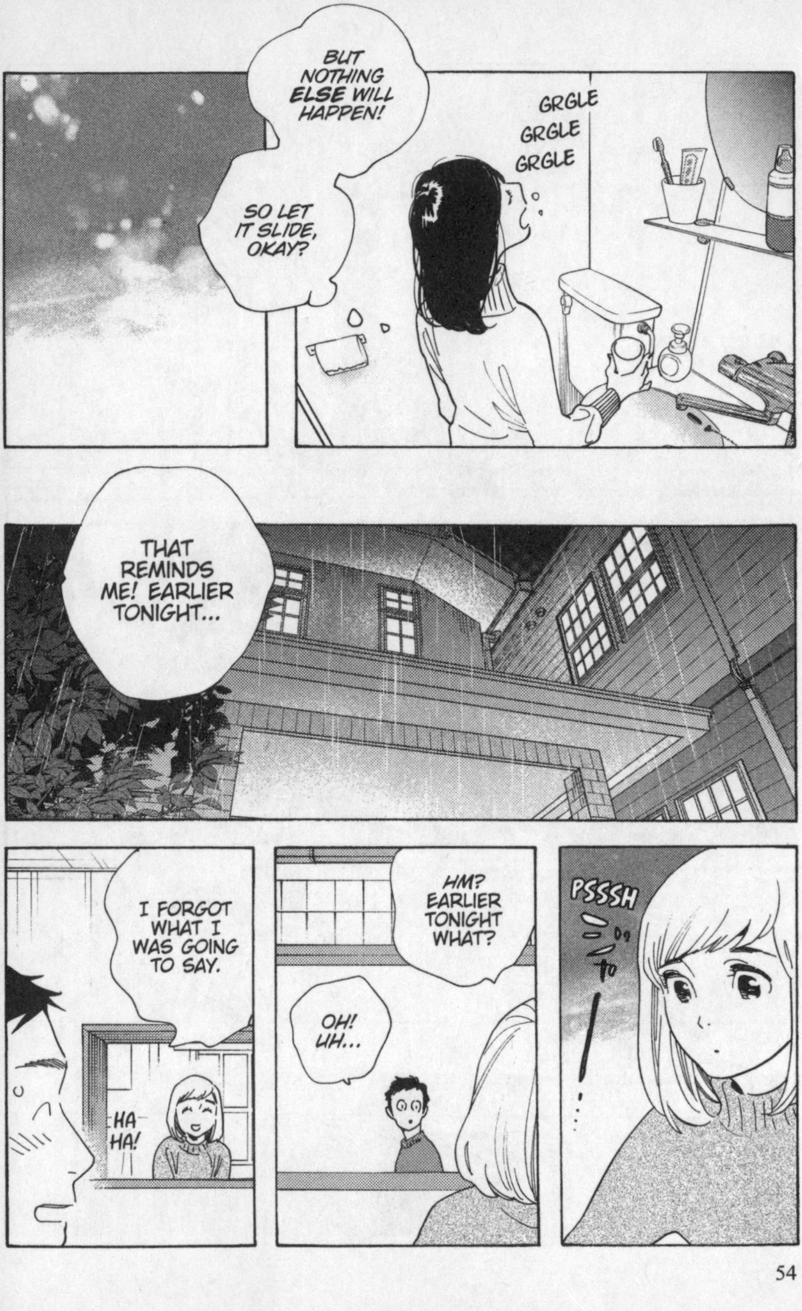
GRGLE
GRGLE
GRGLE
BUT NOTHING ELSE WILL HAPPEN!
SO LET IT SLIDE, OKAY?
THAT REMINDS ME! EARLIER TONIGHT...
PSSSH
HM? EARLIER TONIGHT WHAT?
OH! UH...
I FORGOT WHAT I WAS GOING TO SAY.
HA HA!

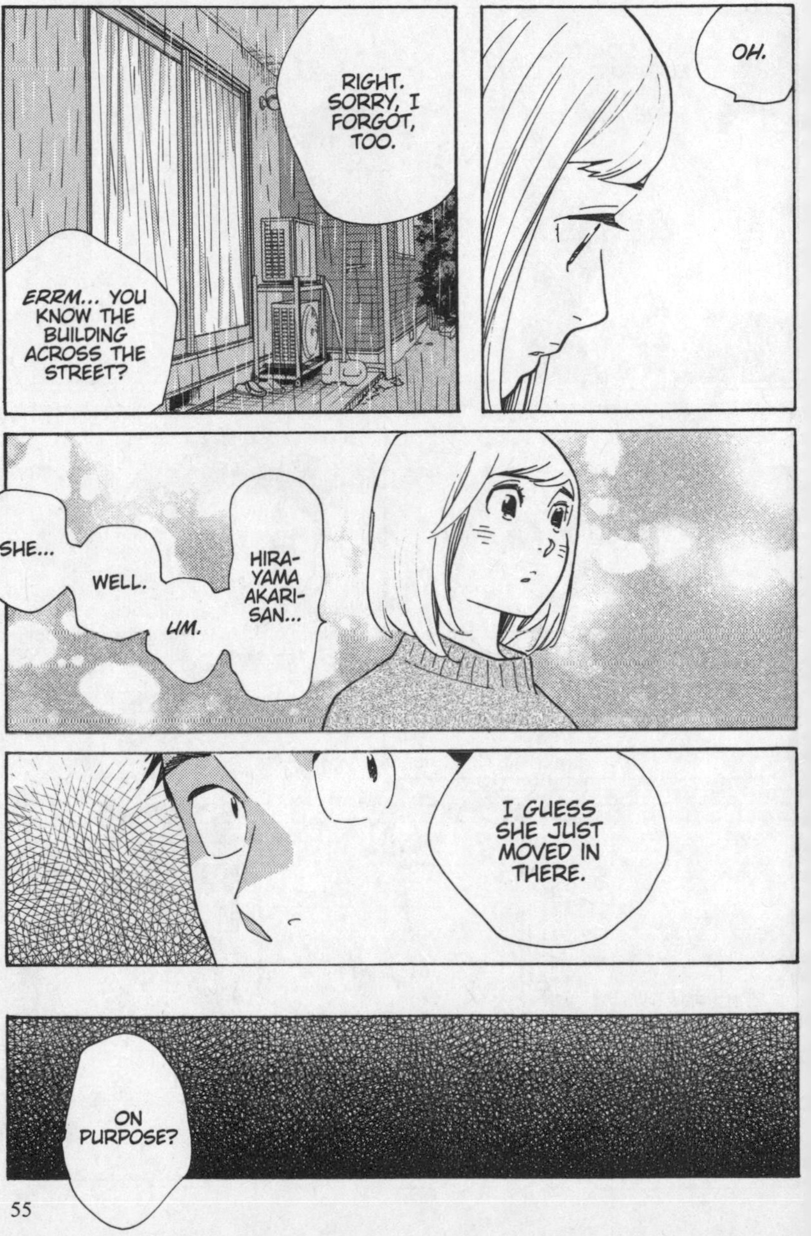
OH.
RIGHT. SORRY, I FORGOT, TOO.
ERRM... YOU KNOW THE BUILDING ACROSS THE STREET?
HIRA-YAMA AKARI-SAN...
UM.
WELL.
SHE...
I GUESS SHE JUST MOVED IN THERE.
ON PURPOSE?

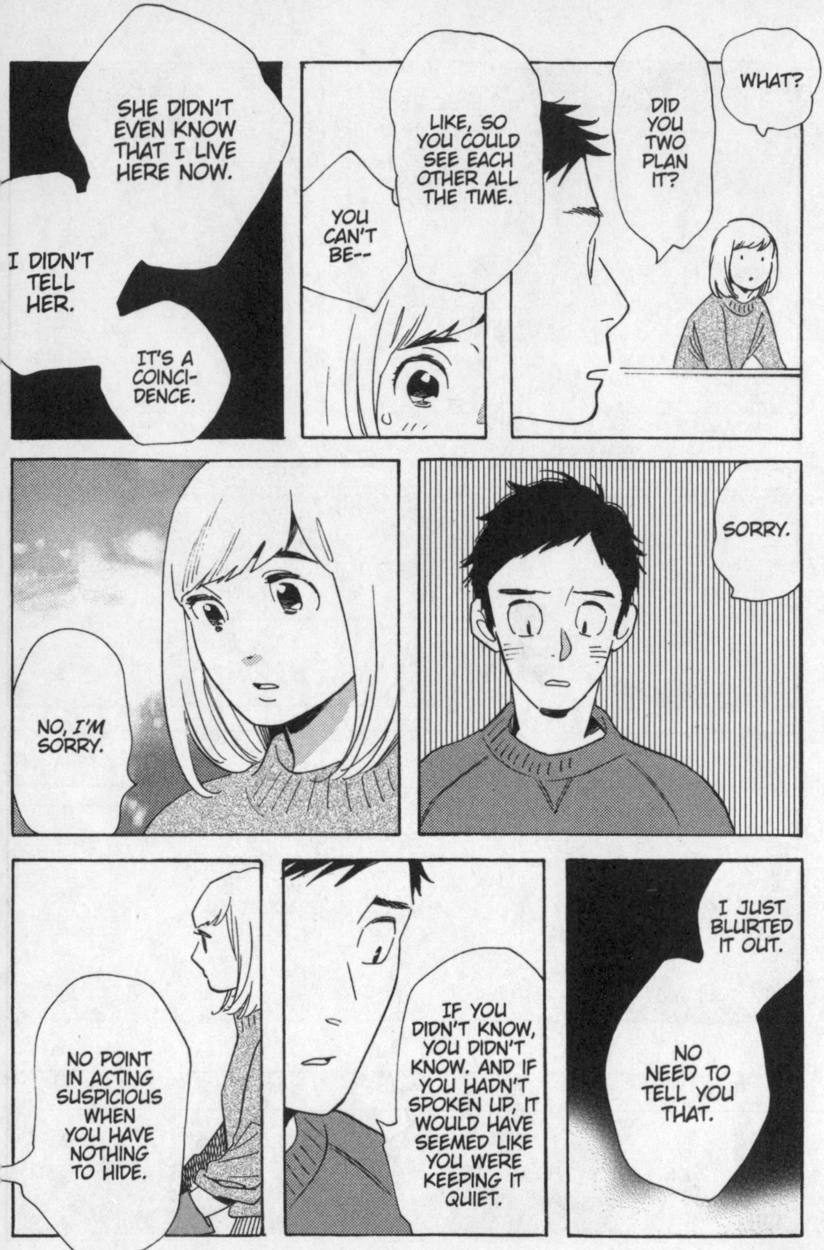
WHAT?
DID YOU TWO PLAN IT?
LIKE, SO YOU COULD SEE EACH OTHER ALL THE TIME.
YOU CAN'T BE--
SHE DIDN'T EVEN KNOW THAT I LIVE HERE NOW.
I DIDN'T TELL HER.
IT'S A COINCIDENCE.
SORRY.
NO, I'M SORRY.
I JUST BLURTED IT OUT.
NO NEED TO TELL YOU THAT.
IF YOU DIDN'T KNOW, YOU DIDN'T KNOW. AND IF YOU HADN'T SPOKEN UP, IT WOULD HAVE SEEMED LIKE YOU WERE KEEPING IT QUIET.
NO POINT IN ACTING SUSPICIOUS WHEN YOU HAVE NOTHING TO HIDE.

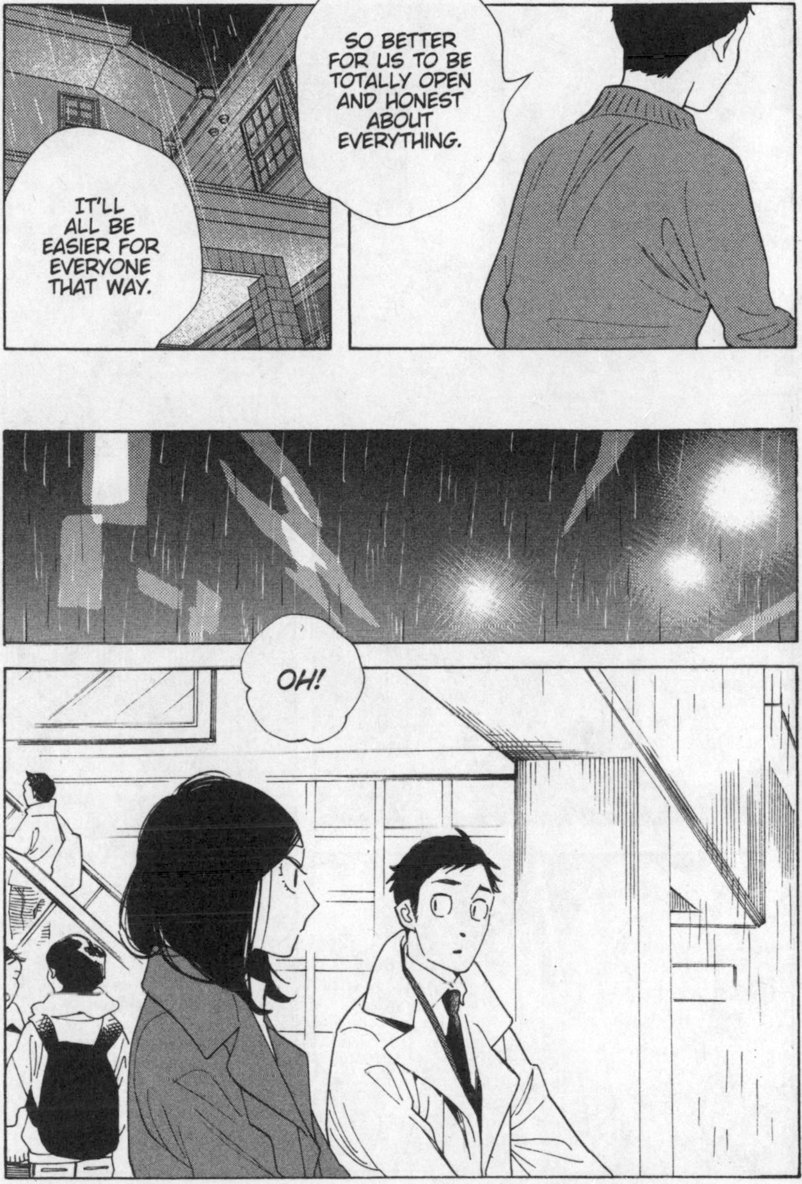
SO BETTER FOR US TO BE TOTALLY OPEN AND HONEST ABOUT EVERYTHING.
IT'LL ALL BE EASIER FOR EVERYONE THAT WAY.
OH!

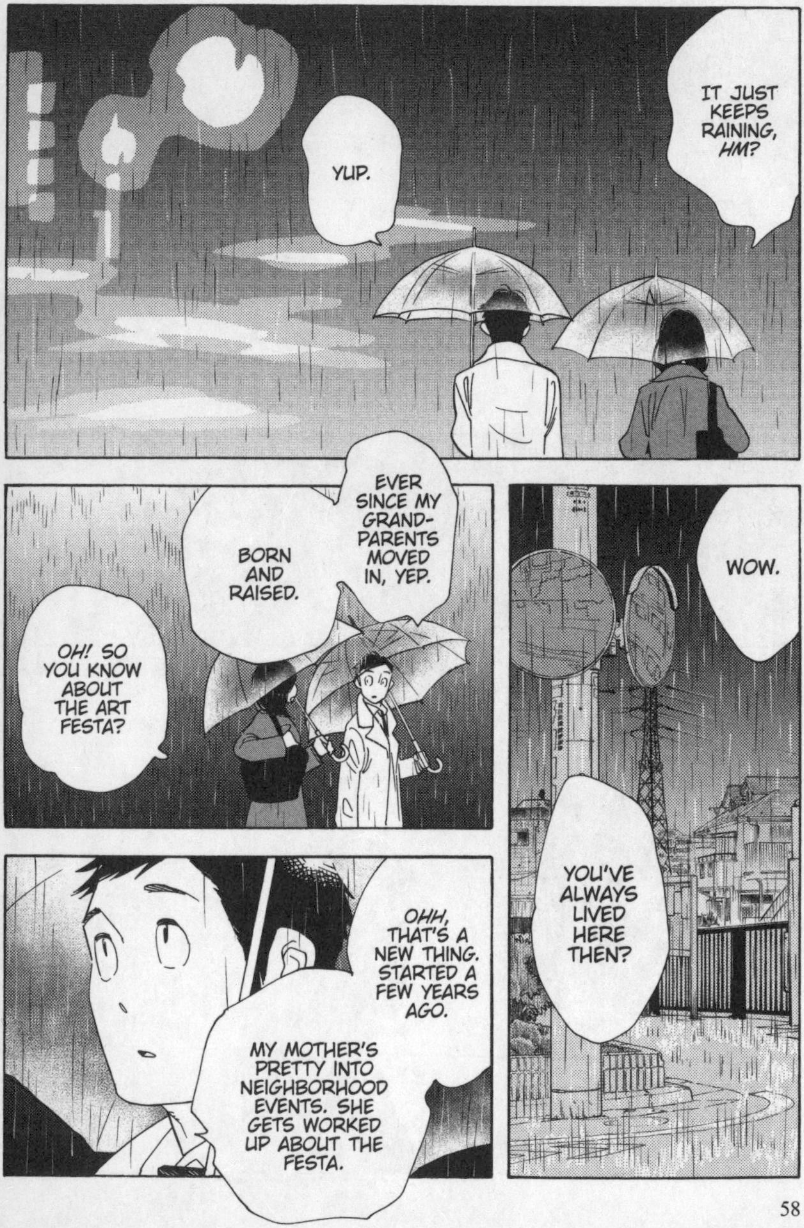

IT JUST KEEPS RAINING, *HM?*
YUP.
WOW.
YOU'VE ALWAYS LIVED HERE THEN?
EVER SINCE MY GRAND-PARENTS MOVED IN, YEP.
BORN AND RAISED.
OH! SO YOU KNOW ABOUT THE ART FESTA?
OHH, THAT'S A NEW THING. STARTED A FEW YEARS AGO.
MY MOTHER'S PRETTY INTO NEIGHBORHOOD EVENTS. SHE GETS WORKED UP ABOUT THE FESTA.

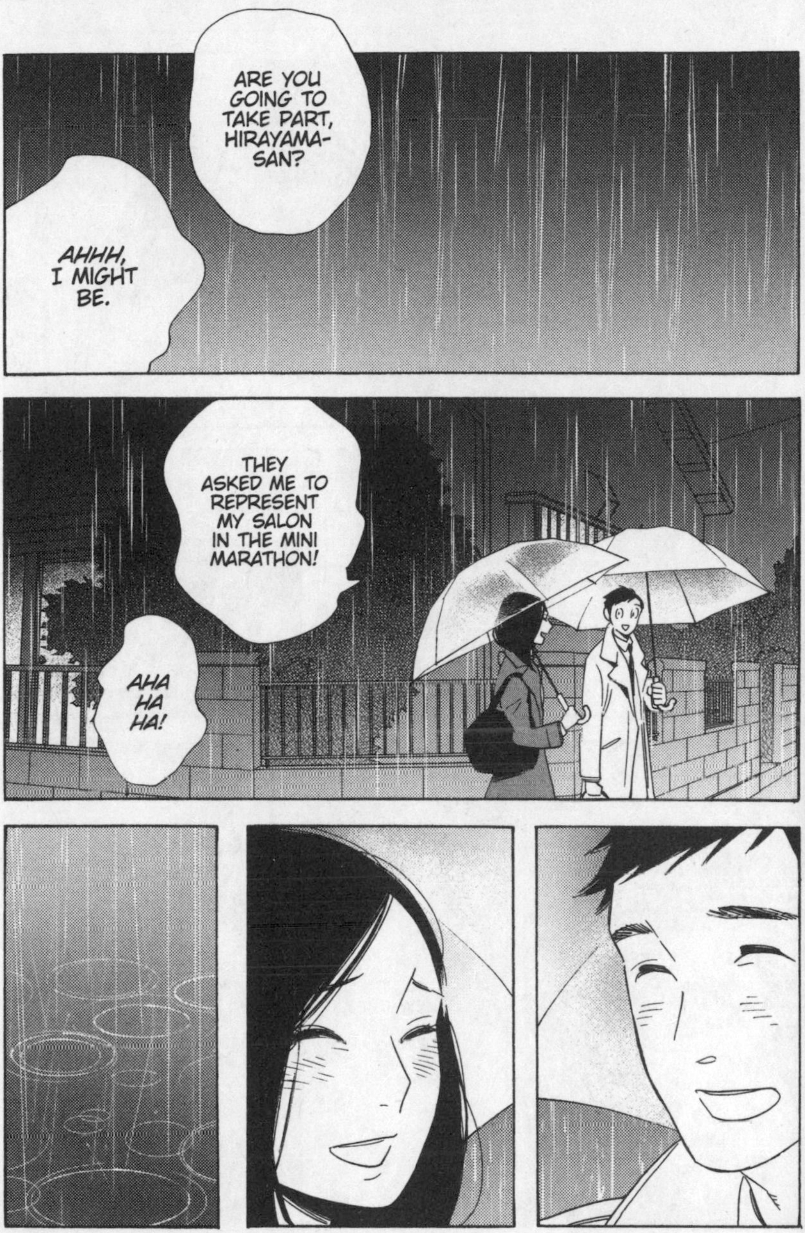
ARE YOU GOING TO TAKE PART, HIRAYAMA-SAN?
AHHH, I MIGHT BE.
THEY ASKED ME TO REPRESENT MY SALON IN THE MINI MARATHON!
AHA HA HA!

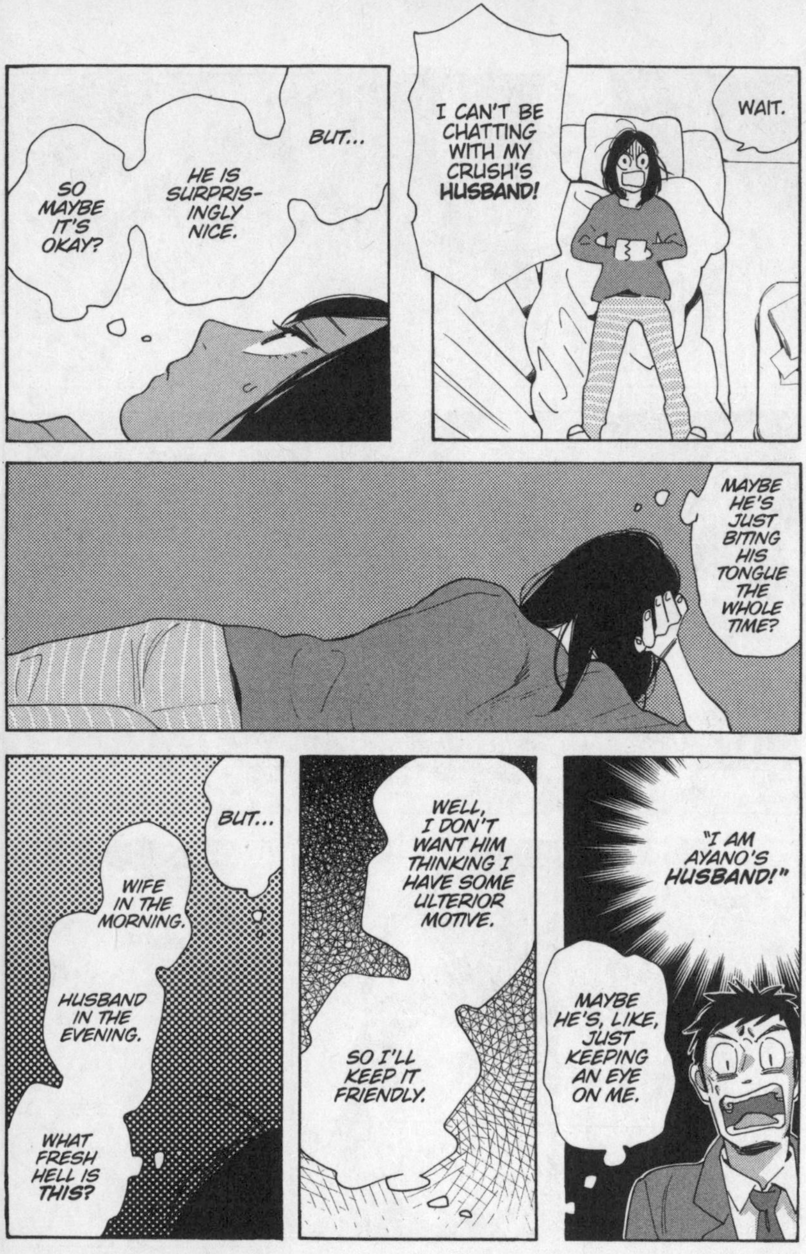
WAIT.
I CAN'T BE CHATTING WITH MY CRUSH'S **HUSBAND**!
BUT...
HE IS SURPRISINGLY NICE.
SO MAYBE IT'S OKAY?
MAYBE HE'S JUST BITING HIS TONGUE THE WHOLE TIME?
"I AM AYANO'S **HUSBAND**!"
MAYBE HE'S, LIKE, JUST KEEPING AN EYE ON ME.
WELL, I DON'T WANT HIM THINKING I HAVE SOME ULTERIOR MOTIVE.
SO I'LL KEEP IT FRIENDLY.
BUT...
WIFE IN THE MORNING.
HUSBAND IN THE EVENING.
WHAT FRESH HELL IS **THIS**?

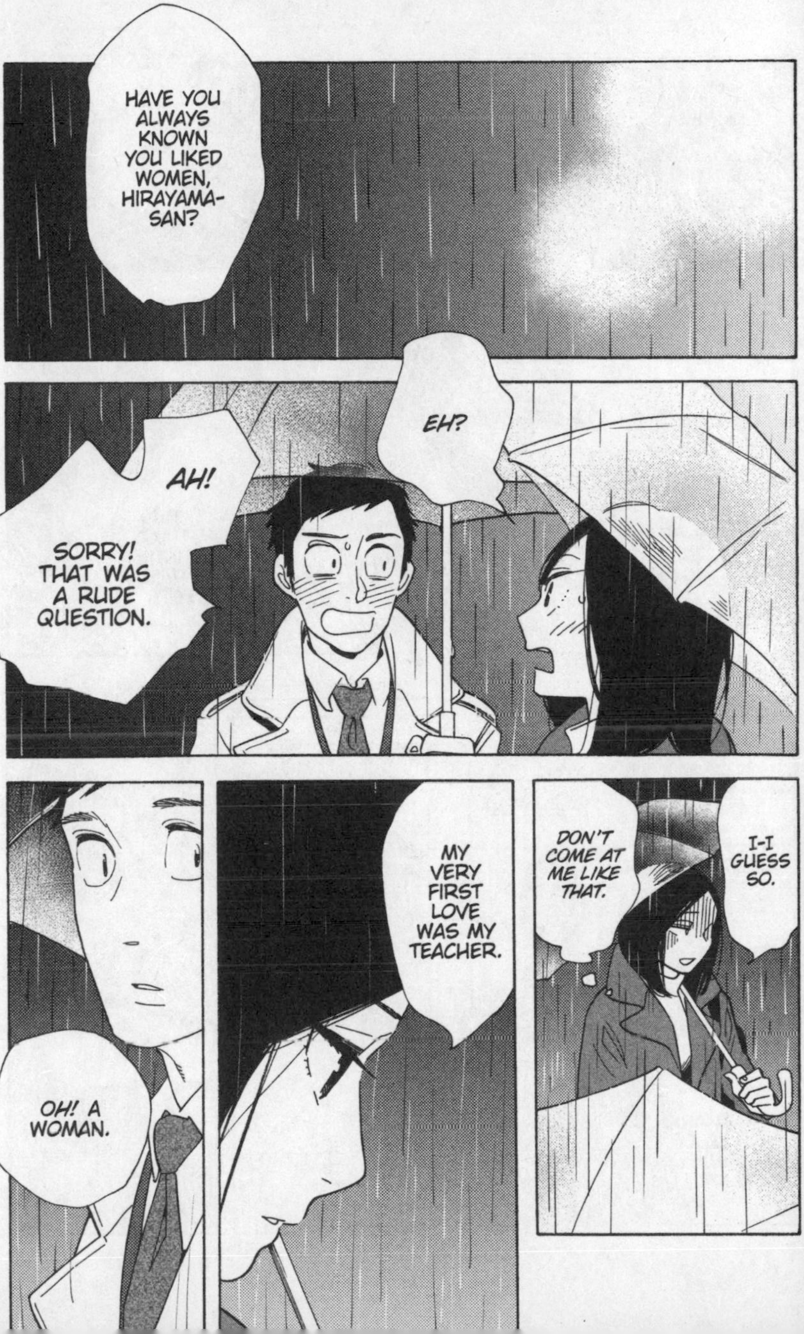
HAVE YOU ALWAYS KNOWN YOU LIKED WOMEN, HIRAYAMA-SAN?
EH?
AH!
SORRY! THAT WAS A RUDE QUESTION.
I-I GUESS SO.
DON'T COME AT ME LIKE THAT.
MY VERY FIRST LOVE WAS MY TEACHER.
OH! A WOMAN.

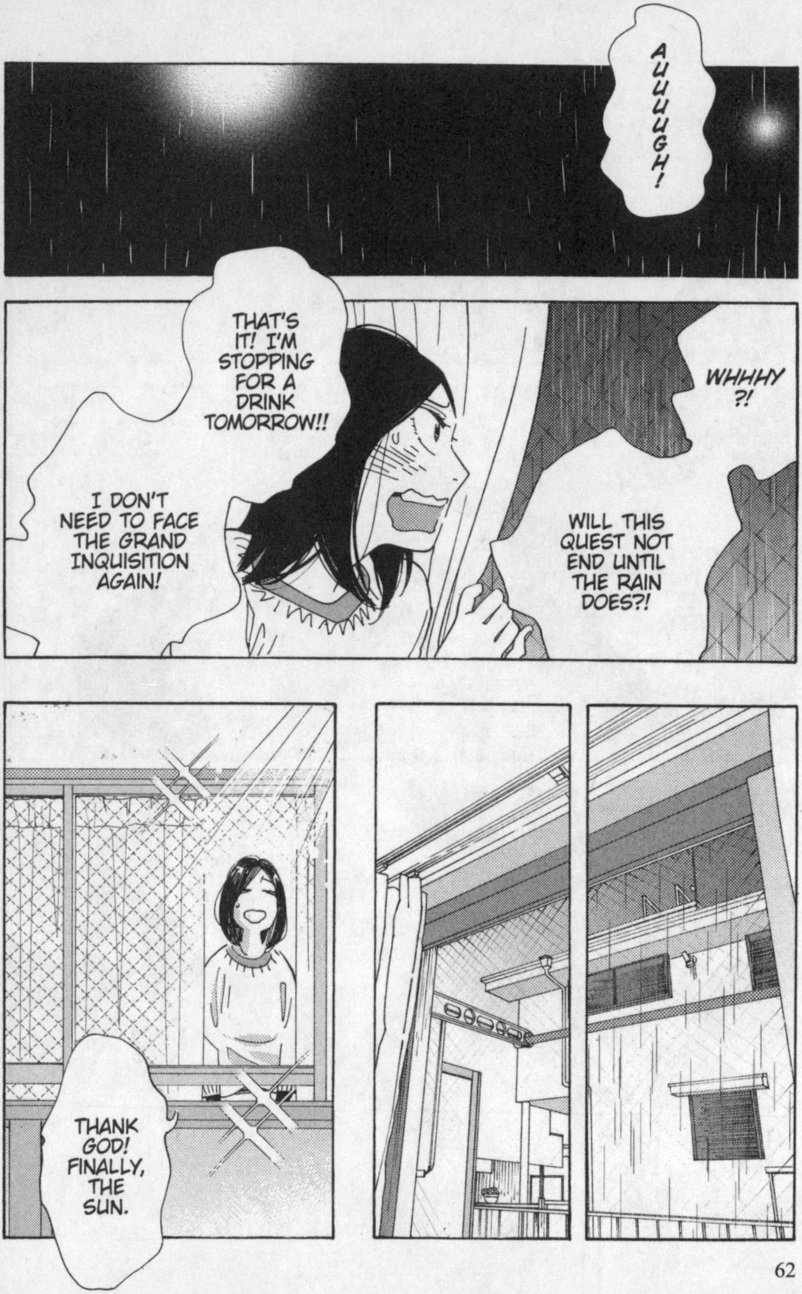
AUUUUGH!
WHHHY ?!
WILL THIS QUEST NOT END UNTIL THE RAIN DOES?!
THAT'S IT! I'M STOPPING FOR A DRINK TOMORROW!!
I DON'T NEED TO FACE THE GRAND INQUISITION AGAIN!
THANK GOD! FINALLY, THE SUN.

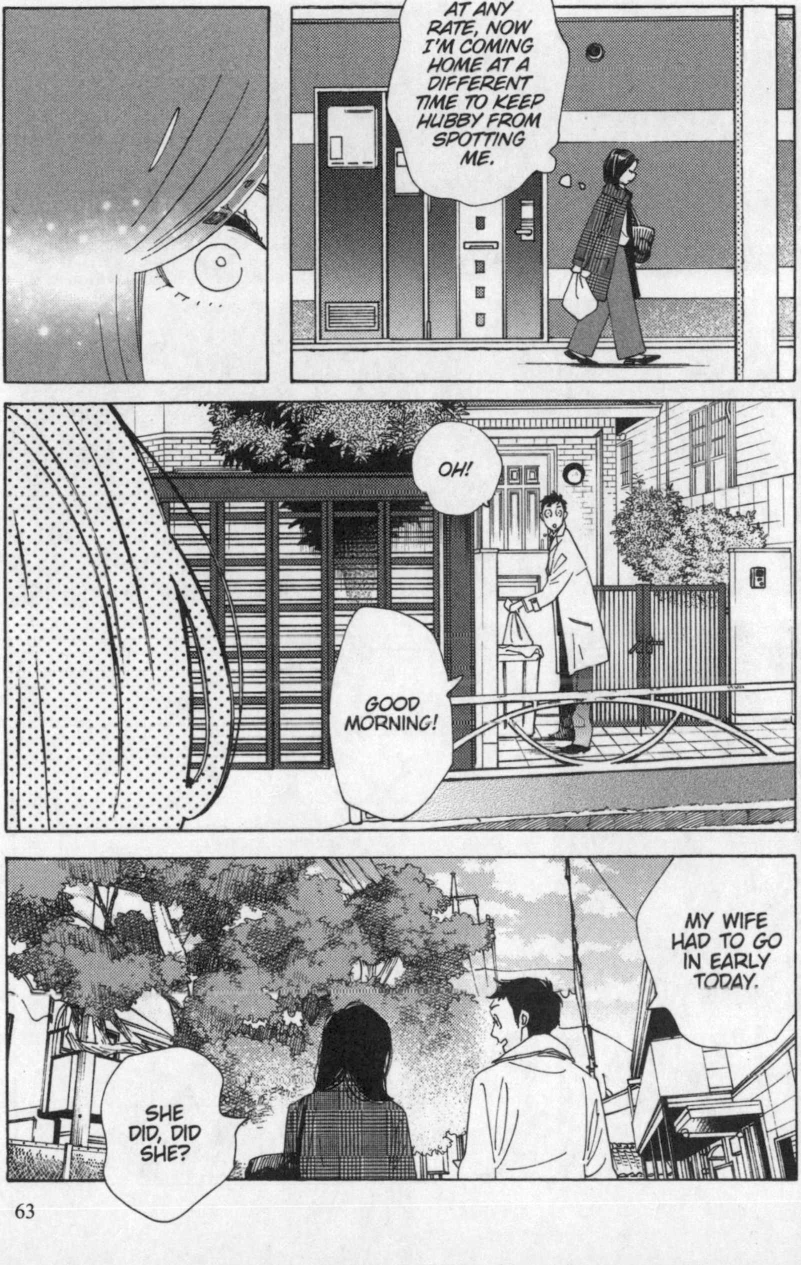
AT ANY RATE, NOW I'M COMING HOME AT A DIFFERENT TIME TO KEEP HUBBY FROM SPOTTING ME.
OH!
GOOD MORNING!
MY WIFE HAD TO GO IN EARLY TODAY.
SHE DID, DID SHE?

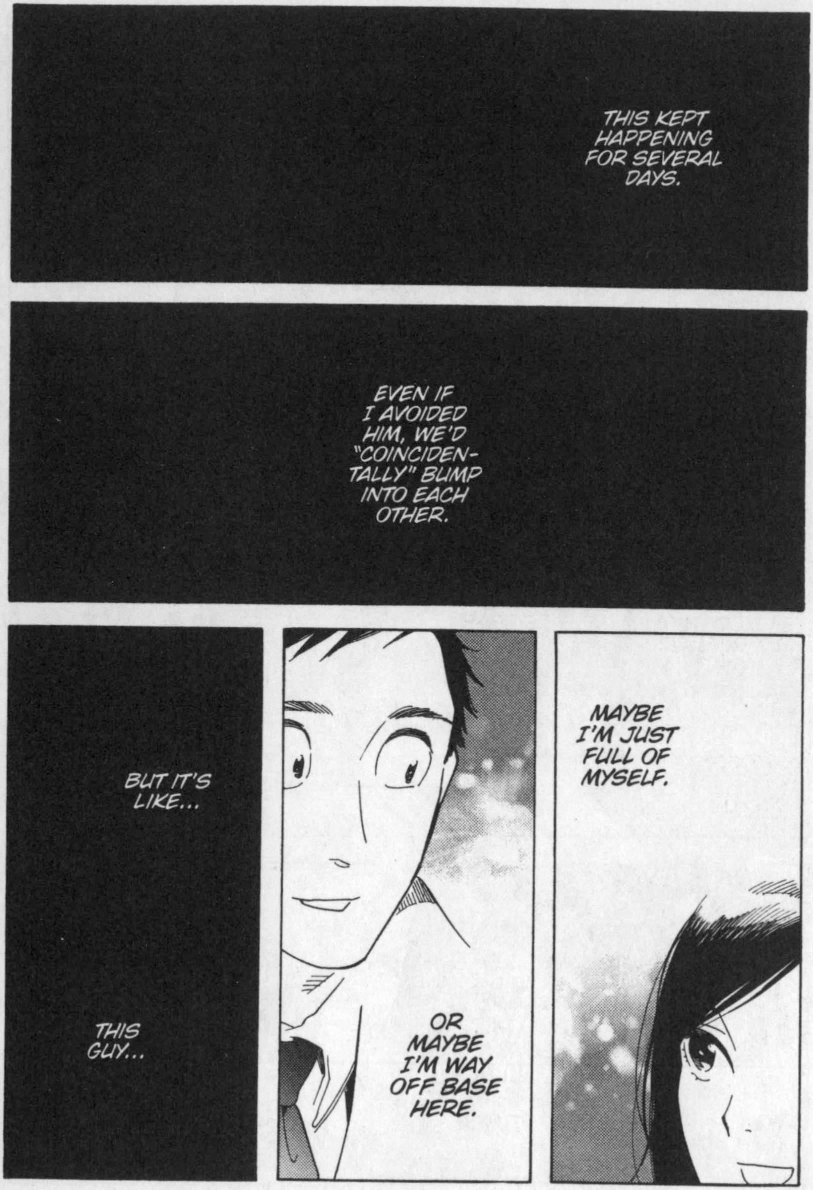
THIS KEPT HAPPENING FOR SEVERAL DAYS.
EVEN IF I AVOIDED HIM, WE'D "COINCIDENTALLY" BUMP INTO EACH OTHER.
MAYBE I'M JUST FULL OF MYSELF.
OR MAYBE I'M WAY OFF BASE HERE.
BUT IT'S LIKE...
THIS GUY...

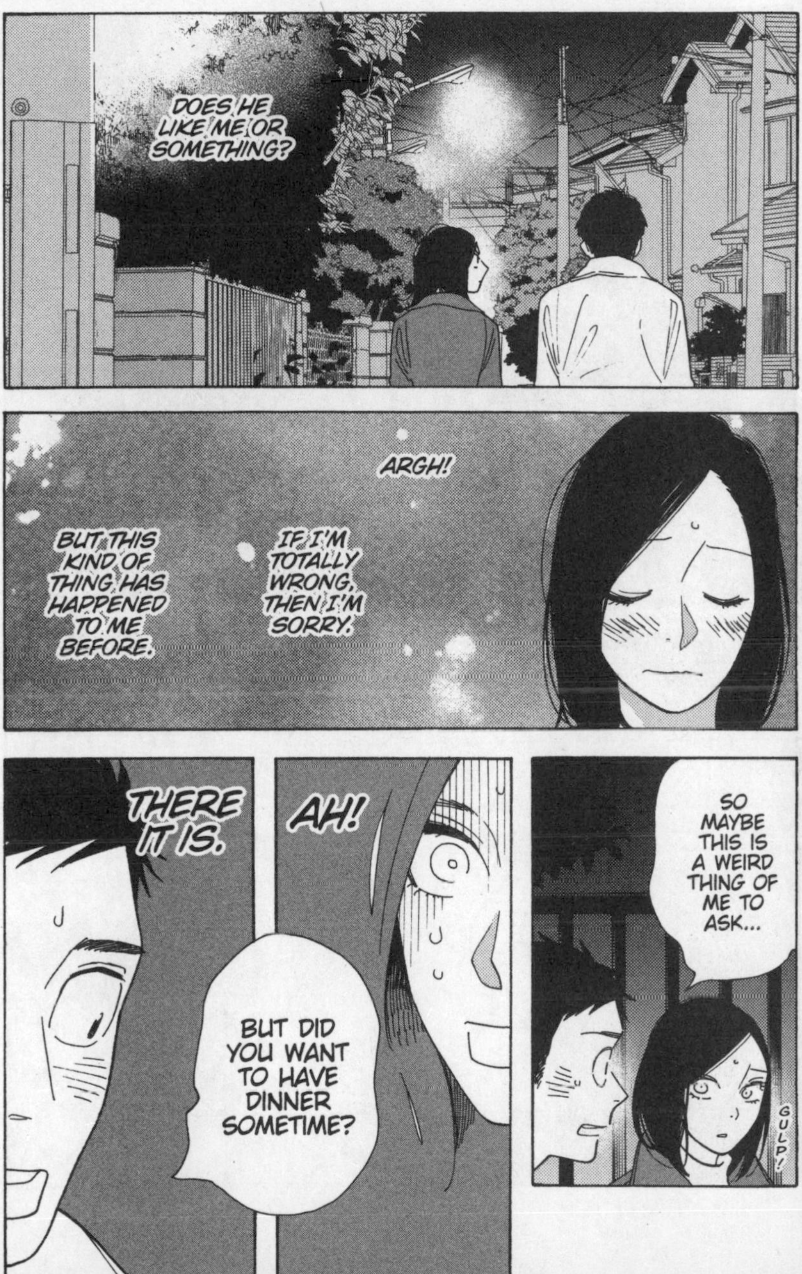
DOES HE LIKE ME OR SOMETHING?
ARGH!
IF I'M TOTALLY WRONG, THEN I'M SORRY.
BUT THIS KIND OF THING HAS HAPPENED TO ME BEFORE.
SO MAYBE THIS IS A WEIRD THING OF ME TO ASK...
GULP!
AH!
BUT DID YOU WANT TO HAVE DINNER SOMETIME?
THERE IT IS.

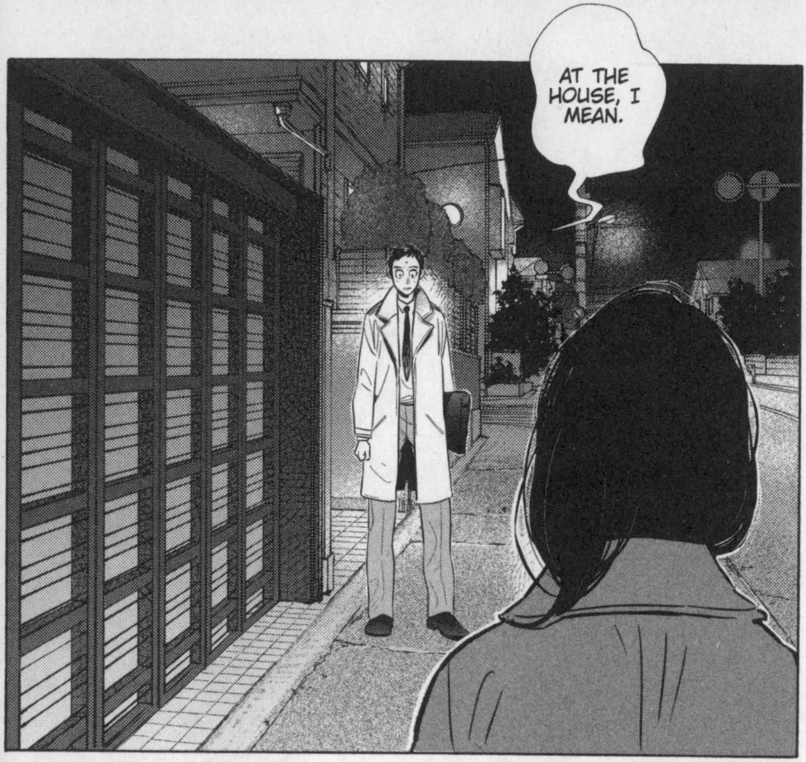
AT THE HOUSE, I MEAN.

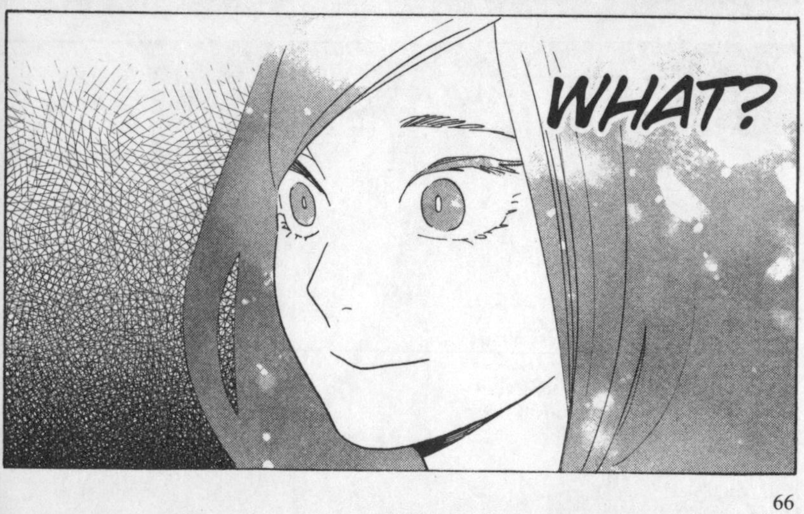
WHAT?

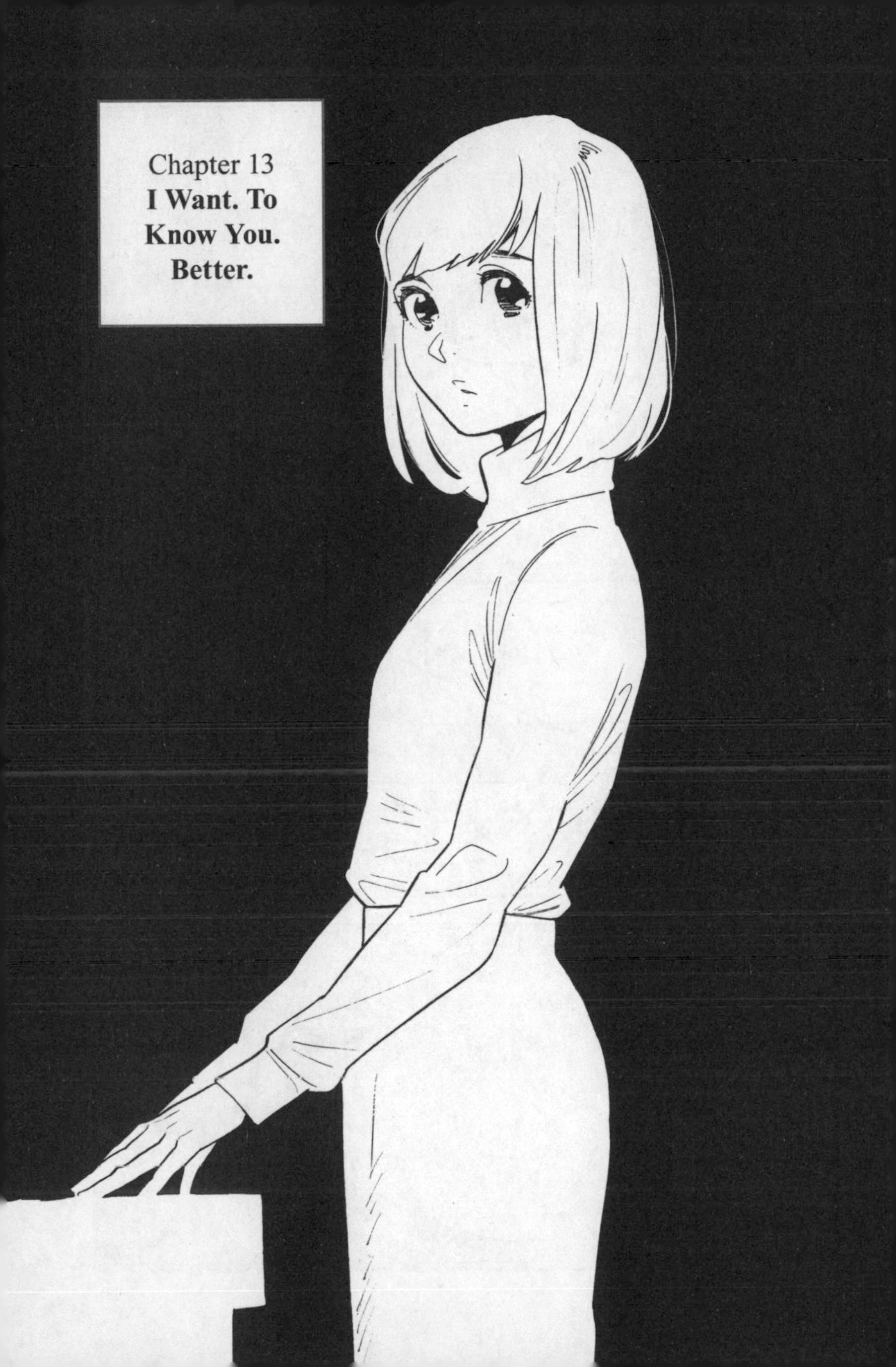
Chapter 13
I Want. To Know You. Better.

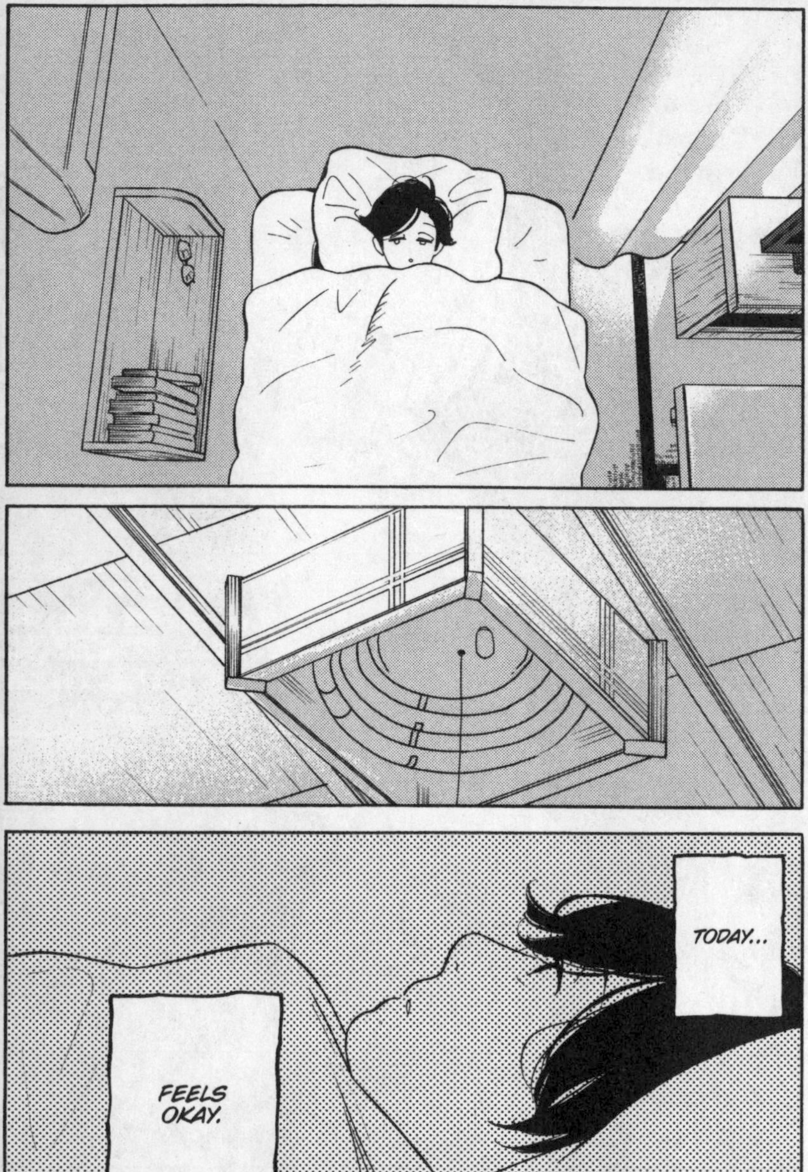
TODAY...
FEELS OKAY.

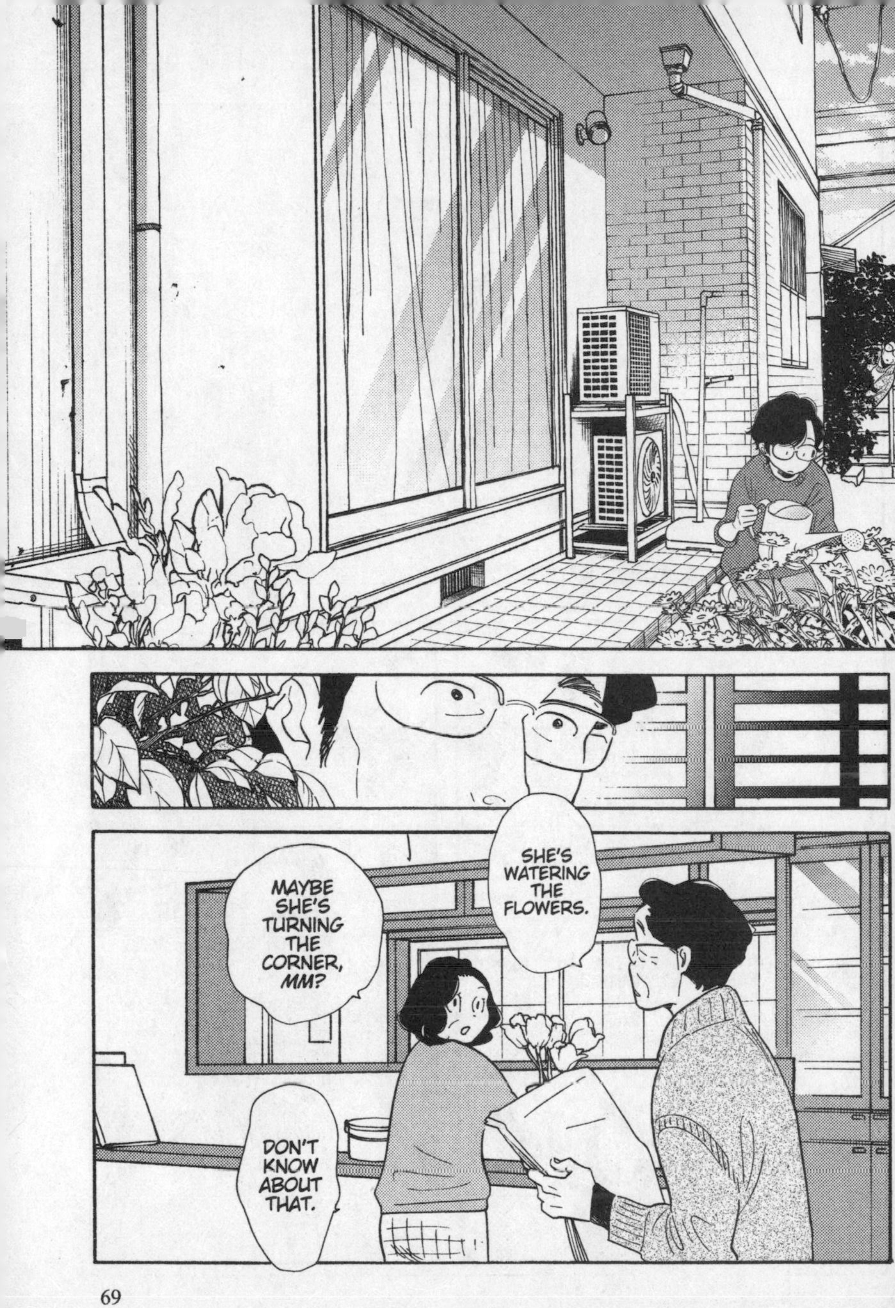
SHE'S WATERING THE FLOWERS.
MAYBE SHE'S TURNING THE CORNER, MM?
DON'T KNOW ABOUT THAT.

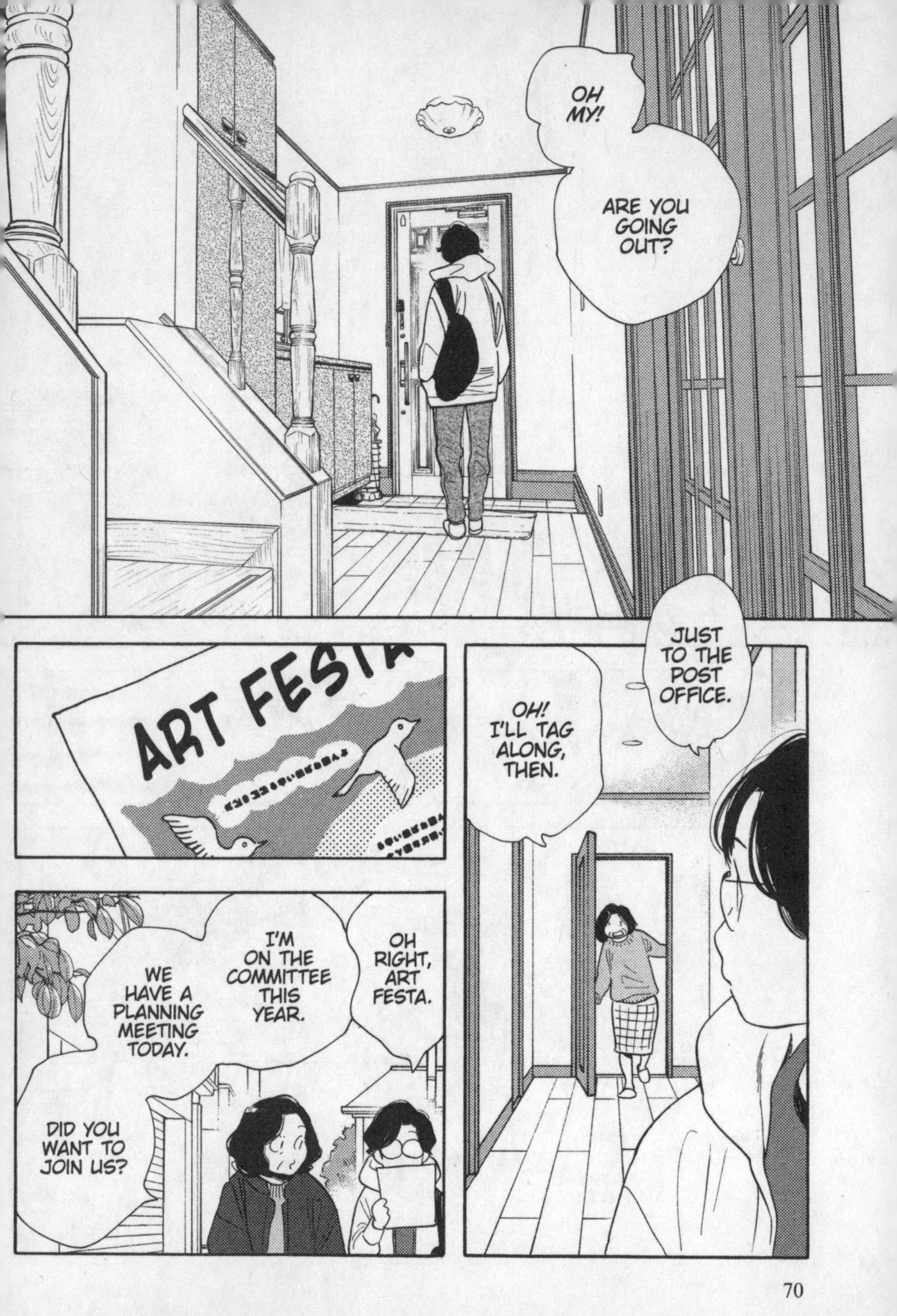
OH MY!
ARE YOU GOING OUT?
JUST TO THE POST OFFICE.
OH! I'LL TAG ALONG, THEN.
ART FESTA
OH RIGHT, ART FESTA.
I'M ON THE COMMITTEE THIS YEAR.
WE HAVE A PLANNING MEETING TODAY.
DID YOU WANT TO JOIN US?

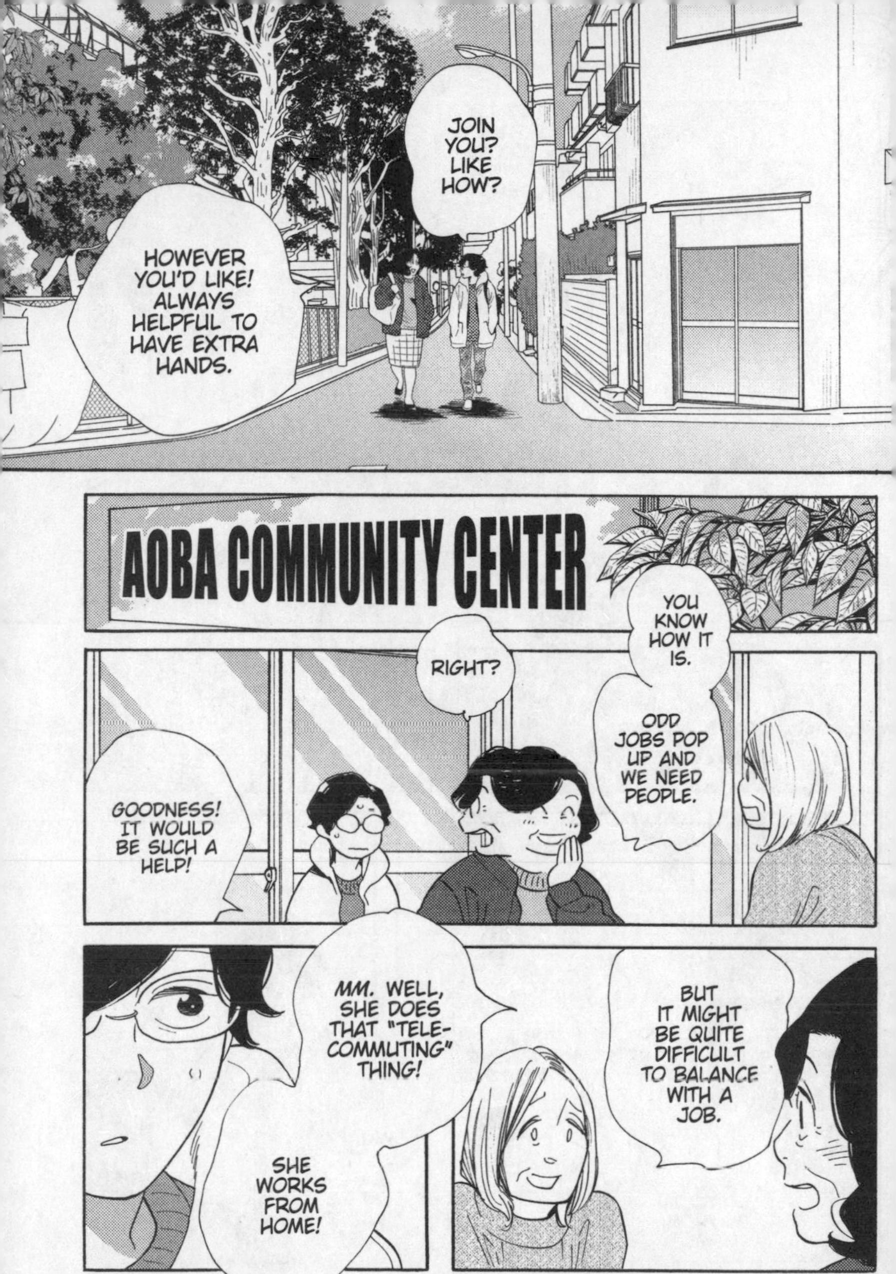
JOIN YOU? LIKE HOW?
HOWEVER YOU'D LIKE! ALWAYS HELPFUL TO HAVE EXTRA HANDS.
AOBA COMMUNITY CENTER
YOU KNOW HOW IT IS.
ODD JOBS POP UP AND WE NEED PEOPLE.
RIGHT?
GOODNESS! IT WOULD BE SUCH A HELP!
BUT IT MIGHT BE QUITE DIFFICULT TO BALANCE WITH A JOB.
MM. WELL, SHE DOES THAT "TELE-COMMUTING" THING!
SHE WORKS FROM HOME!

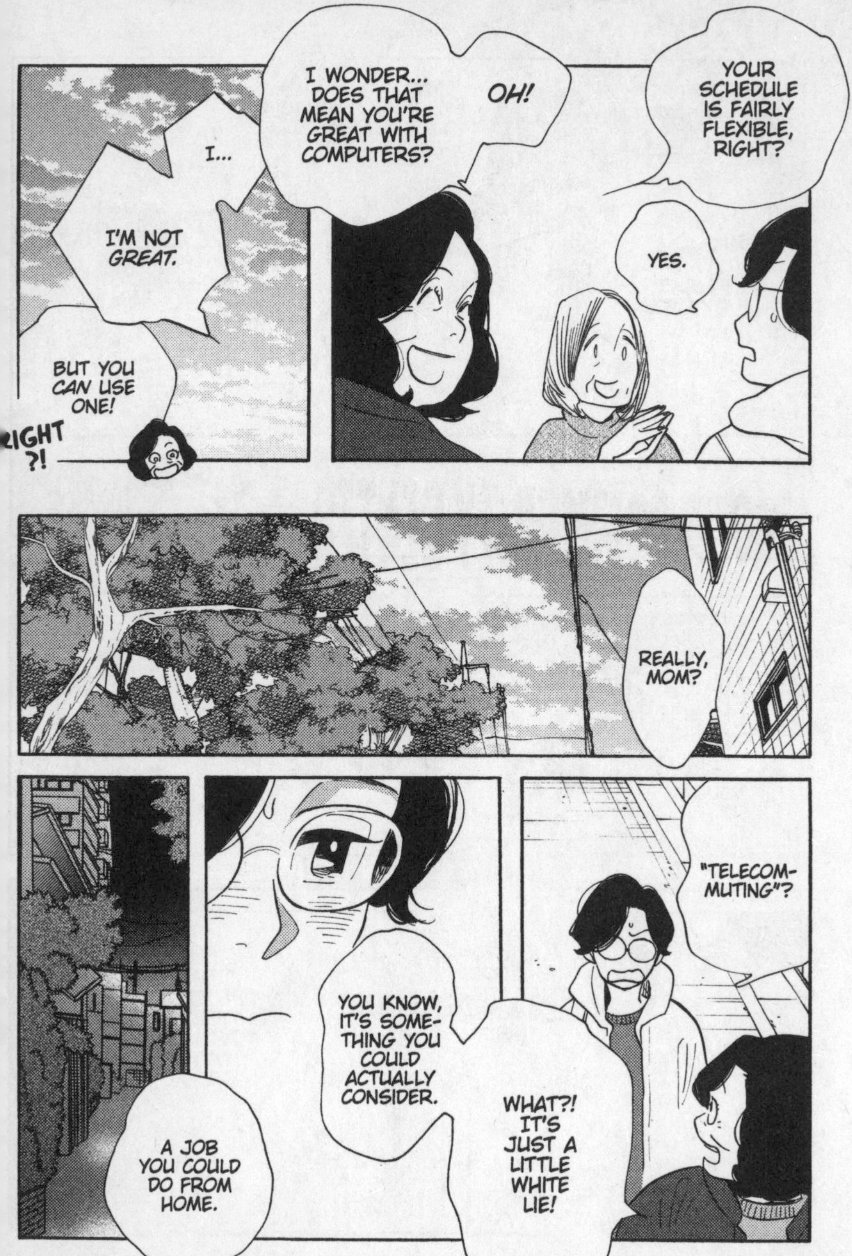
YOUR SCHEDULE IS FAIRLY FLEXIBLE, RIGHT?
YES.
OH!
I WONDER... DOES THAT MEAN YOU'RE GREAT WITH COMPUTERS?
I...
I'M NOT GREAT.
BUT YOU CAN USE ONE!
RIGHT?!
REALLY, MOM?
"TELECOM-MUTING"?
WHAT?! IT'S JUST A LITTLE WHITE LIE!
YOU KNOW, IT'S SOME-THING YOU COULD ACTUALLY CONSIDER.
A JOB YOU COULD DO FROM HOME.

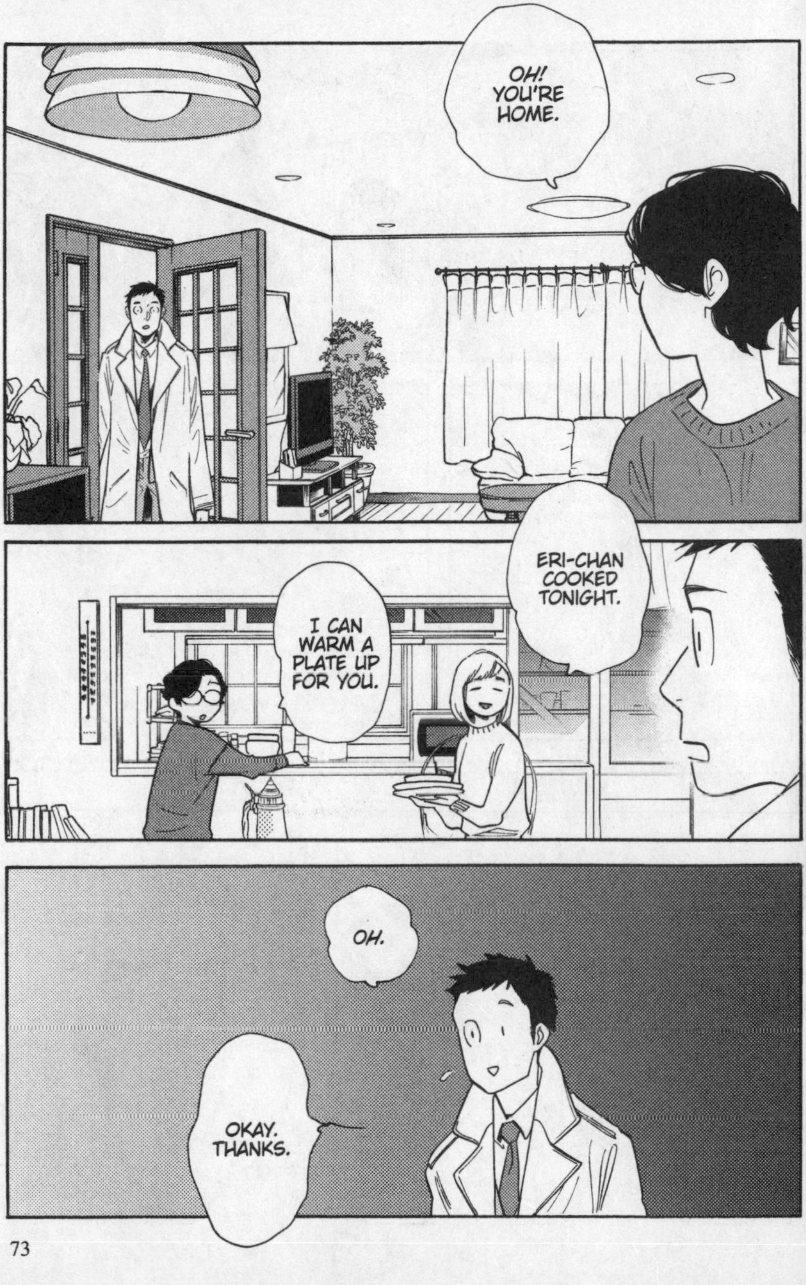
OH! YOU'RE HOME.
ERI-CHAN COOKED TONIGHT.
I CAN WARM A PLATE UP FOR YOU.
OH.
OKAY. THANKS.

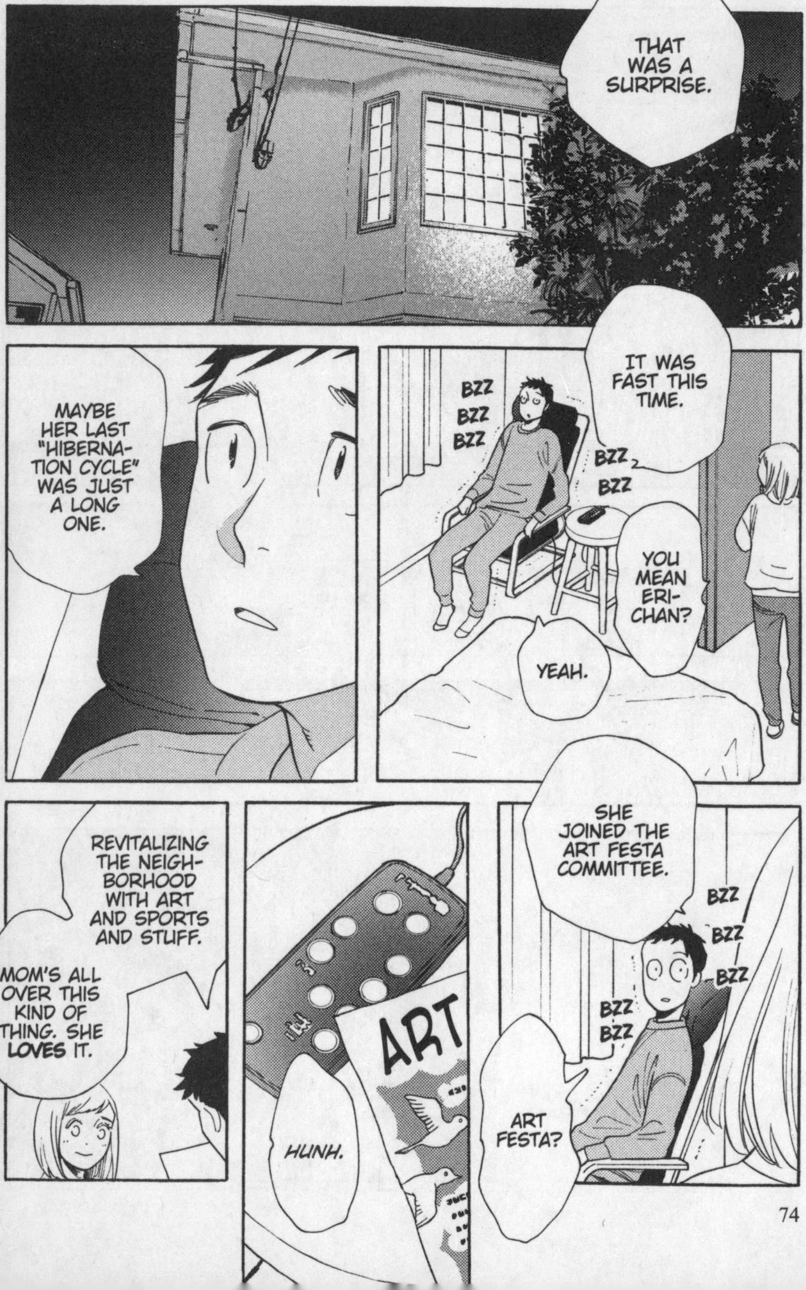
THAT WAS A SURPRISE.
IT WAS FAST THIS TIME.
BZZ BZZ BZZ
BZZ BZZ
YOU MEAN ERI-CHAN?
YEAH.
MAYBE HER LAST "HIBERNATION CYCLE" WAS JUST A LONG ONE.
SHE JOINED THE ART FESTA COMMITTEE.
BZZ BZZ BZZ
BZZ BZZ
ART FESTA?
ART
HUNH.
REVITALIZING THE NEIGHBORHOOD WITH ART AND SPORTS AND STUFF.
MOM'S ALL OVER THIS KIND OF THING. SHE LOVES IT.

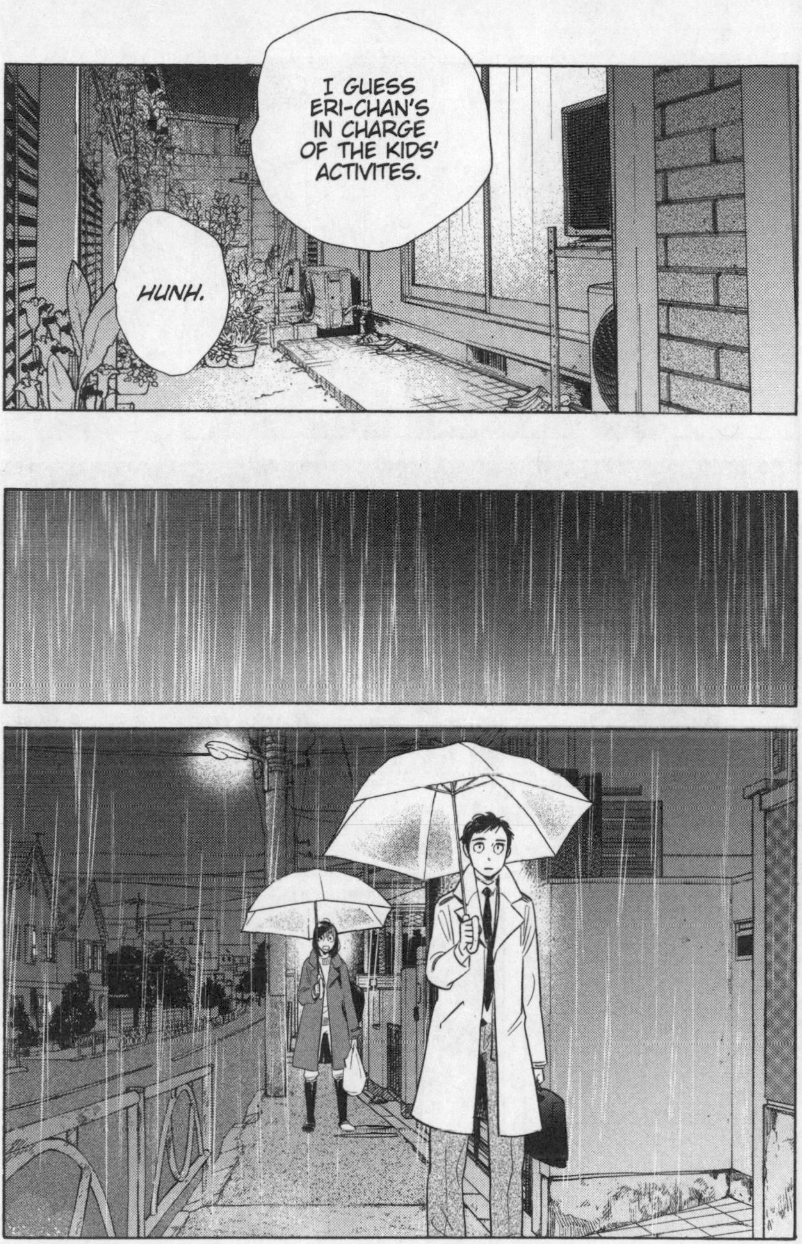
I GUESS ERI-CHAN'S IN CHARGE OF THE KIDS' ACTIVITES.
HUNH.

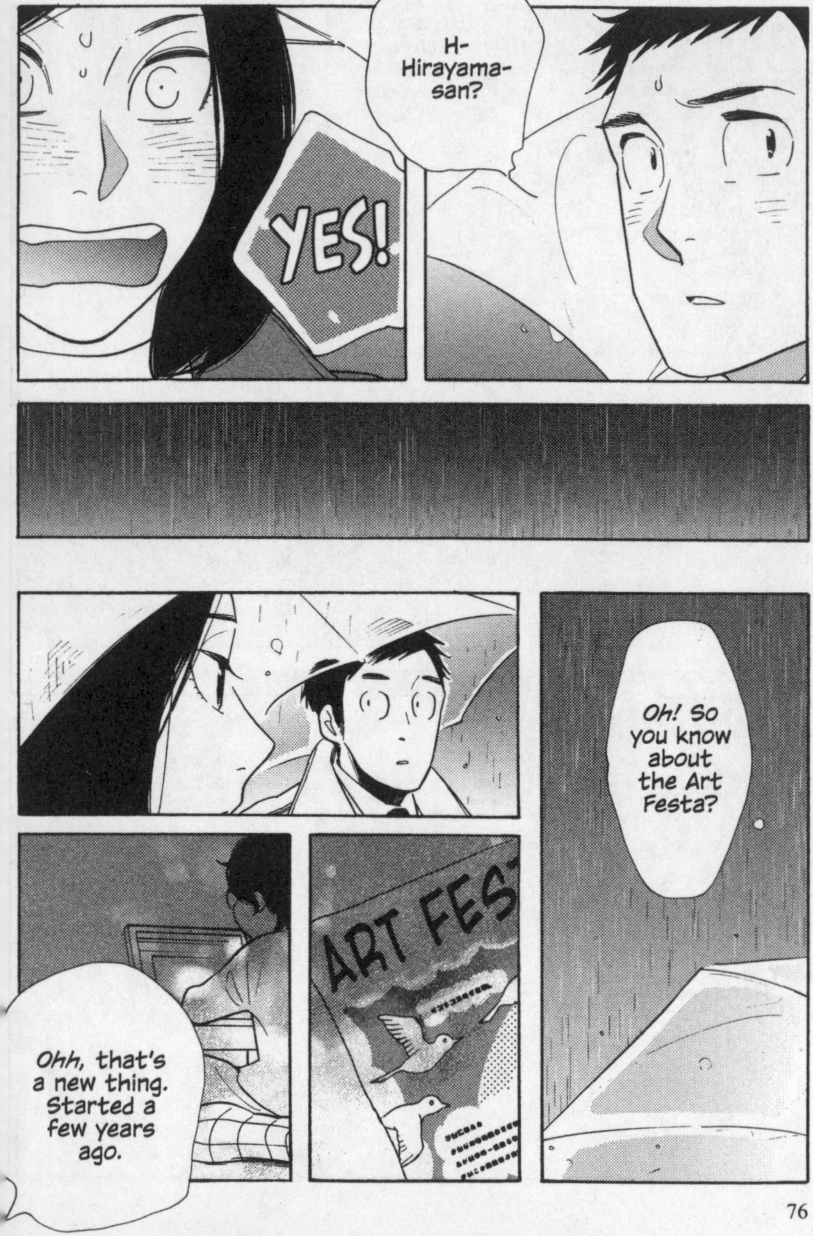
H- Hirayama-san?
YES!
Oh! So you know about the Art Festa?
ART FEST
Ohh, that's a new thing. Started a few years ago.

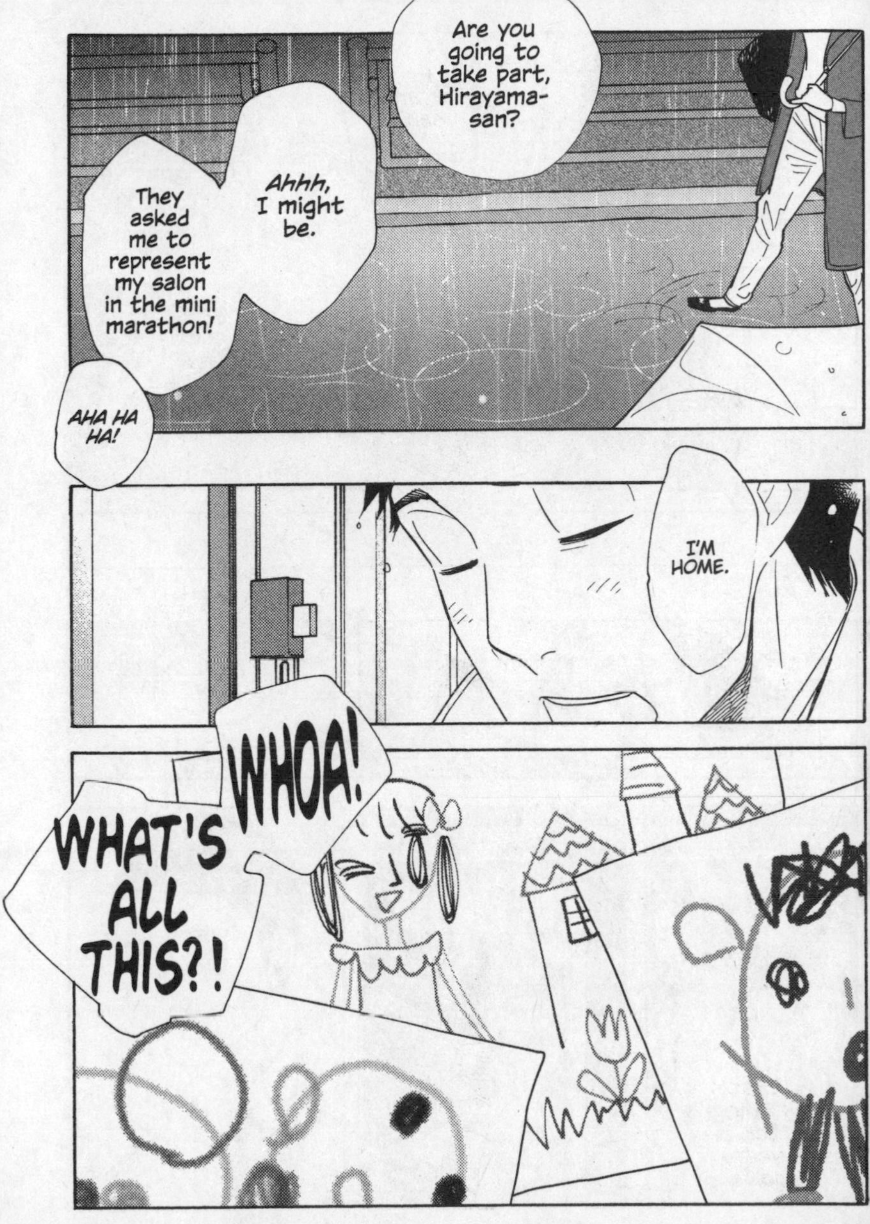
Are you going to take part, Hirayama-san?
Ahhh, I might be.
They asked me to represent my salon in the mini marathon!
AHA HA HA!
I'M HOME.
WHOA!
WHAT'S ALL THIS?!

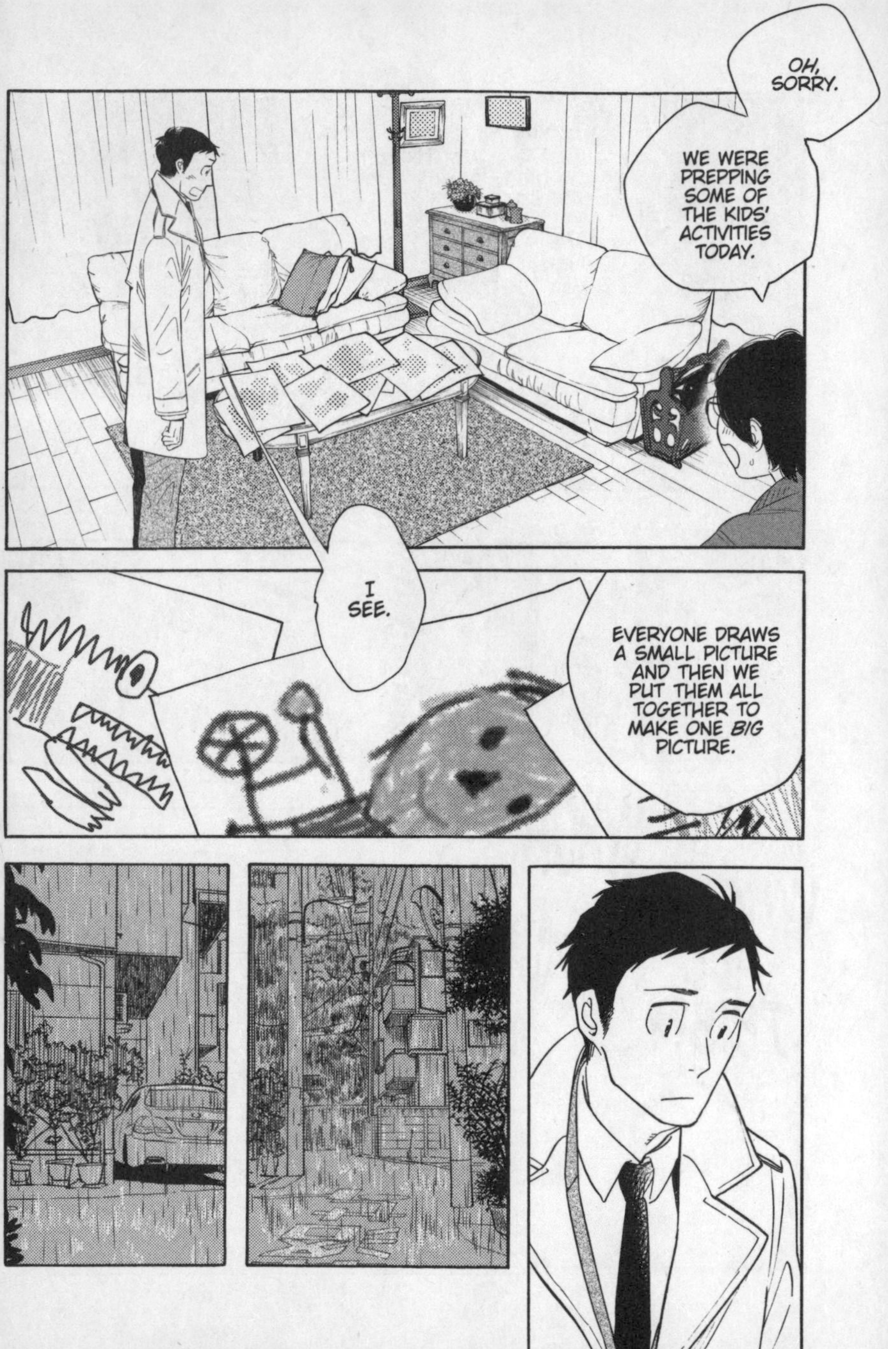
OH, SORRY.
WE WERE PREPPING SOME OF THE KIDS' ACTIVITIES TODAY.
I SEE.
EVERYONE DRAWS A SMALL PICTURE AND THEN WE PUT THEM ALL TOGETHER TO MAKE ONE *BIG* PICTURE.

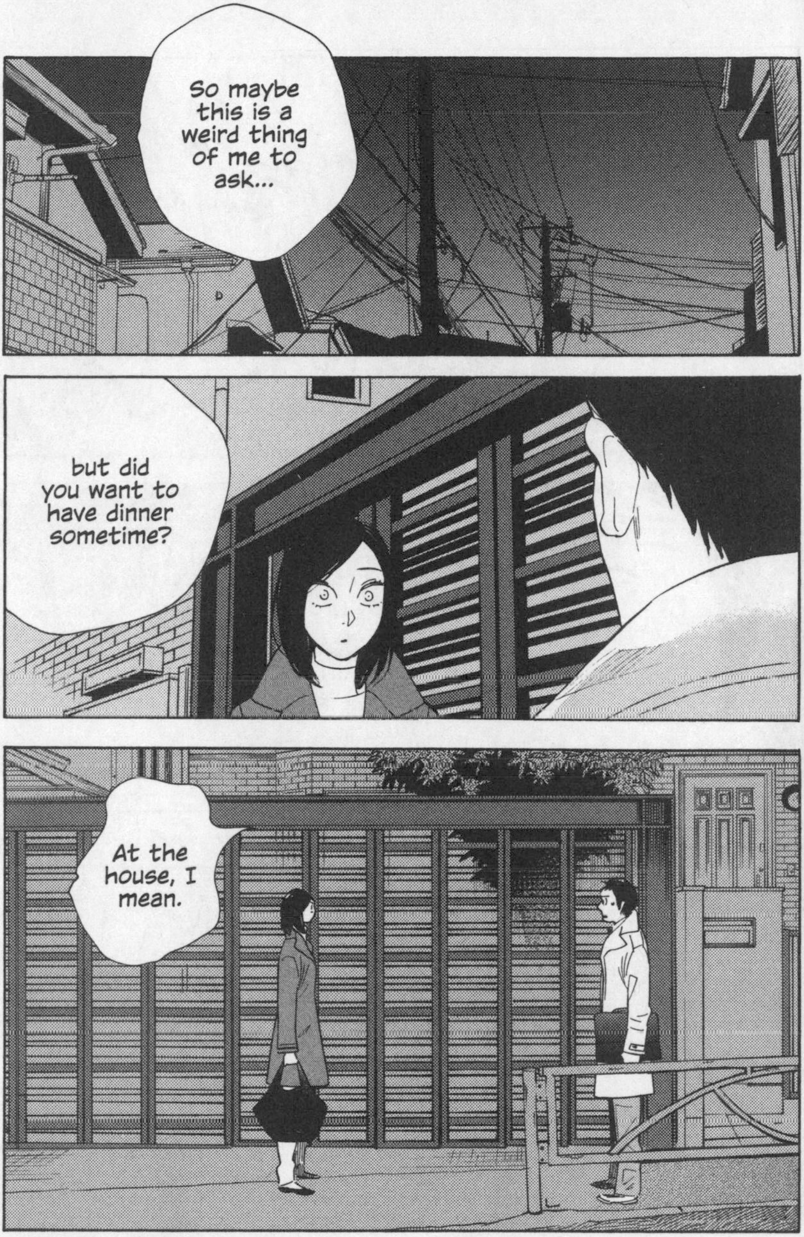
So maybe this is a weird thing of me to ask...
but did you want to have dinner sometime?
At the house, I mean.

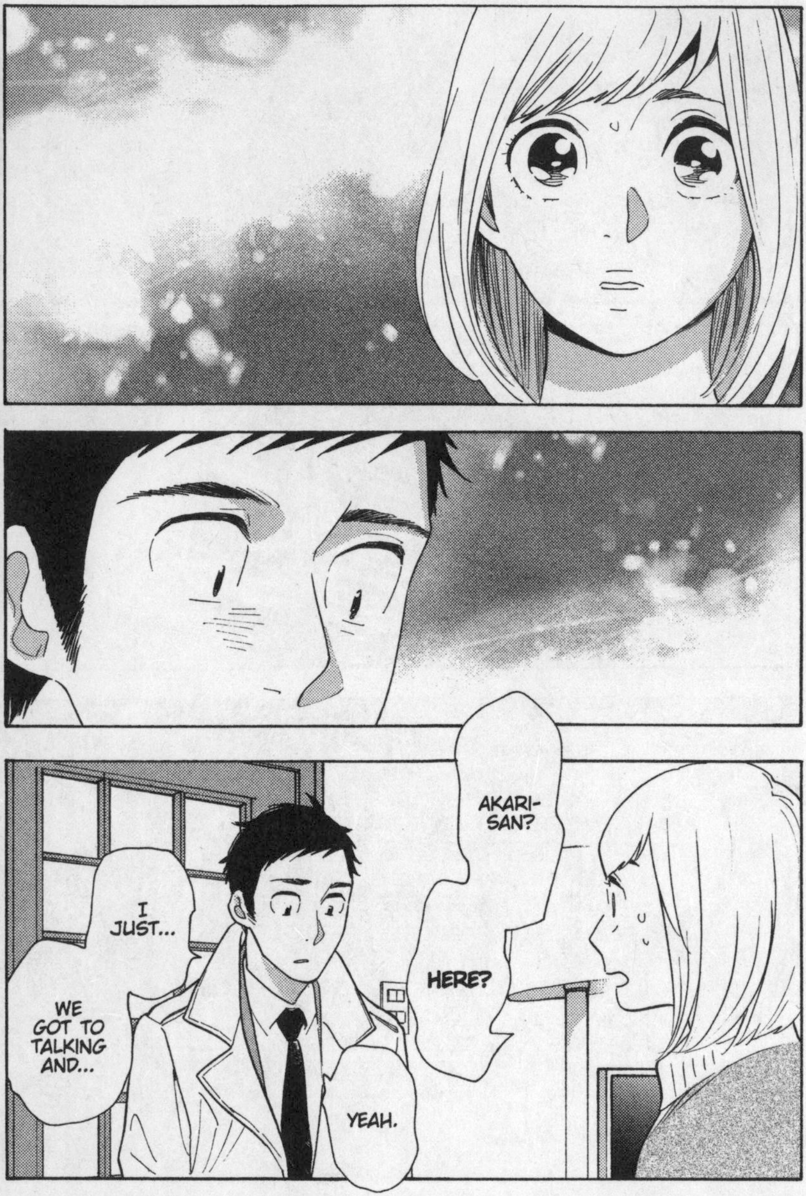
AKARI-SAN?
HERE?
YEAH.
I JUST...
WE GOT TO TALKING AND...

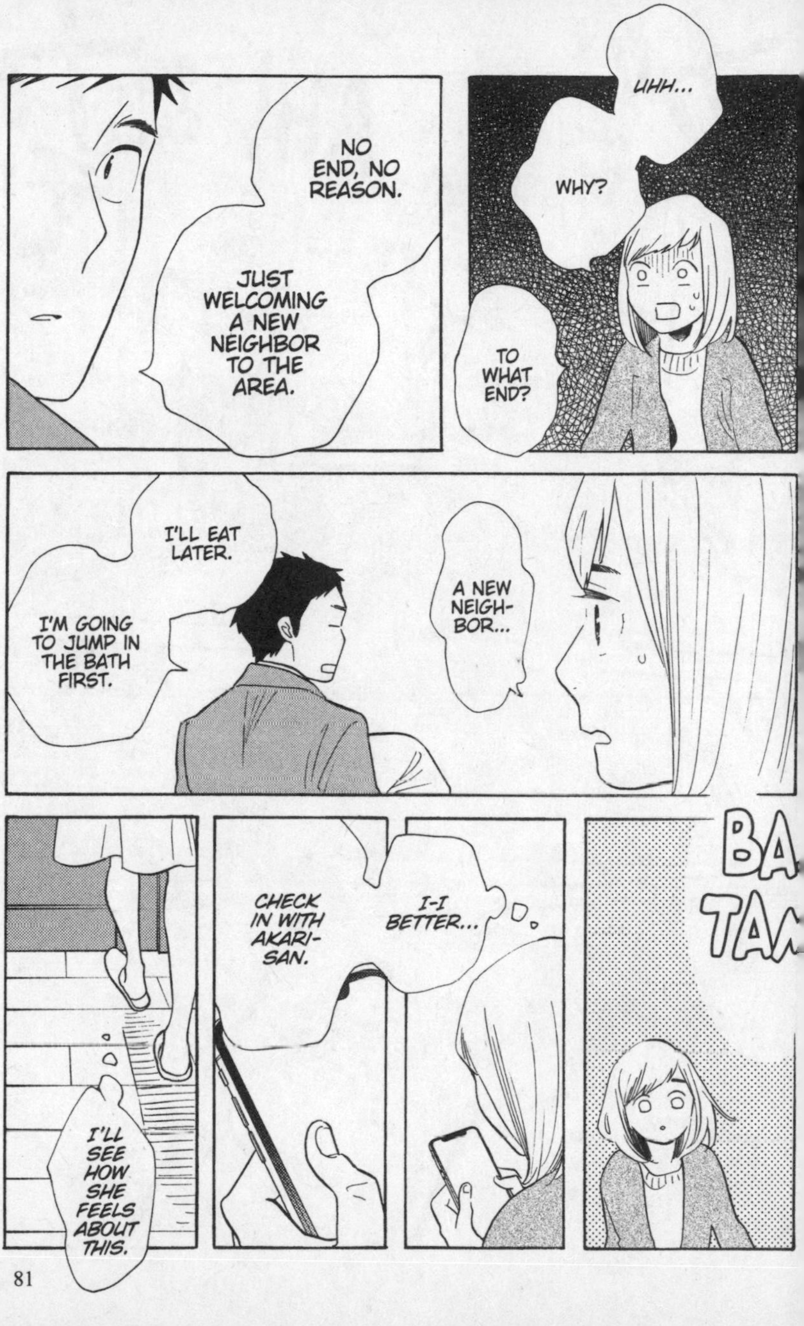
UHH...
WHY?
TO WHAT END?
NO END, NO REASON.
JUST WELCOMING A NEW NEIGHBOR TO THE AREA.
A NEW NEIGH-BOR...
I'LL EAT LATER.
I'M GOING TO JUMP IN THE BATH FIRST.
I-I BETTER...
CHECK IN WITH AKARI-SAN.
I'LL SEE HOW SHE FEELS ABOUT THIS.

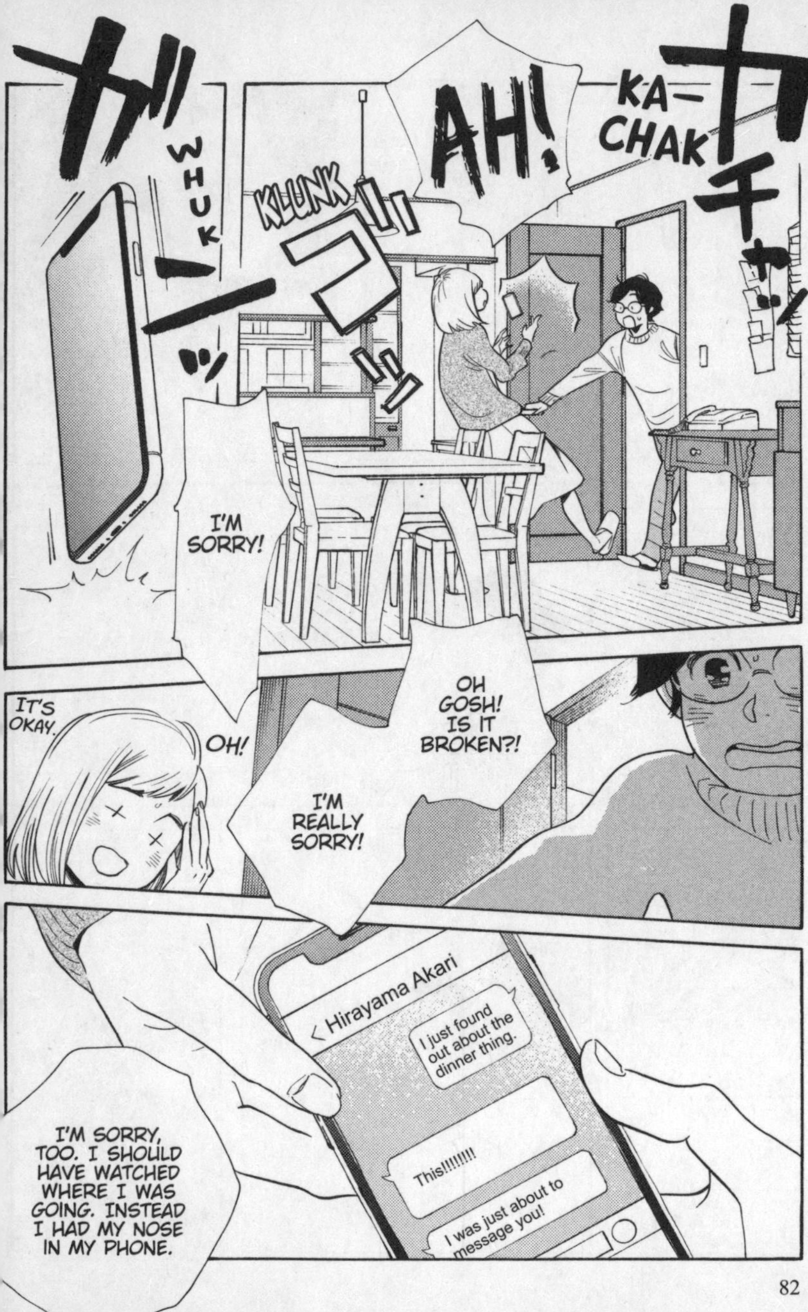
KA-CHAK
AH!
KLUNK
WHUK
I'M SORRY!
OH GOSH! IS IT BROKEN?!
I'M REALLY SORRY!
OH!
IT'S OKAY.
Hirayama Akari
I just found out about the dinner thing.
This!!!!!!!!
I was just about to message you!
I'M SORRY, TOO. I SHOULD HAVE WATCHED WHERE I WAS GOING. INSTEAD I HAD MY NOSE IN MY PHONE.

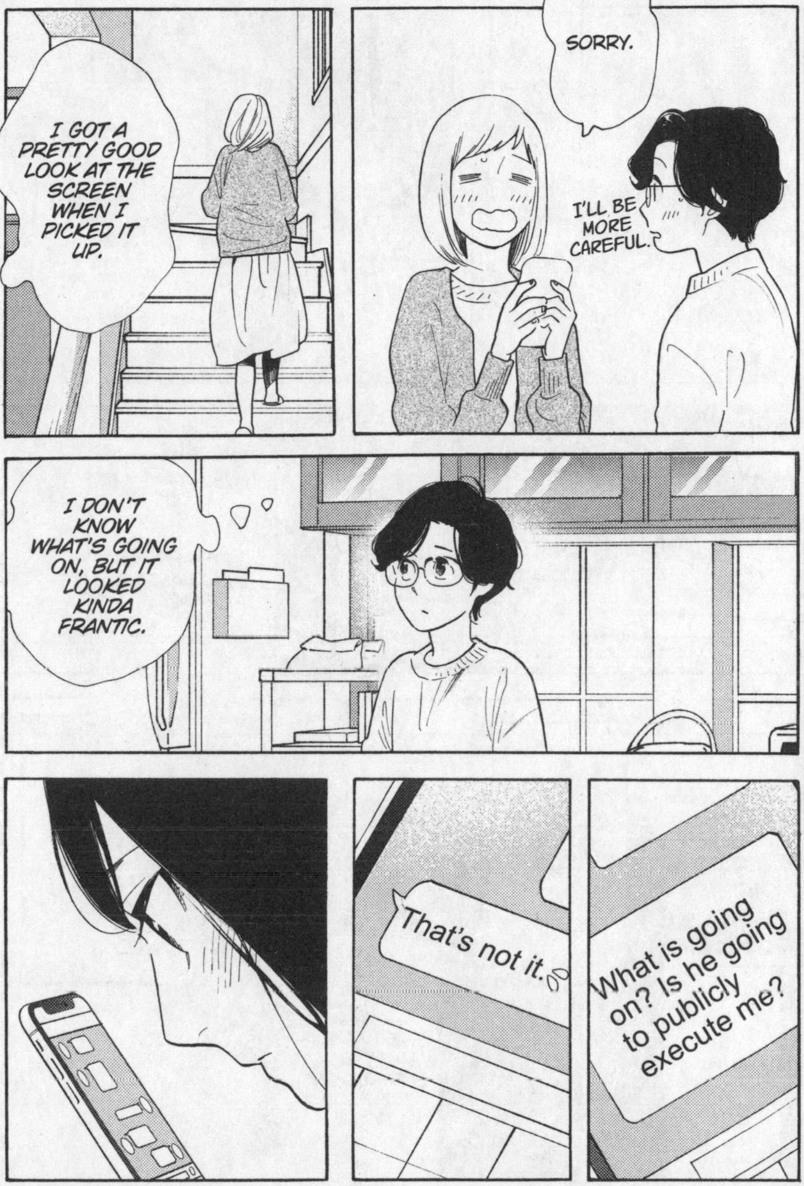
SORRY.
I'LL BE MORE CAREFUL.
I GOT A PRETTY GOOD LOOK AT THE SCREEN WHEN I PICKED IT UP.
I DON'T KNOW WHAT'S GOING ON, BUT IT LOOKED KINDA FRANTIC.
What is going on? Is he going to publicly execute me?
That's not it.

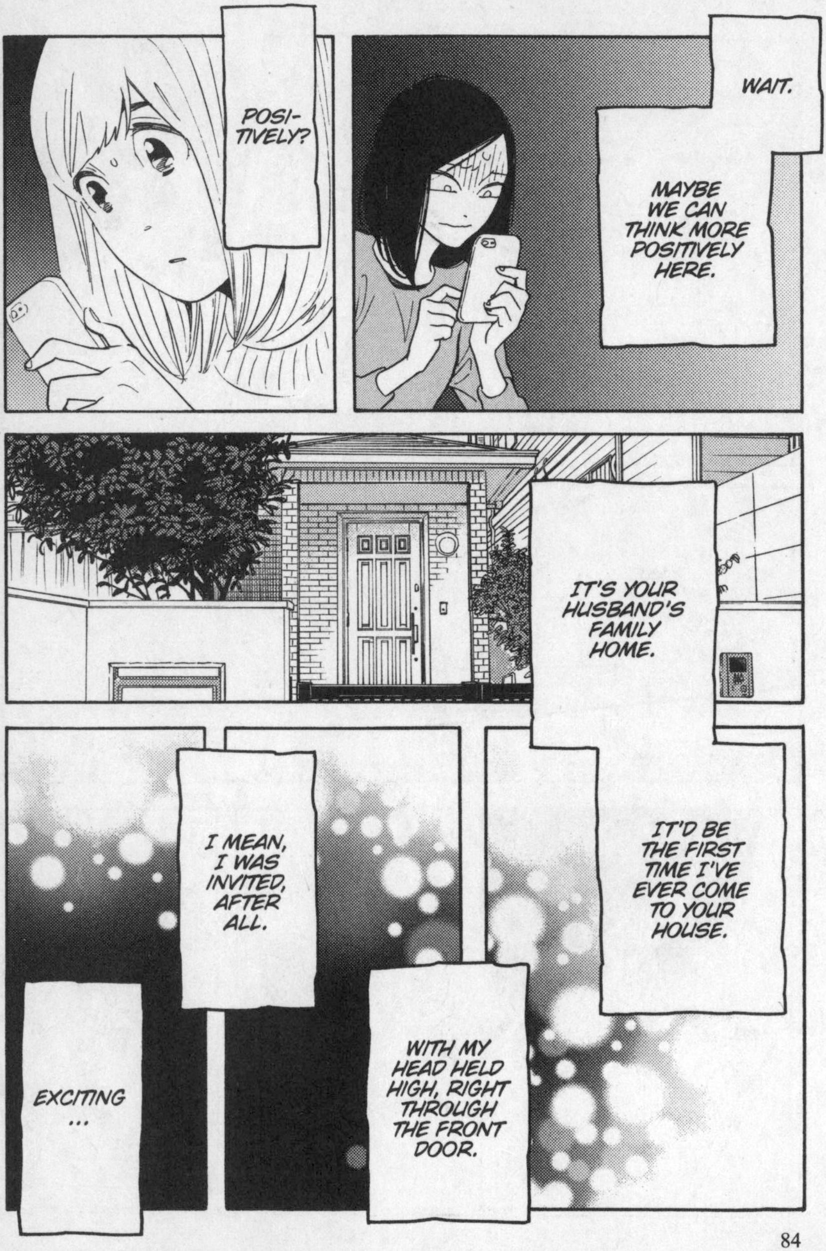
WAIT.
MAYBE WE CAN THINK MORE POSITIVELY HERE.
POSI-TIVELY?
IT'S YOUR HUSBAND'S FAMILY HOME.
IT'D BE THE FIRST TIME I'VE EVER COME TO YOUR HOUSE.
I MEAN, I WAS INVITED, AFTER ALL.
WITH MY HEAD HELD HIGH, RIGHT THROUGH THE FRONT DOOR.
EXCITING ...

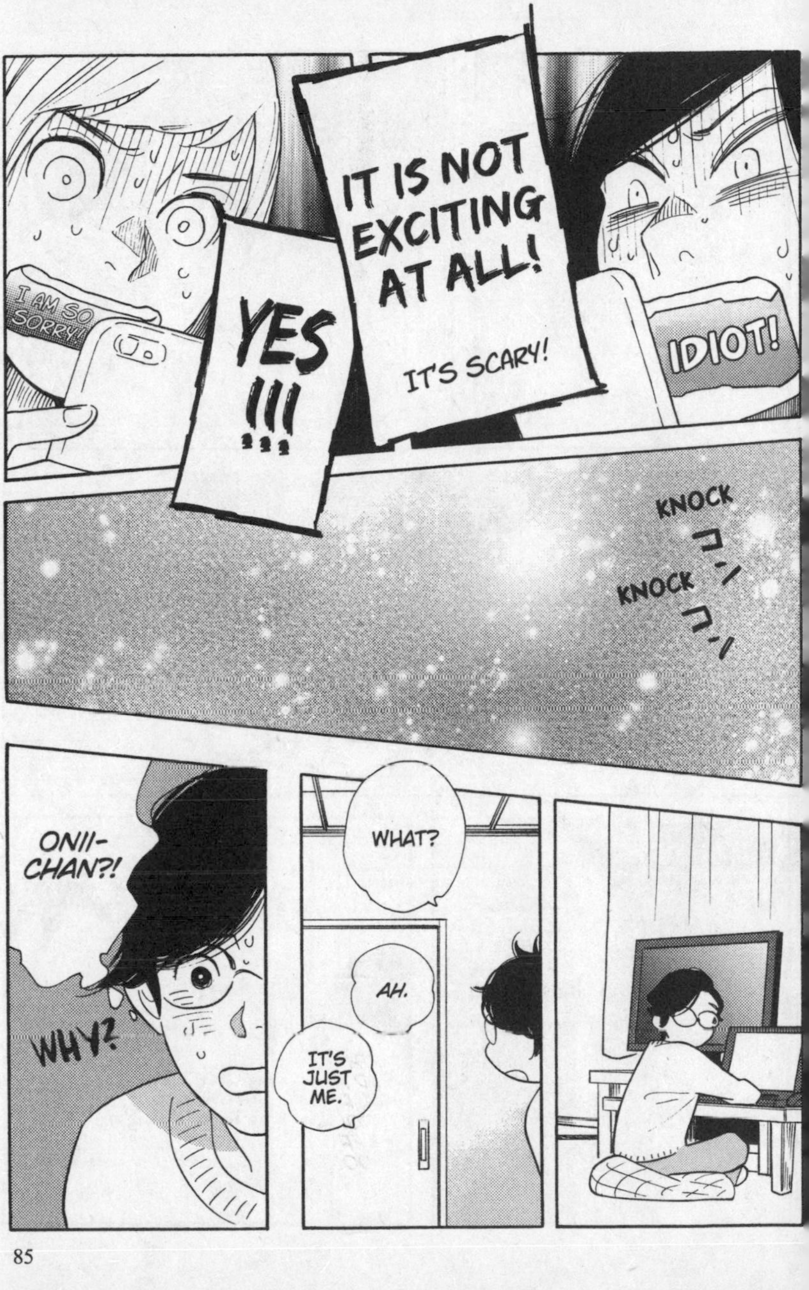
IDIOT!
IT IS NOT EXCITING AT ALL!
IT'S SCARY!
I AM SO SORRY!
YES !!!
KNOCK
コン
KNOCK
コン
WHAT?
AH.
IT'S JUST ME.
ONII-CHAN?!
WHY?

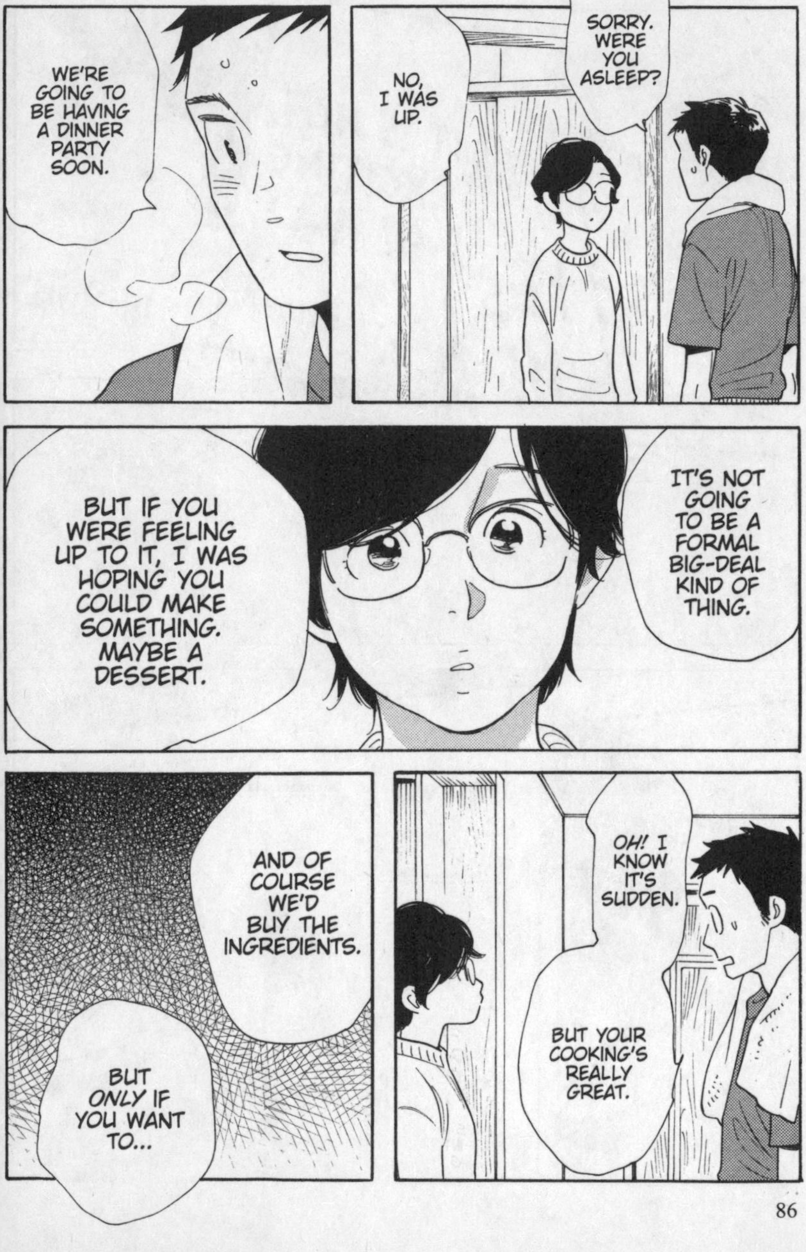
SORRY. WERE YOU ASLEEP?
NO, I WAS UP.
WE'RE GOING TO BE HAVING A DINNER PARTY SOON.
IT'S NOT GOING TO BE A FORMAL BIG-DEAL KIND OF THING.
BUT IF YOU WERE FEELING UP TO IT, I WAS HOPING YOU COULD MAKE SOMETHING. MAYBE A DESSERT.
OH! I KNOW IT'S SUDDEN.
BUT YOUR COOKING'S REALLY GREAT.
AND OF COURSE WE'D BUY THE INGREDIENTS.
BUT *ONLY* IF YOU WANT TO...

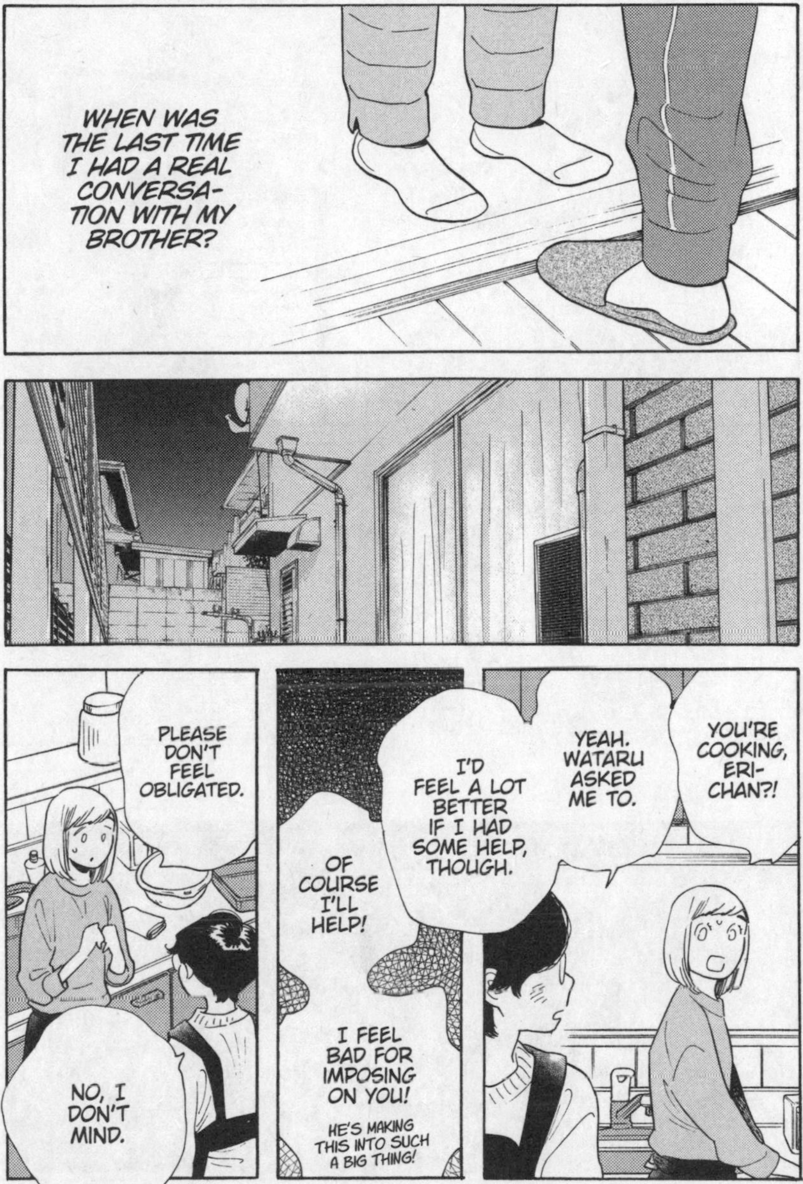
WHEN WAS THE LAST TIME I HAD A REAL CONVERSATION WITH MY BROTHER?
YOU'RE COOKING, ERI-CHAN?!
YEAH. WATARU ASKED ME TO.
I'D FEEL A LOT BETTER IF I HAD SOME HELP, THOUGH.
OF COURSE I'LL HELP!
I FEEL BAD FOR IMPOSING ON YOU!
HE'S MAKING THIS INTO SUCH A BIG THING!
PLEASE DON'T FEEL OBLIGATED.
NO, I DON'T MIND.

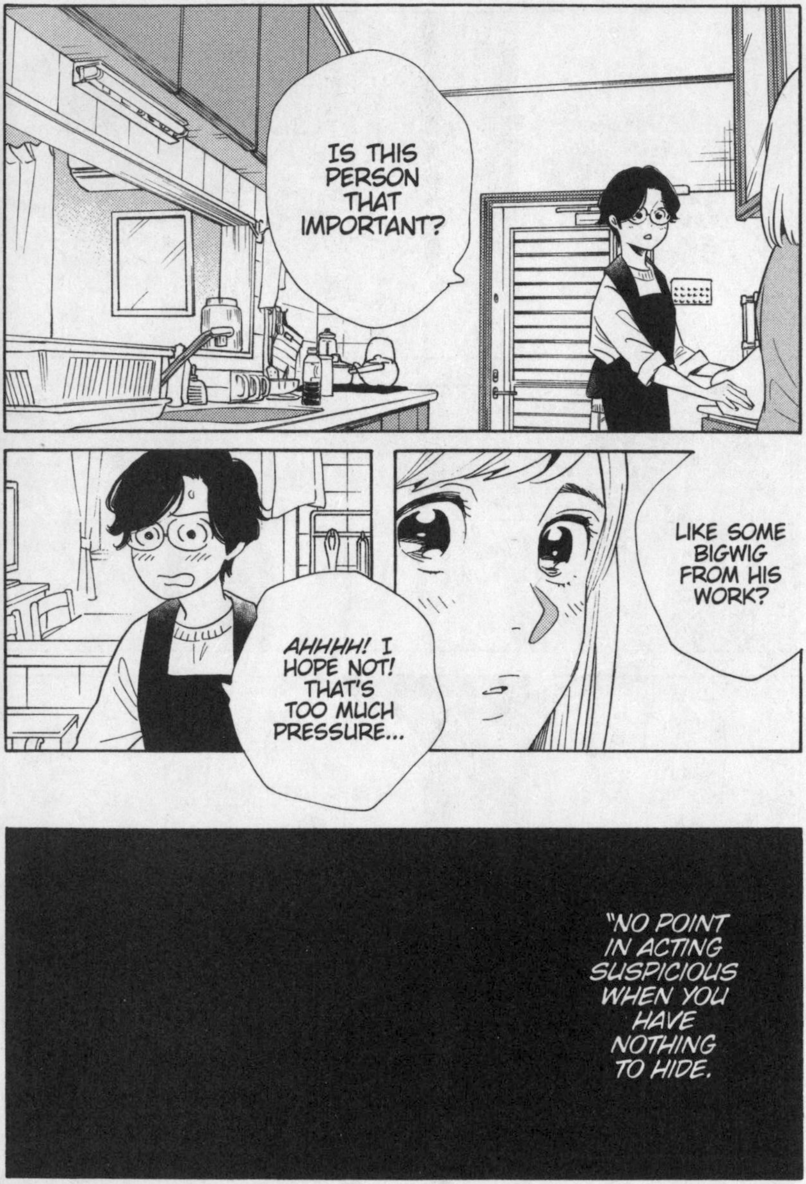
IS THIS PERSON THAT IMPORTANT?
LIKE SOME BIGWIG FROM HIS WORK?
AHHHH! I HOPE NOT! THAT'S TOO MUCH PRESSURE...
"NO POINT IN ACTING SUSPICIOUS WHEN YOU HAVE NOTHING TO HIDE.

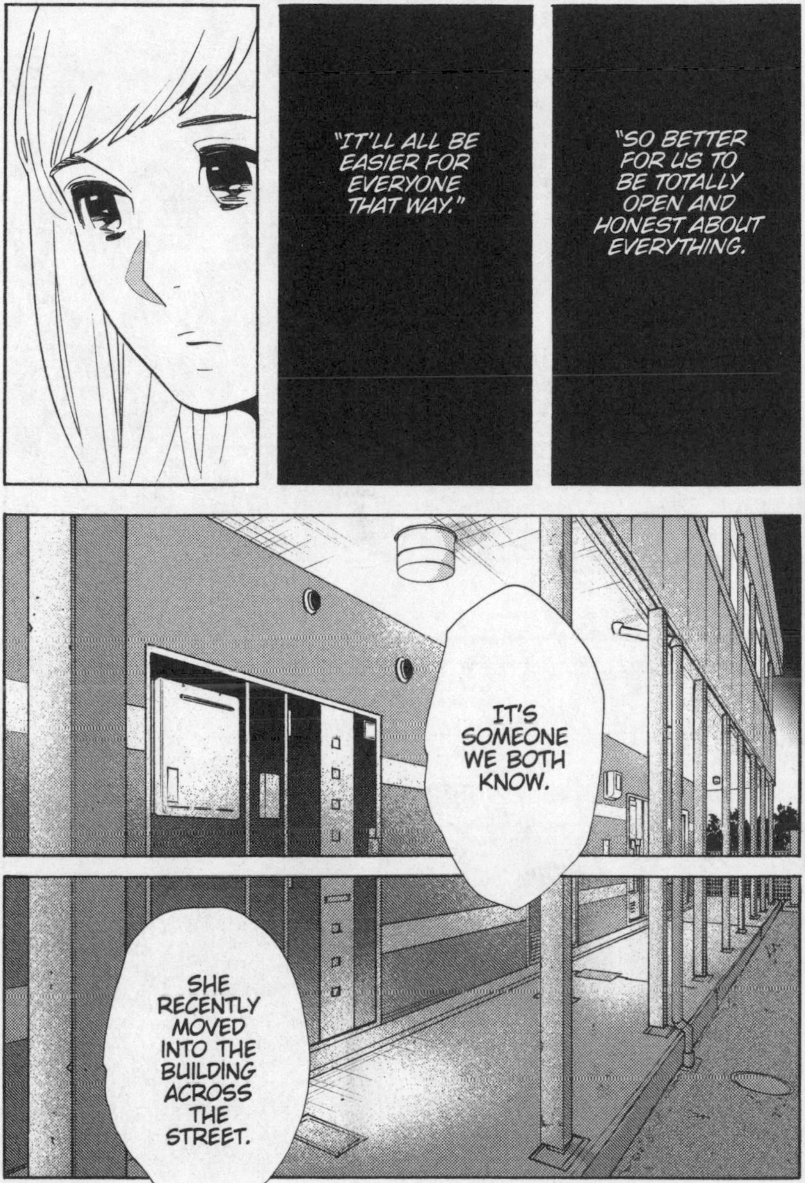
"SO BETTER FOR US TO BE TOTALLY OPEN AND HONEST ABOUT EVERYTHING.
"IT'LL ALL BE EASIER FOR EVERYONE THAT WAY."
IT'S SOMEONE WE BOTH KNOW.
SHE RECENTLY MOVED INTO THE BUILDING ACROSS THE STREET.

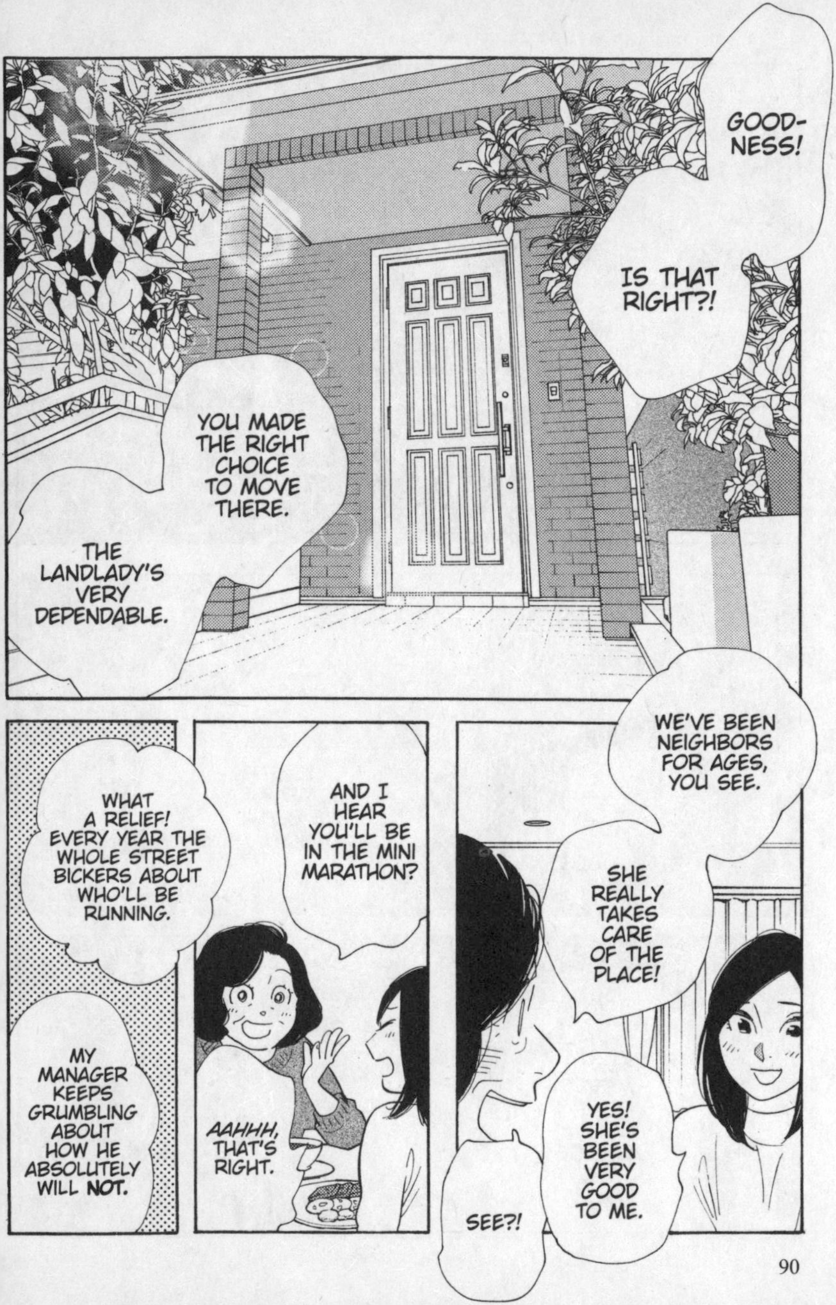
GOOD-NESS!
IS THAT RIGHT?!
YOU MADE THE RIGHT CHOICE TO MOVE THERE.
THE LANDLADY'S VERY DEPENDABLE.
WE'VE BEEN NEIGHBORS FOR AGES, YOU SEE.
SHE REALLY TAKES CARE OF THE PLACE!
YES! SHE'S BEEN VERY GOOD TO ME.
SEE?!
AND I HEAR YOU'LL BE IN THE MINI MARATHON?
AAHHH, THAT'S RIGHT.
WHAT A RELIEF! EVERY YEAR THE WHOLE STREET BICKERS ABOUT WHO'LL BE RUNNING.
MY MANAGER KEEPS GRUMBLING ABOUT HOW HE ABSOLUTELY WILL **NOT**.

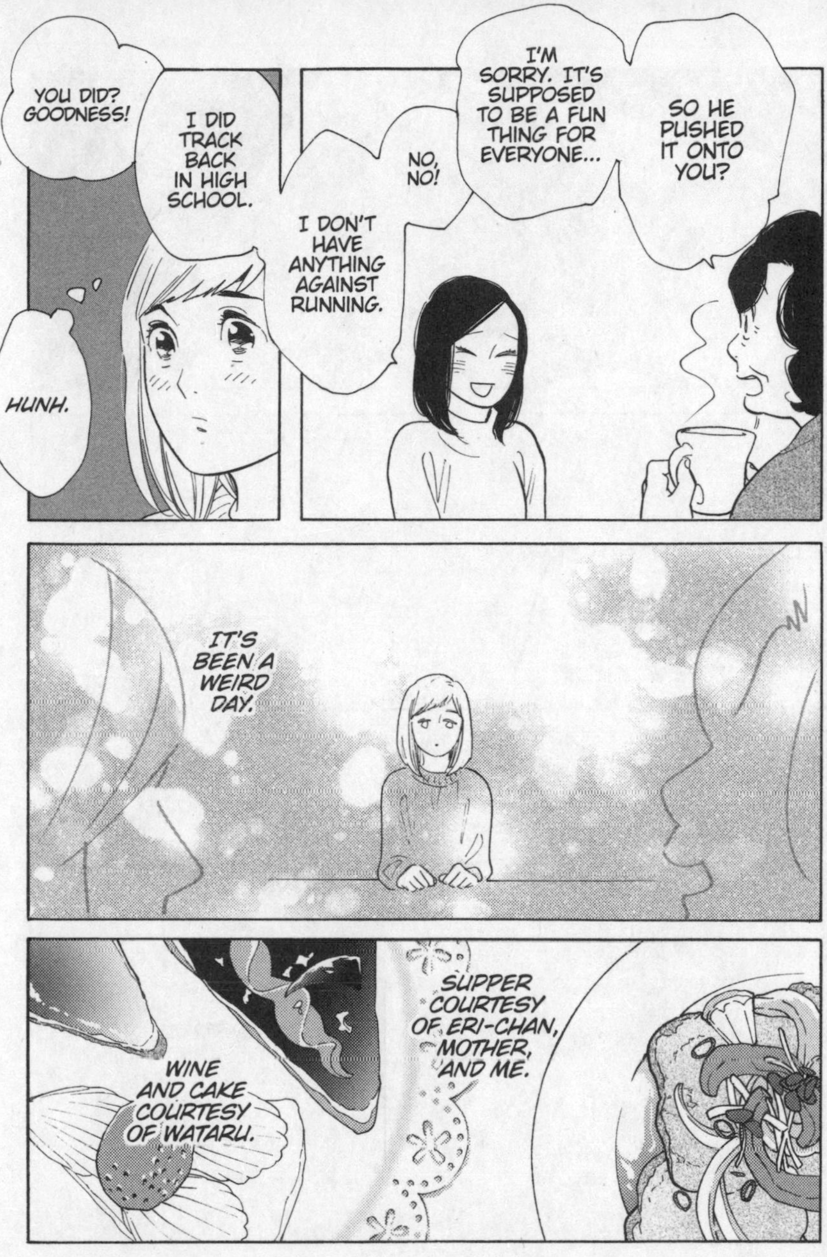
SO HE PUSHED IT ONTO YOU?
I'M SORRY. IT'S SUPPOSED TO BE A FUN THING FOR EVERYONE...
NO, NO!
I DON'T HAVE ANYTHING AGAINST RUNNING.
I DID TRACK BACK IN HIGH SCHOOL.
YOU DID? GOODNESS!
HUNH.
IT'S BEEN A WEIRD DAY.
SUPPER COURTESY OF ERI-CHAN, MOTHER, AND ME.
WINE AND CAKE COURTESY OF WATARU.

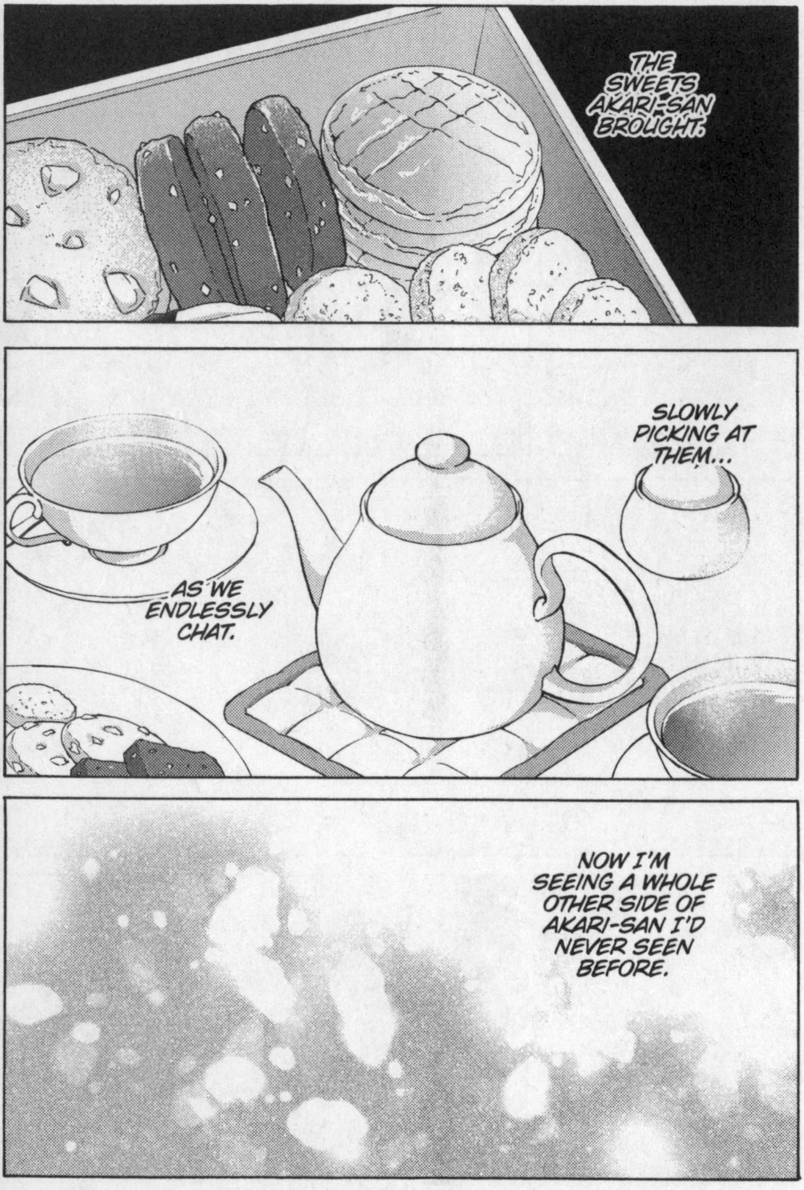
THE SWEETS AKARI-SAN BROUGHT.
SLOWLY PICKING AT THEM...
AS WE ENDLESSLY CHAT.
NOW I'M SEEING A WHOLE OTHER SIDE OF AKARI-SAN I'D NEVER SEEN BEFORE.

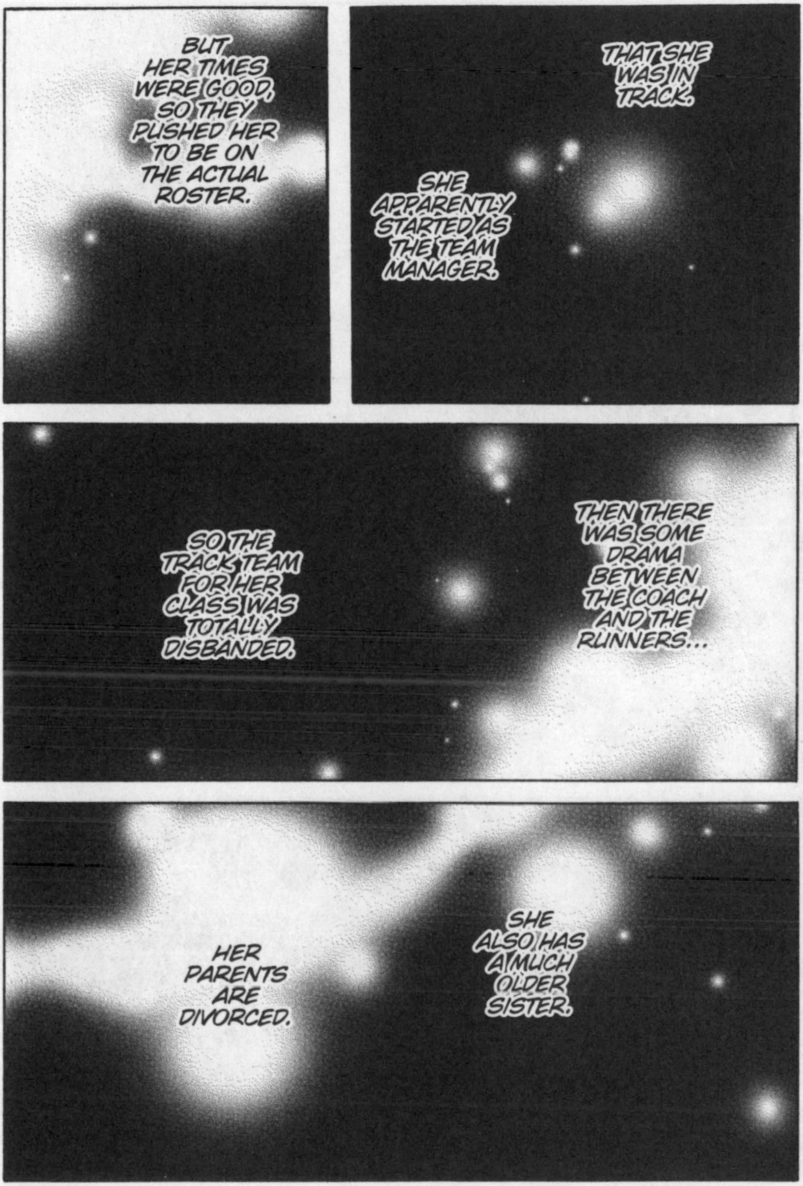
THAT SHE WAS IN TRACK.
SHE APPARENTLY STARTED AS THE TEAM MANAGER.
BUT HER TIMES WERE GOOD, SO THEY PUSHED HER TO BE ON THE ACTUAL ROSTER.
THEN THERE WAS SOME DRAMA BETWEEN THE COACH AND THE RUNNERS...
SO THE TRACK TEAM FOR HER CLASS WAS TOTALLY DISBANDED.
SHE ALSO HAS A MUCH OLDER SISTER.
HER PARENTS ARE DIVORCED.

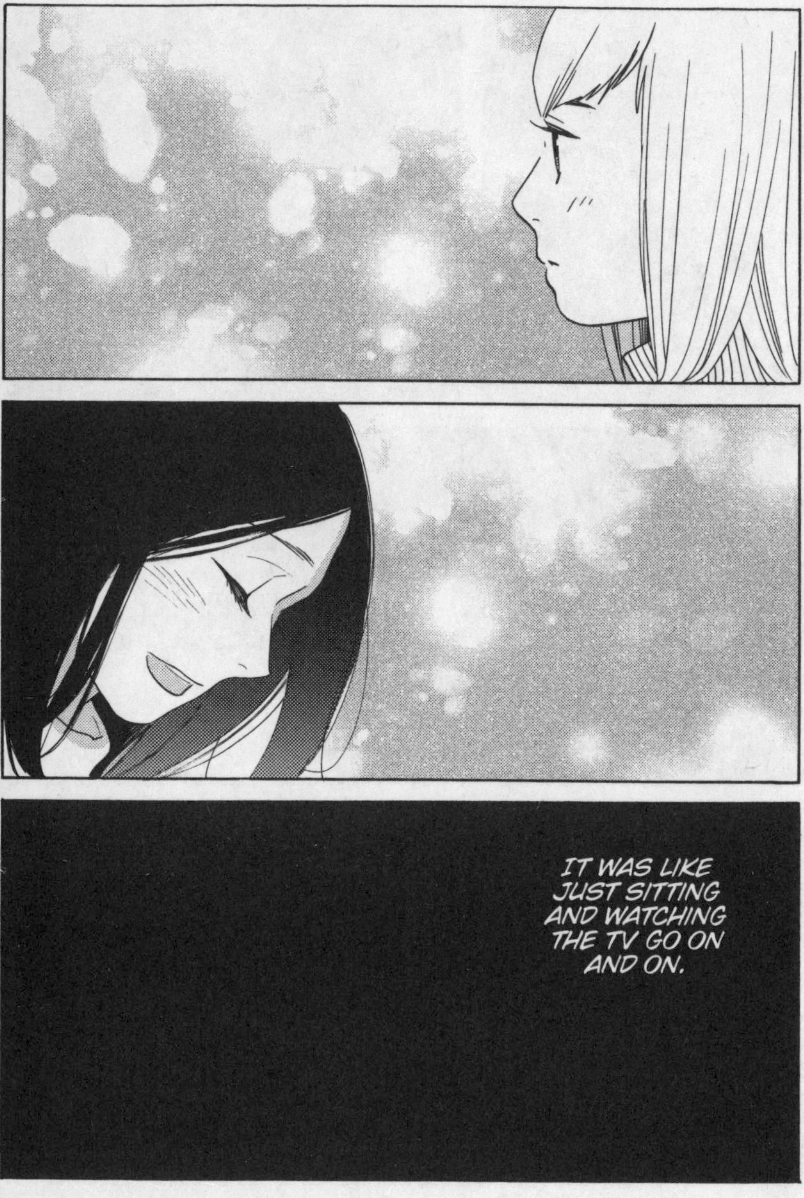
IT WAS LIKE JUST SITTING AND WATCHING THE TV GO ON AND ON.

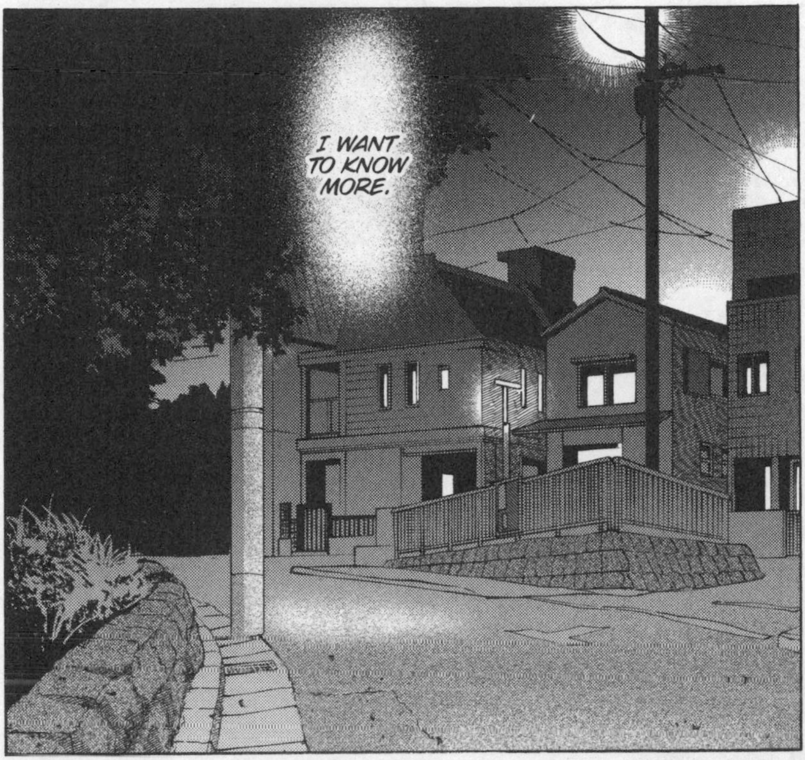
I WANT TO KNOW MORE.

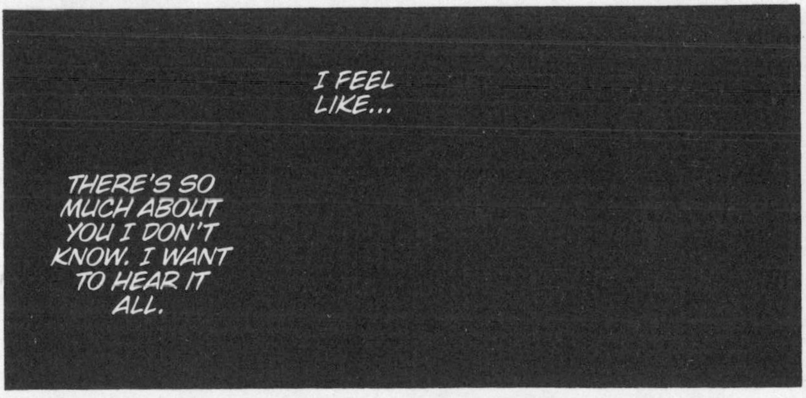
I FEEL LIKE...
THERE'S SO MUCH ABOUT YOU I DON'T KNOW. I WANT TO HEAR IT ALL.

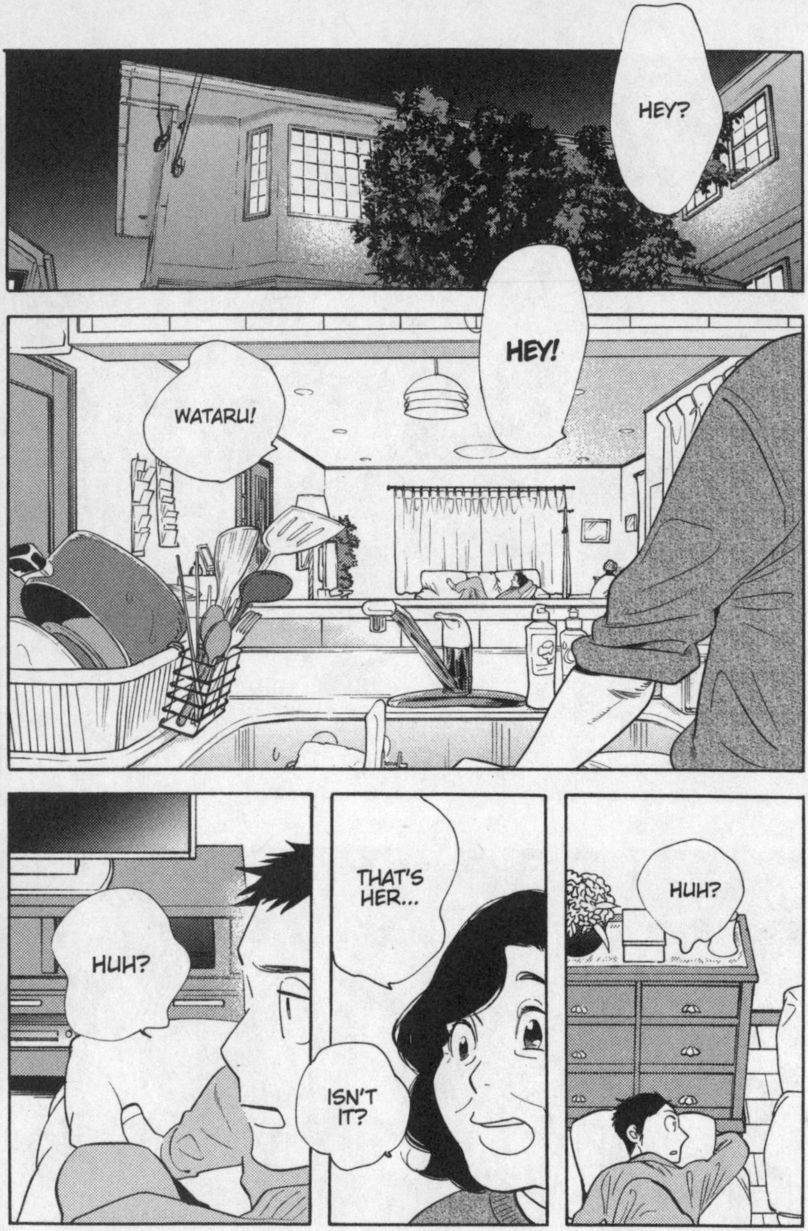
HEY?
HEY!
WATARU!
HUH?
THAT'S HER...
ISN'T IT?
HUH?

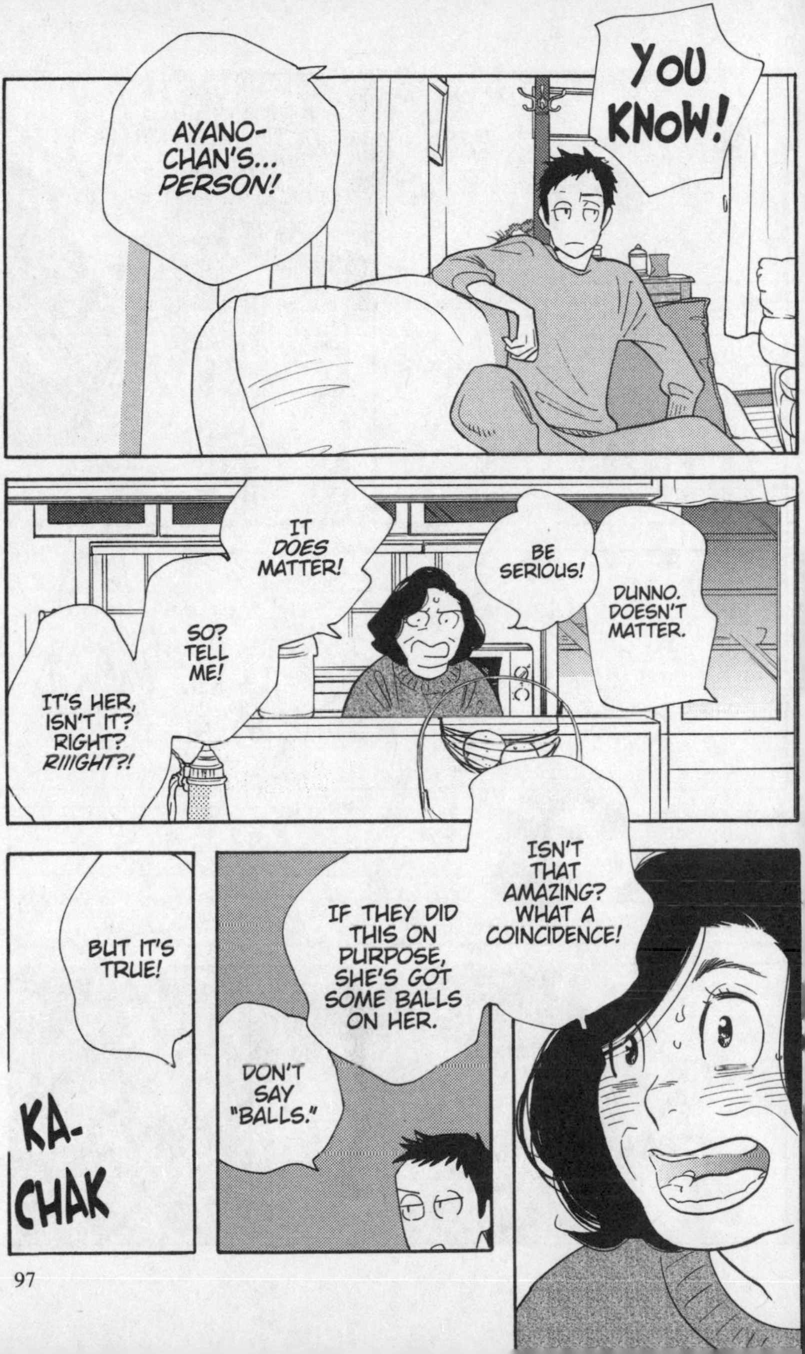
YOU KNOW!
AYANO-CHAN'S... PERSON!
DUNNO. DOESN'T MATTER.
BE SERIOUS!
IT DOES MATTER!
SO? TELL ME!
IT'S HER, ISN'T IT? RIGHT? RIIIGHT?!
ISN'T THAT AMAZING? WHAT A COINCIDENCE!
IF THEY DID THIS ON PURPOSE, SHE'S GOT SOME BALLS ON HER.
DON'T SAY "BALLS."
BUT IT'S TRUE!
KA-CHAK

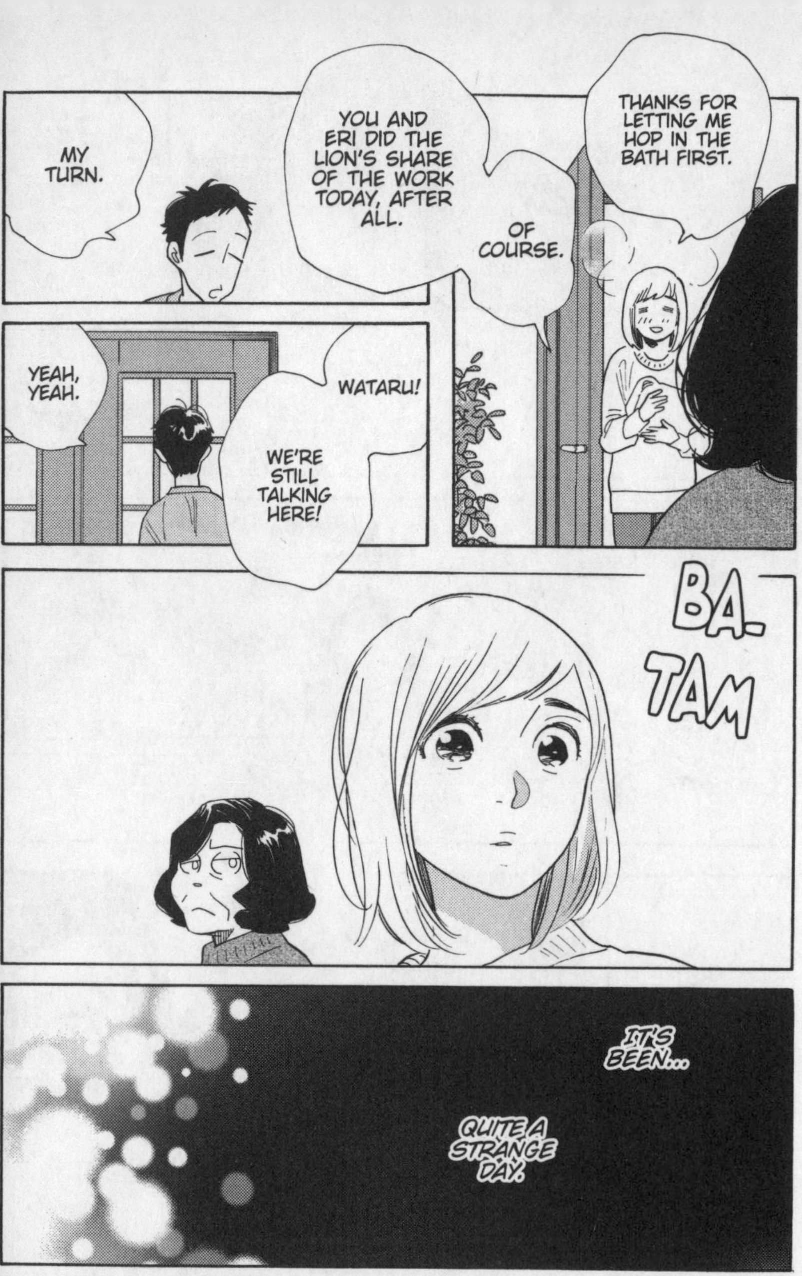
THANKS FOR LETTING ME HOP IN THE BATH FIRST.
OF COURSE.
YOU AND ERI DID THE LION'S SHARE OF THE WORK TODAY, AFTER ALL.
MY TURN.
WATARU!
WE'RE STILL TALKING HERE!
YEAH, YEAH.
BA-TAM
IT'S BEEN...
QUITE A STRANGE DAY.

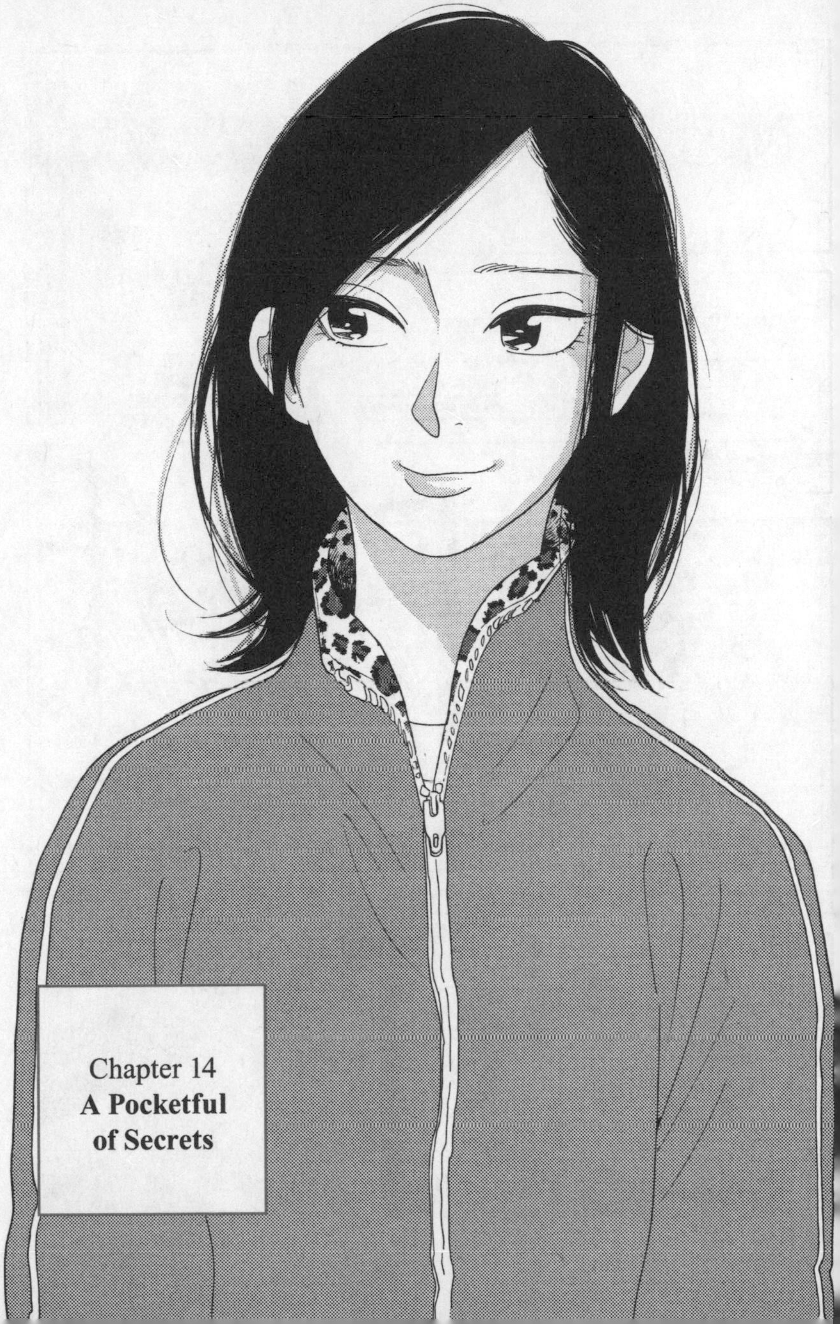
Chapter 14
A Pocketful
of Secrets

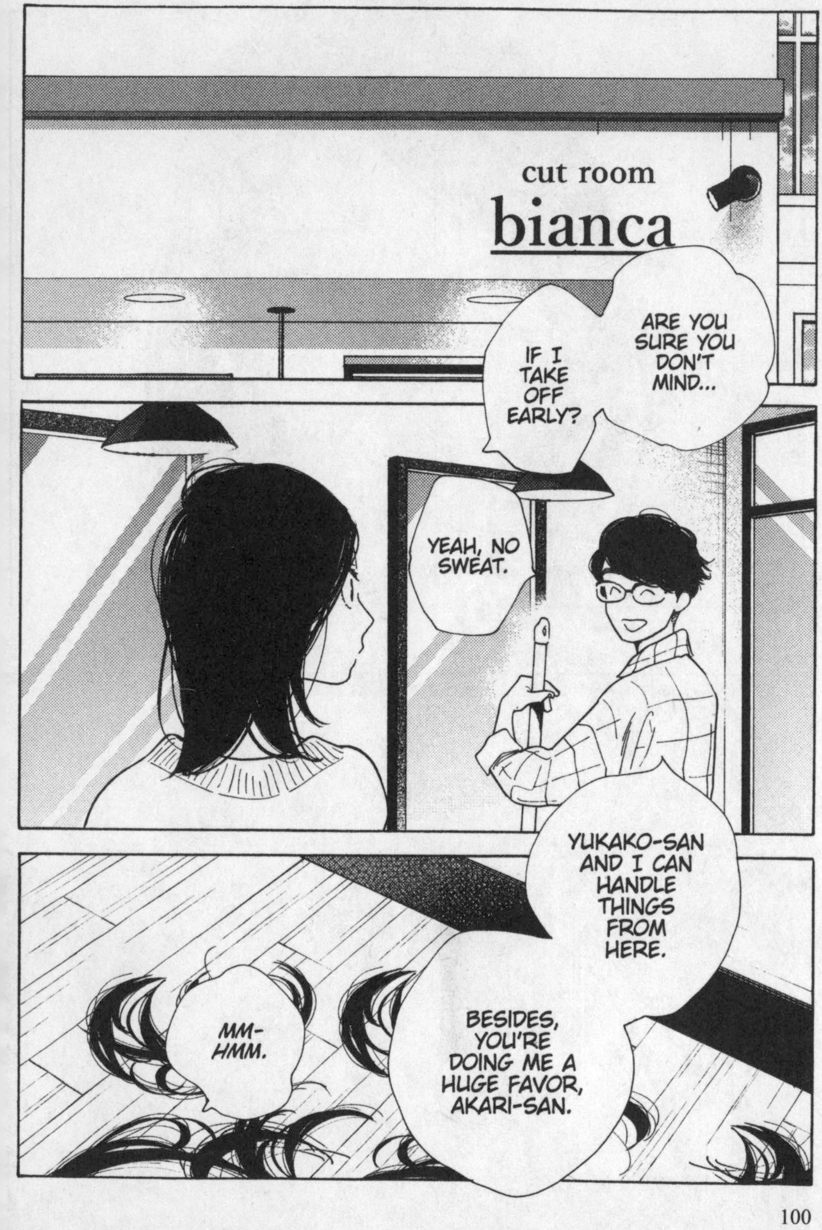
cut room
bianca
ARE YOU SURE YOU DON'T MIND...
IF I TAKE OFF EARLY?
YEAH, NO SWEAT.
YUKAKO-SAN AND I CAN HANDLE THINGS FROM HERE.
BESIDES, YOU'RE DOING ME A HUGE FAVOR, AKARI-SAN.
MM-HMM.

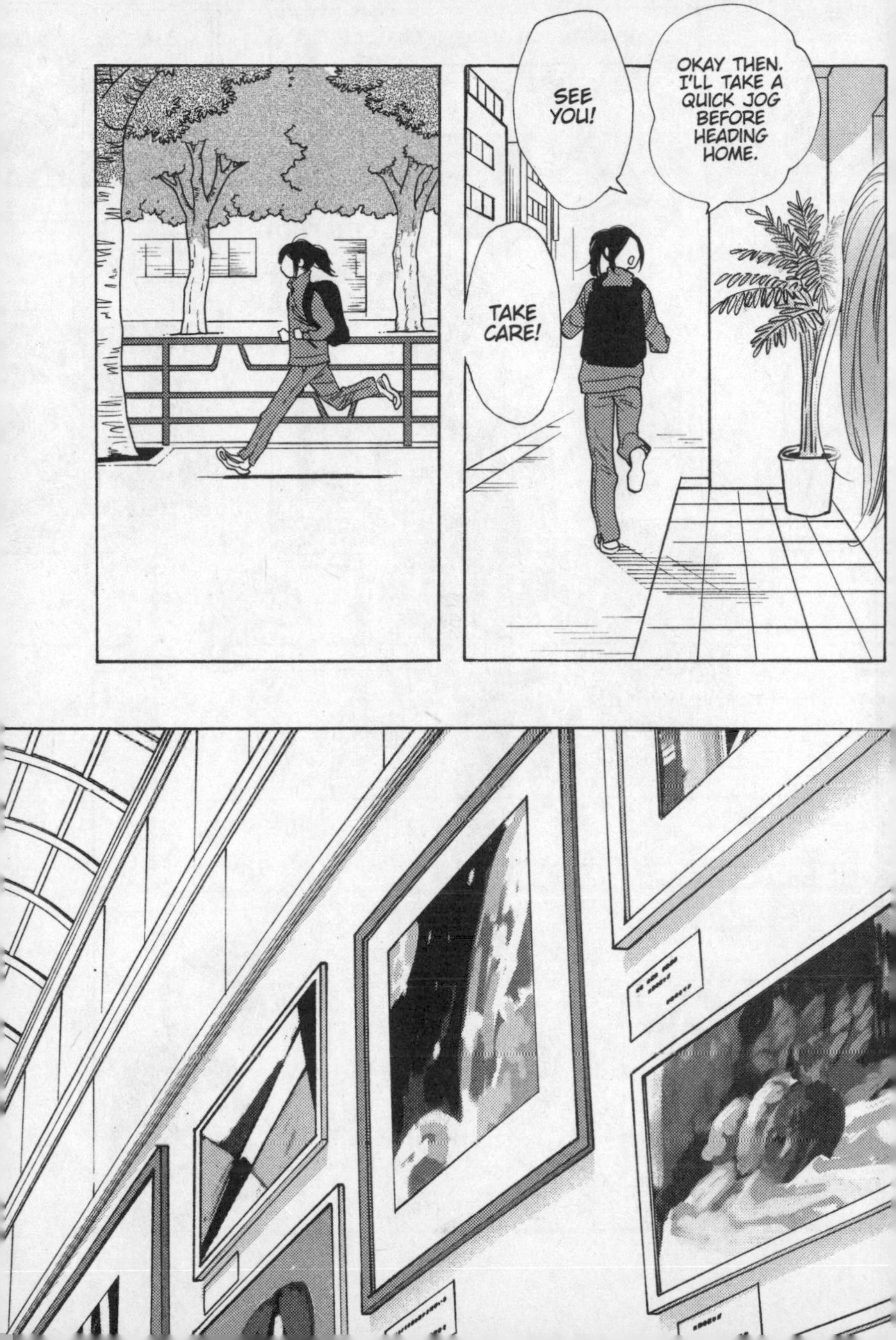
OKAY THEN. I'LL TAKE A QUICK JOG BEFORE HEADING HOME.
SEE YOU!
TAKE CARE!

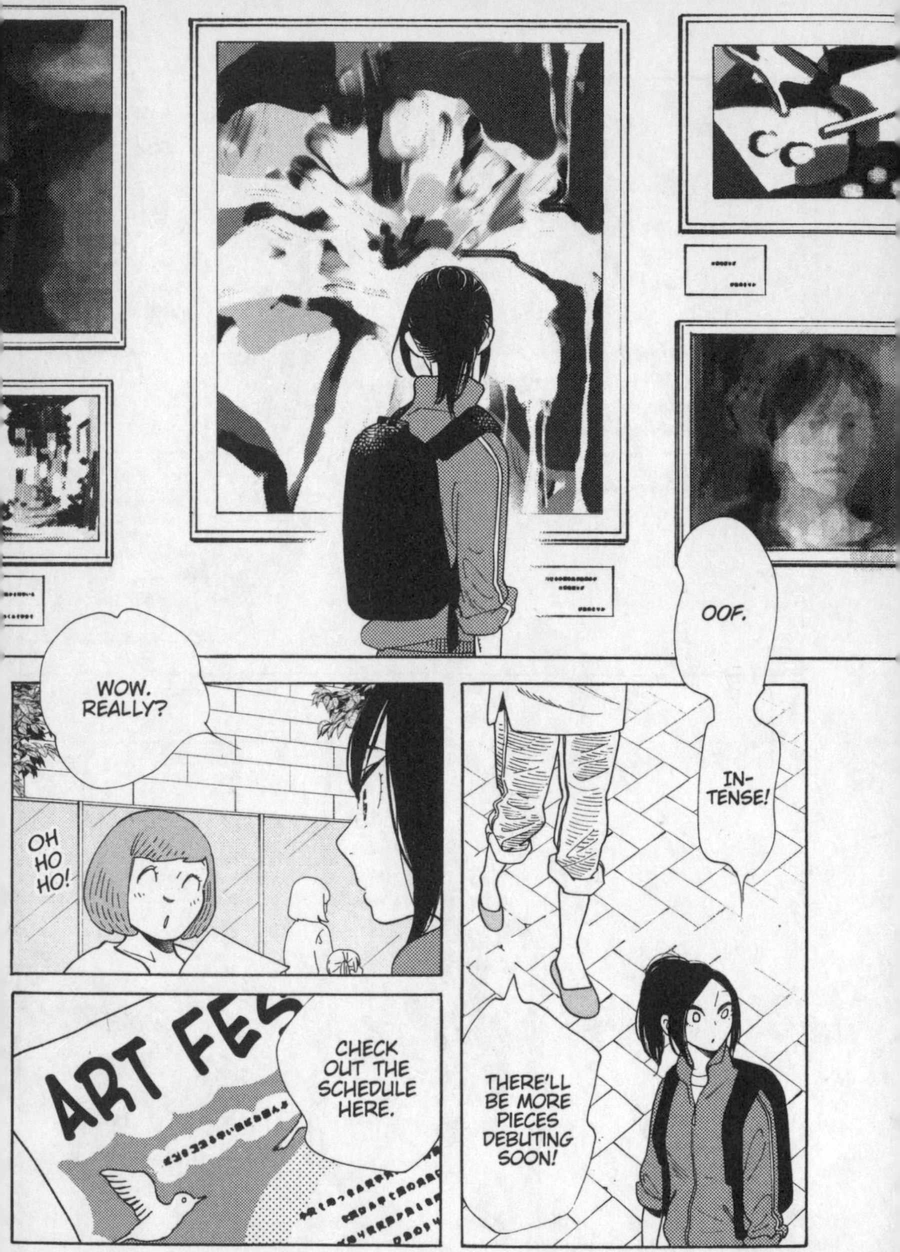
OOF.
IN-TENSE!
THERE'LL BE MORE PIECES DEBUTING SOON!
WOW. REALLY?
OH HO HO!
CHECK OUT THE SCHEDULE HERE.
ART FES

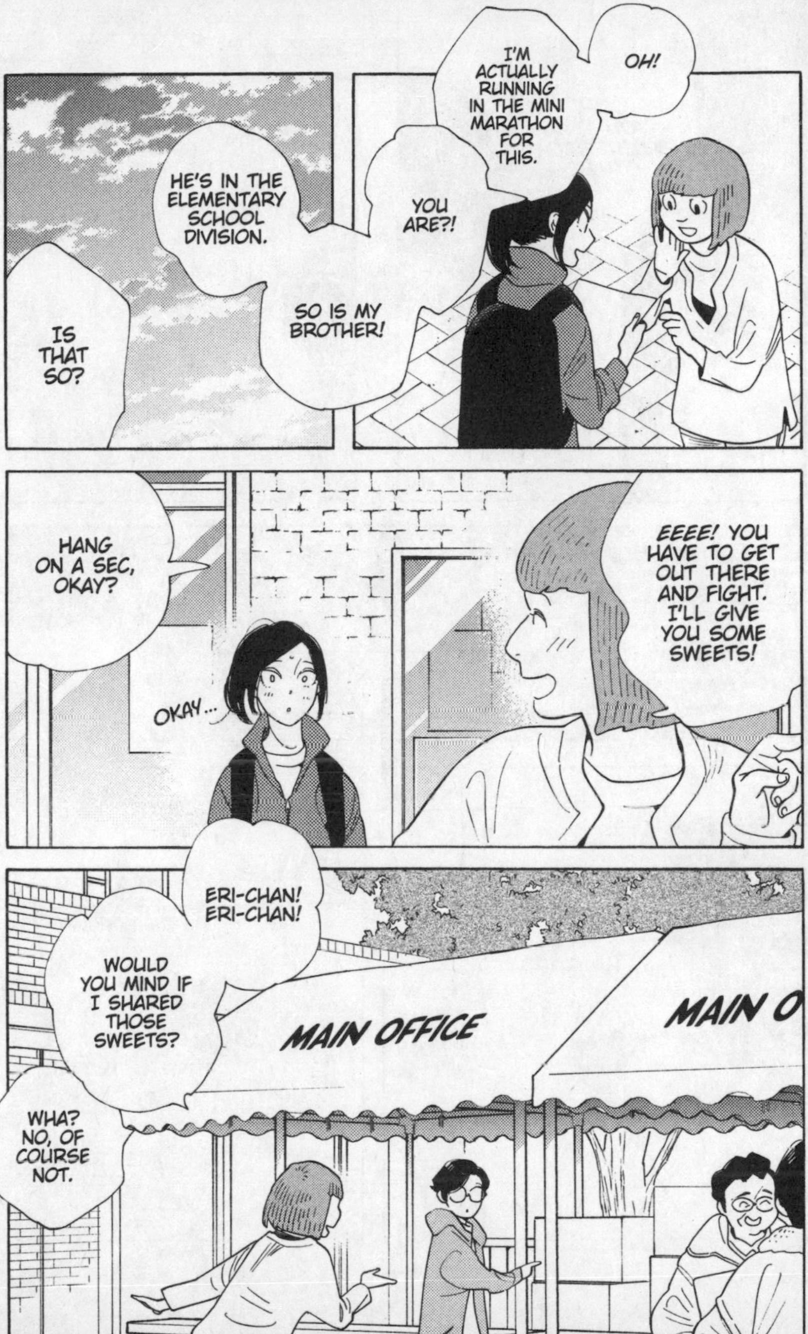
OH!
I'M ACTUALLY RUNNING IN THE MINI MARATHON FOR THIS.
YOU ARE?!
SO IS MY BROTHER!
HE'S IN THE ELEMENTARY SCHOOL DIVISION.
IS THAT SO?
EEEE! YOU HAVE TO GET OUT THERE AND FIGHT. I'LL GIVE YOU SOME SWEETS!
HANG ON A SEC, OKAY?
OKAY...
MAIN OFFICE
ERI-CHAN! ERI-CHAN!
WOULD YOU MIND IF I SHARED THOSE SWEETS?
WHA? NO, OF COURSE NOT.

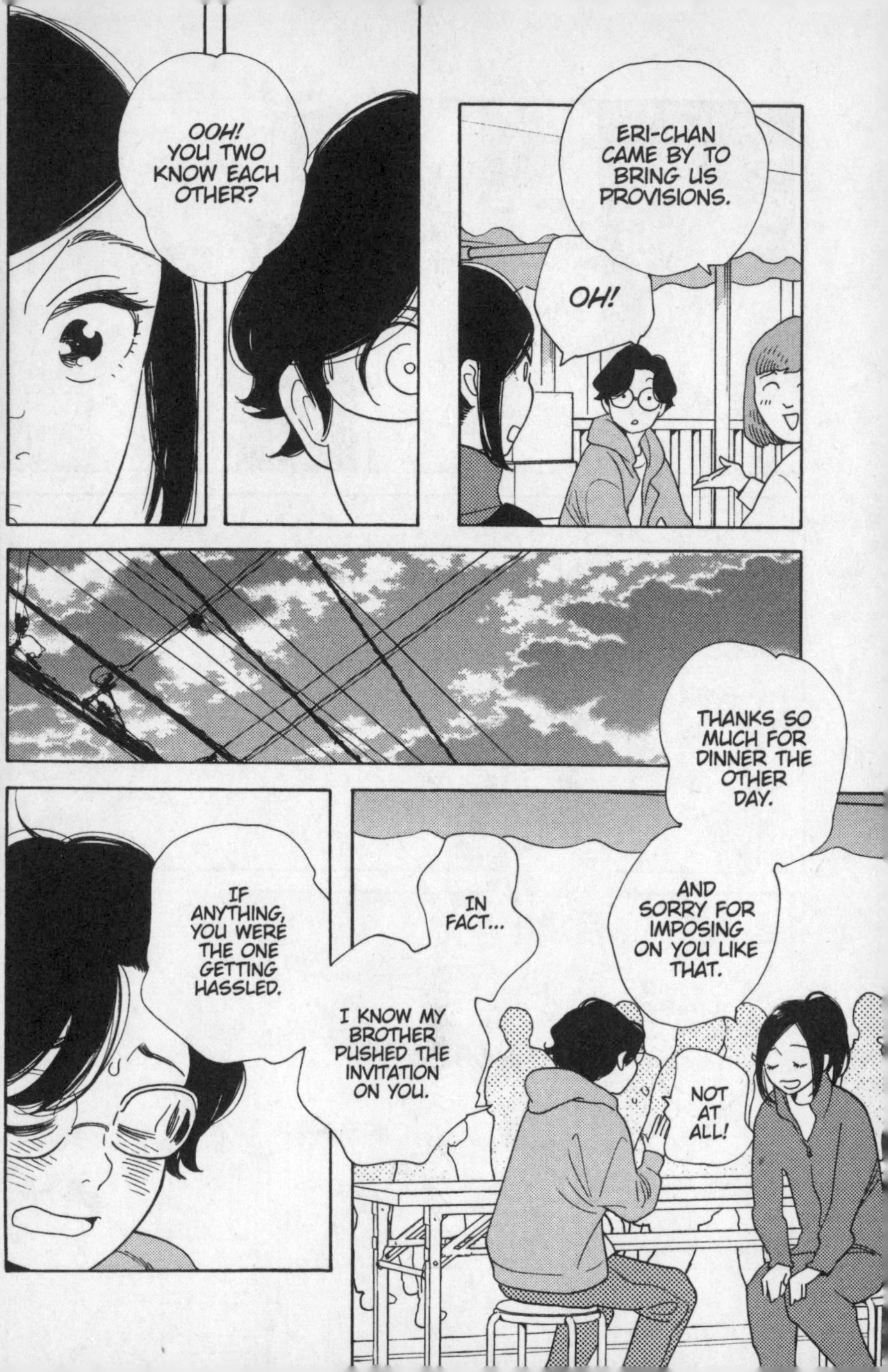
ERI-CHAN CAME BY TO BRING US PROVISIONS.
OH!
OOH! YOU TWO KNOW EACH OTHER?
THANKS SO MUCH FOR DINNER THE OTHER DAY.
AND SORRY FOR IMPOSING ON YOU LIKE THAT.
NOT AT ALL!
IN FACT...
I KNOW MY BROTHER PUSHED THE INVITATION ON YOU.
IF ANYTHING, YOU WERE THE ONE GETTING HASSLED.

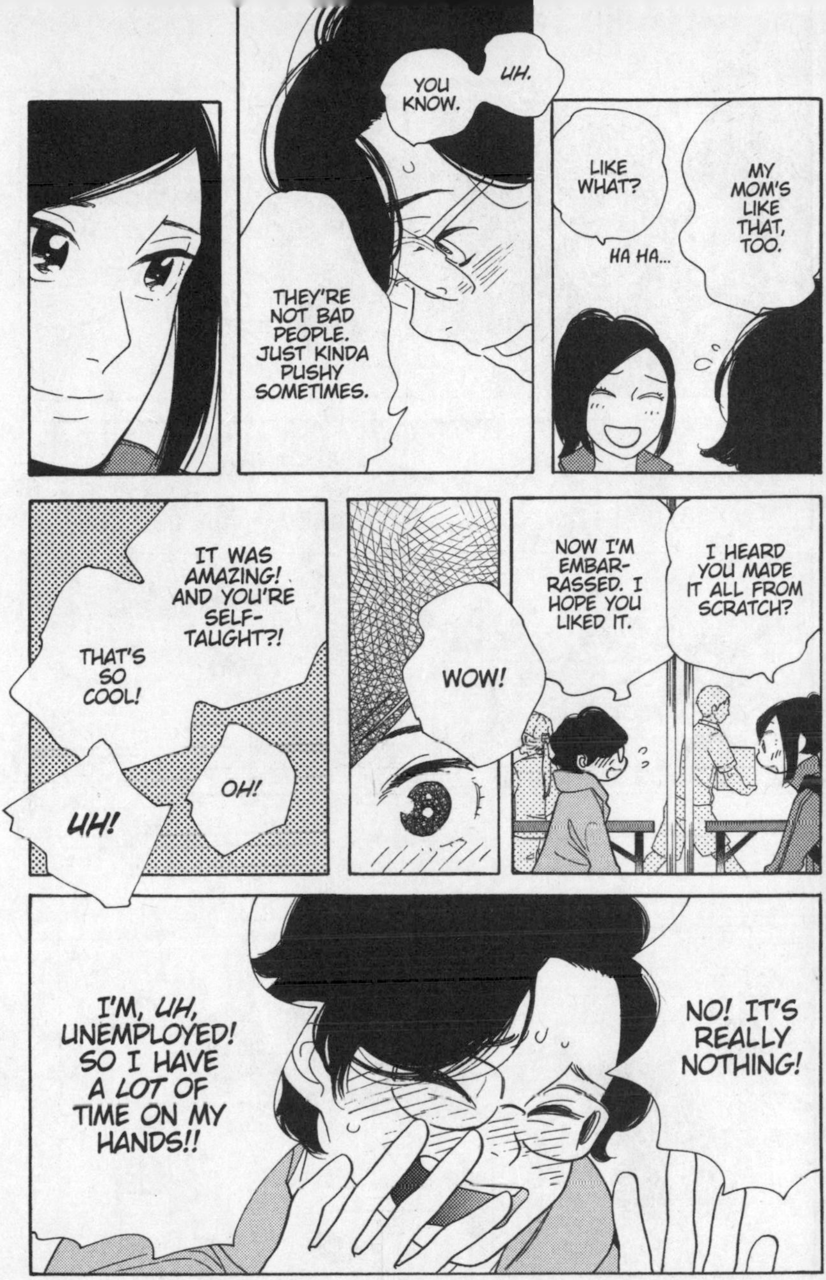
MY MOM'S LIKE THAT, TOO.
LIKE WHAT?
HA HA...
UH.
YOU KNOW.
THEY'RE NOT BAD PEOPLE. JUST KINDA PUSHY SOMETIMES.
I HEARD YOU MADE IT ALL FROM SCRATCH?
NOW I'M EMBAR-RASSED. I HOPE YOU LIKED IT.
WOW!
IT WAS AMAZING! AND YOU'RE SELF-TAUGHT?!
THAT'S SO COOL!
OH!
UH!
NO! IT'S REALLY NOTHING!
I'M, UH, UNEMPLOYED! SO I HAVE A LOT OF TIME ON MY HANDS!!

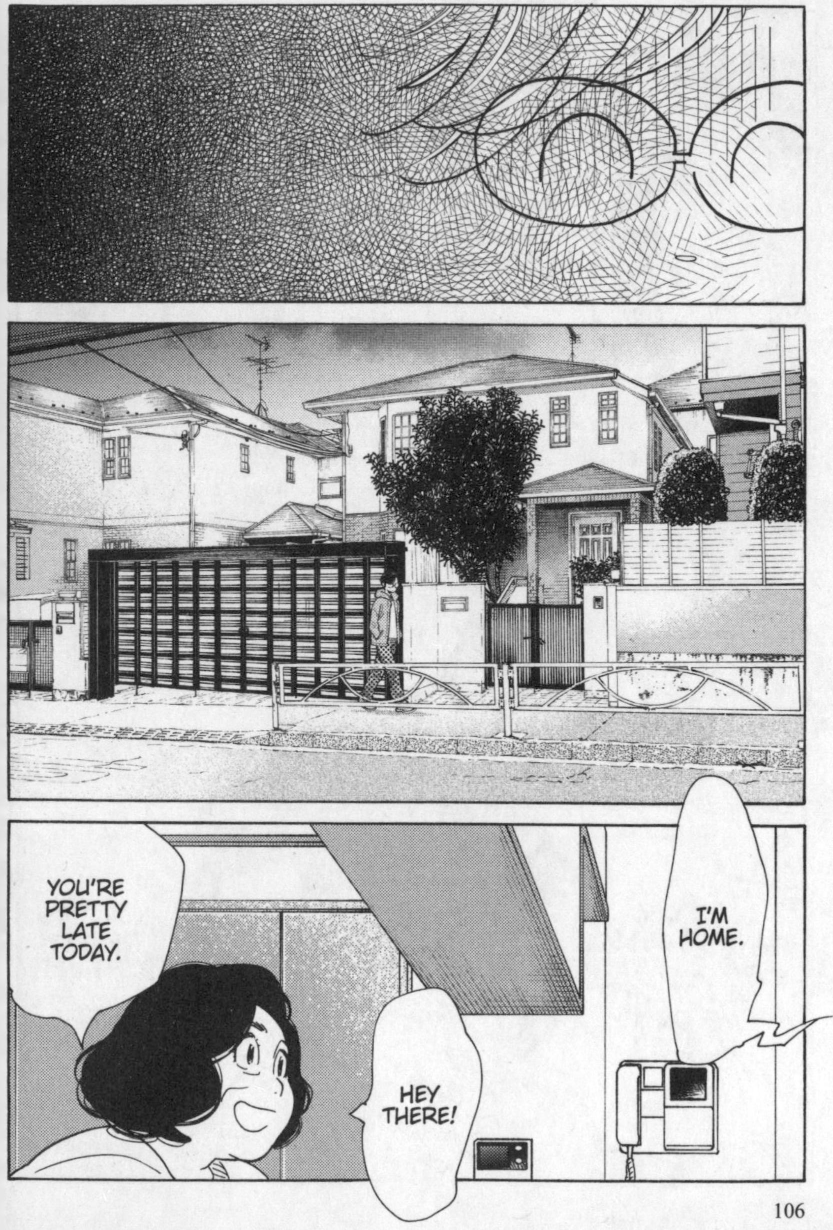
I'M HOME.
HEY THERE!
YOU'RE PRETTY LATE TODAY.

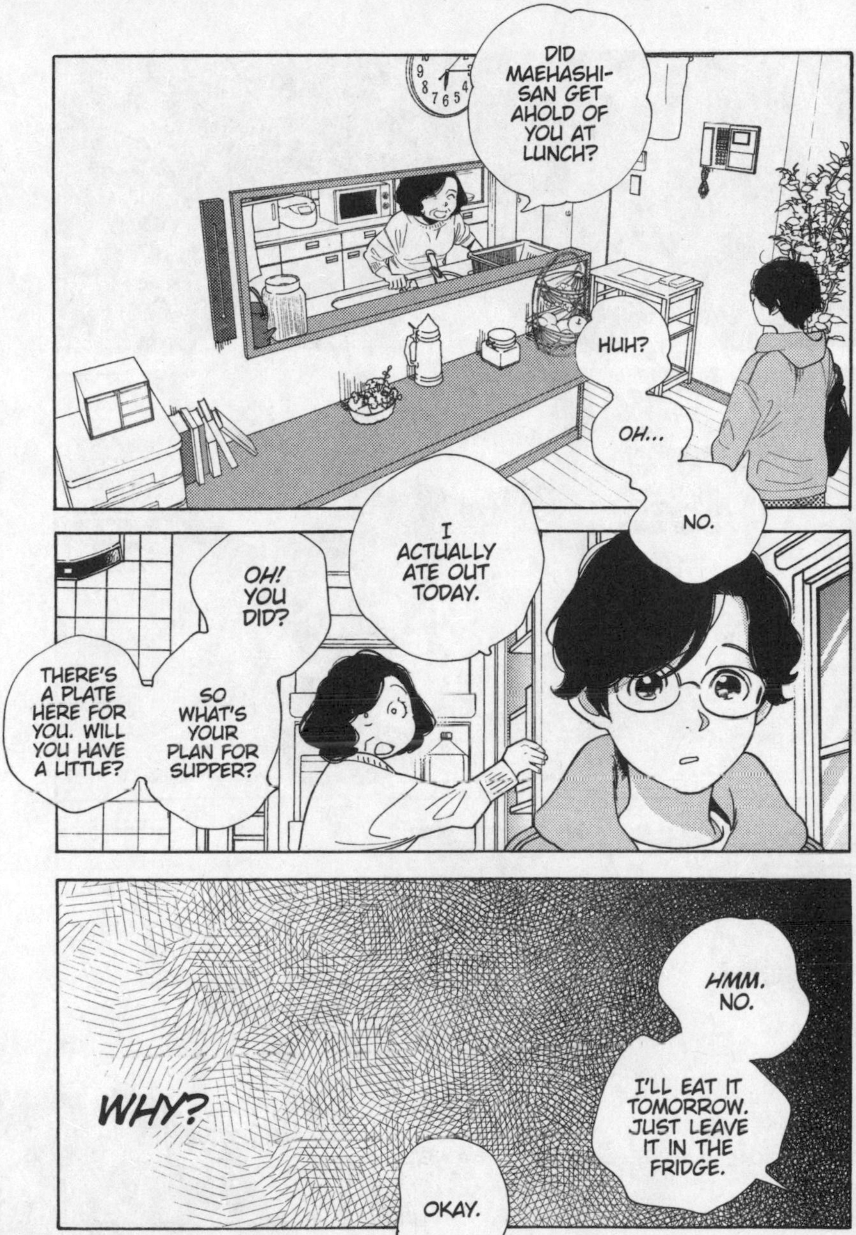
DID MAEHASHI-SAN GET AHOLD OF YOU AT LUNCH?
HUH?
OH...
NO.
I ACTUALLY ATE OUT TODAY.
OH! YOU DID?
SO WHAT'S YOUR PLAN FOR SUPPER?
THERE'S A PLATE HERE FOR YOU. WILL YOU HAVE A LITTLE?
HMM. NO.
I'LL EAT IT TOMORROW. JUST LEAVE IT IN THE FRIDGE.
OKAY.
WHY?

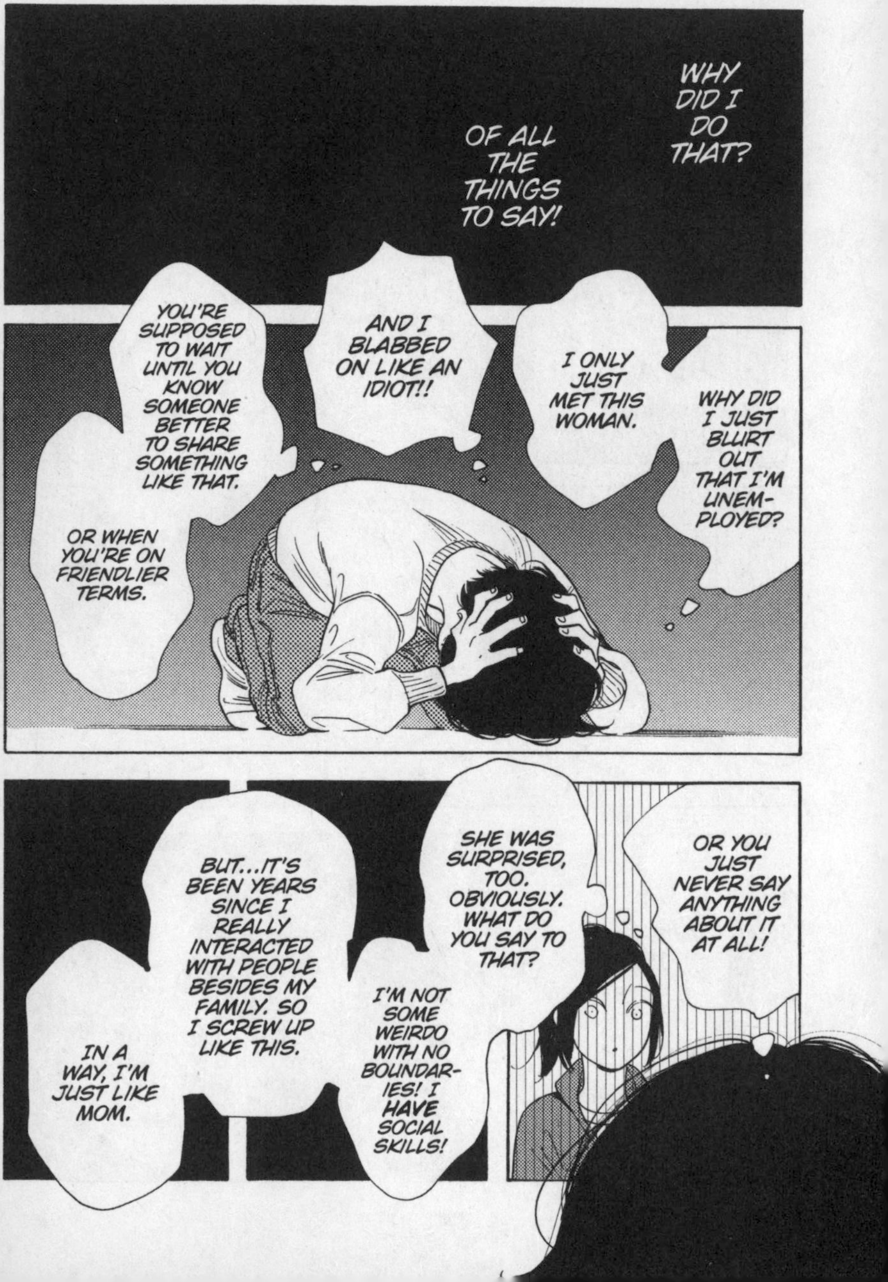

WHY DID I DO THAT?
OF ALL THE THINGS TO SAY!
I ONLY JUST MET THIS WOMAN.
WHY DID I JUST BLURT OUT THAT I'M UNEMPLOYED?
AND I BLABBED ON LIKE AN IDIOT!!
YOU'RE SUPPOSED TO WAIT UNTIL YOU KNOW SOMEONE BETTER TO SHARE SOMETHING LIKE THAT.
OR WHEN YOU'RE ON FRIENDLIER TERMS.
OR YOU JUST NEVER SAY ANYTHING ABOUT IT AT ALL!
SHE WAS SURPRISED, TOO. OBVIOUSLY. WHAT DO YOU SAY TO THAT?
I'M NOT SOME WEIRDO WITH NO BOUNDARIES! I HAVE SOCIAL SKILLS!
BUT...IT'S BEEN YEARS SINCE I REALLY INTERACTED WITH PEOPLE BESIDES MY FAMILY. SO I SCREW UP LIKE THIS.
IN A WAY, I'M JUST LIKE MOM.

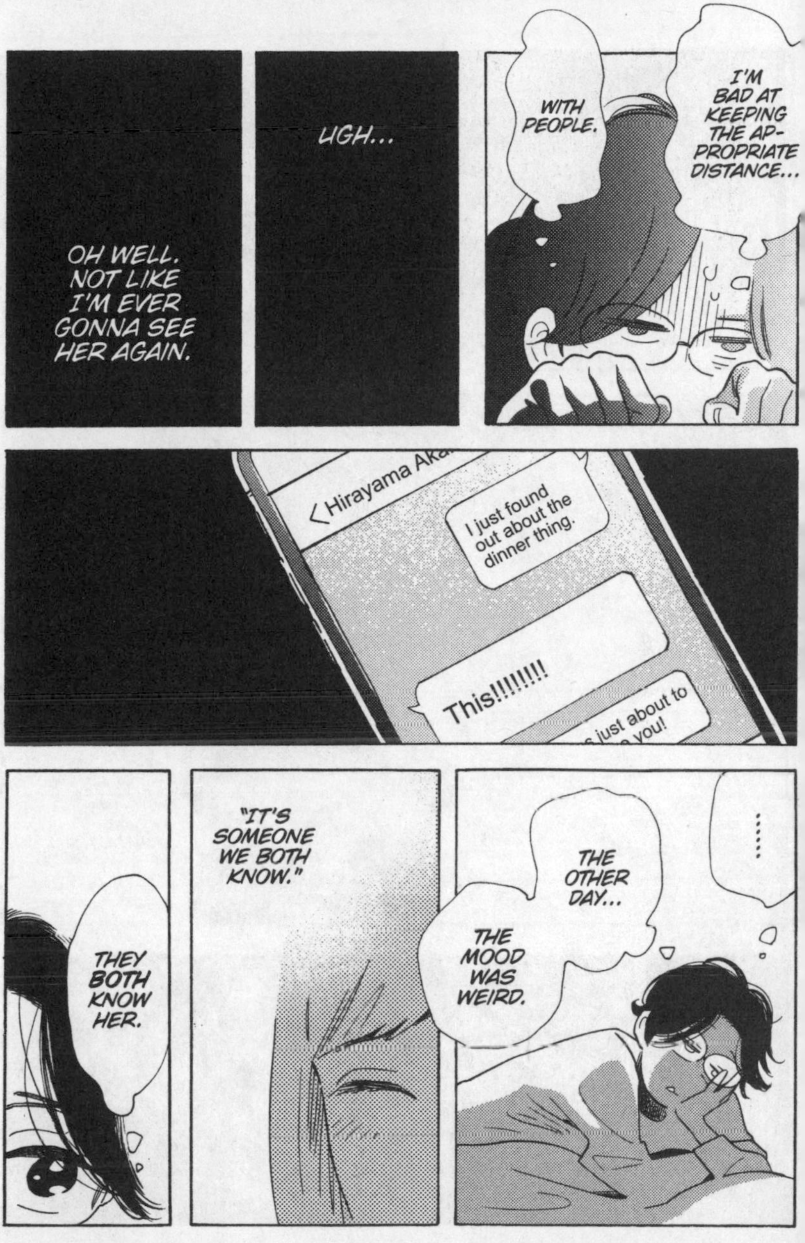
I'M BAD AT KEEPING THE AP-PROPRIATE DISTANCE...
WITH PEOPLE.
UGH...
OH WELL. NOT LIKE I'M EVER GONNA SEE HER AGAIN.
I just found out about the dinner thing.
This!!!!!!!!
......
THE OTHER DAY...
THE MOOD WAS WEIRD.
"IT'S SOMEONE WE BOTH KNOW."
THEY BOTH KNOW HER.

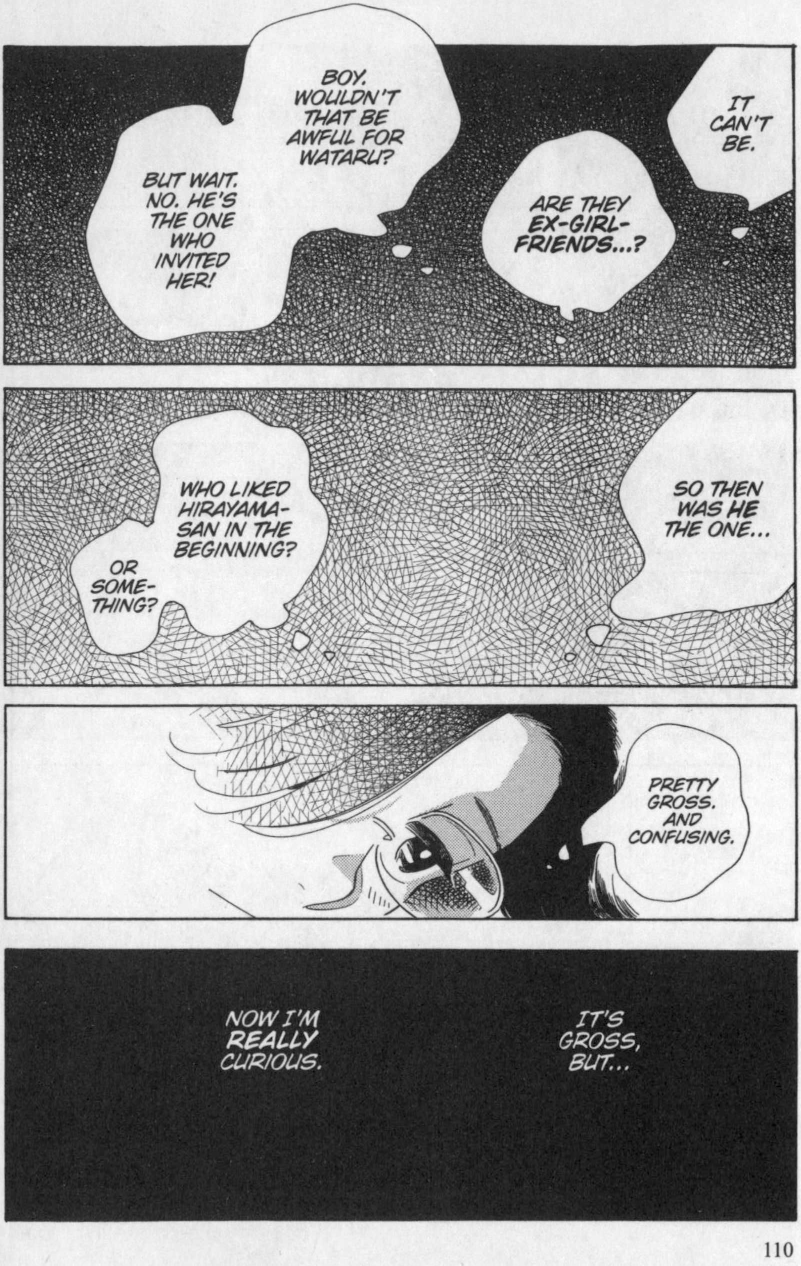
IT CAN'T BE.
ARE THEY EX-GIRL-FRIENDS...?
BOY. WOULDN'T THAT BE AWFUL FOR WATARU?
BUT WAIT. NO. HE'S THE ONE WHO INVITED HER!
SO THEN WAS HE THE ONE...
WHO LIKED HIRAYAMA-SAN IN THE BEGINNING?
OR SOME-THING?
PRETTY GROSS. AND CONFUSING.
IT'S GROSS, BUT...
NOW I'M REALLY CURIOUS.

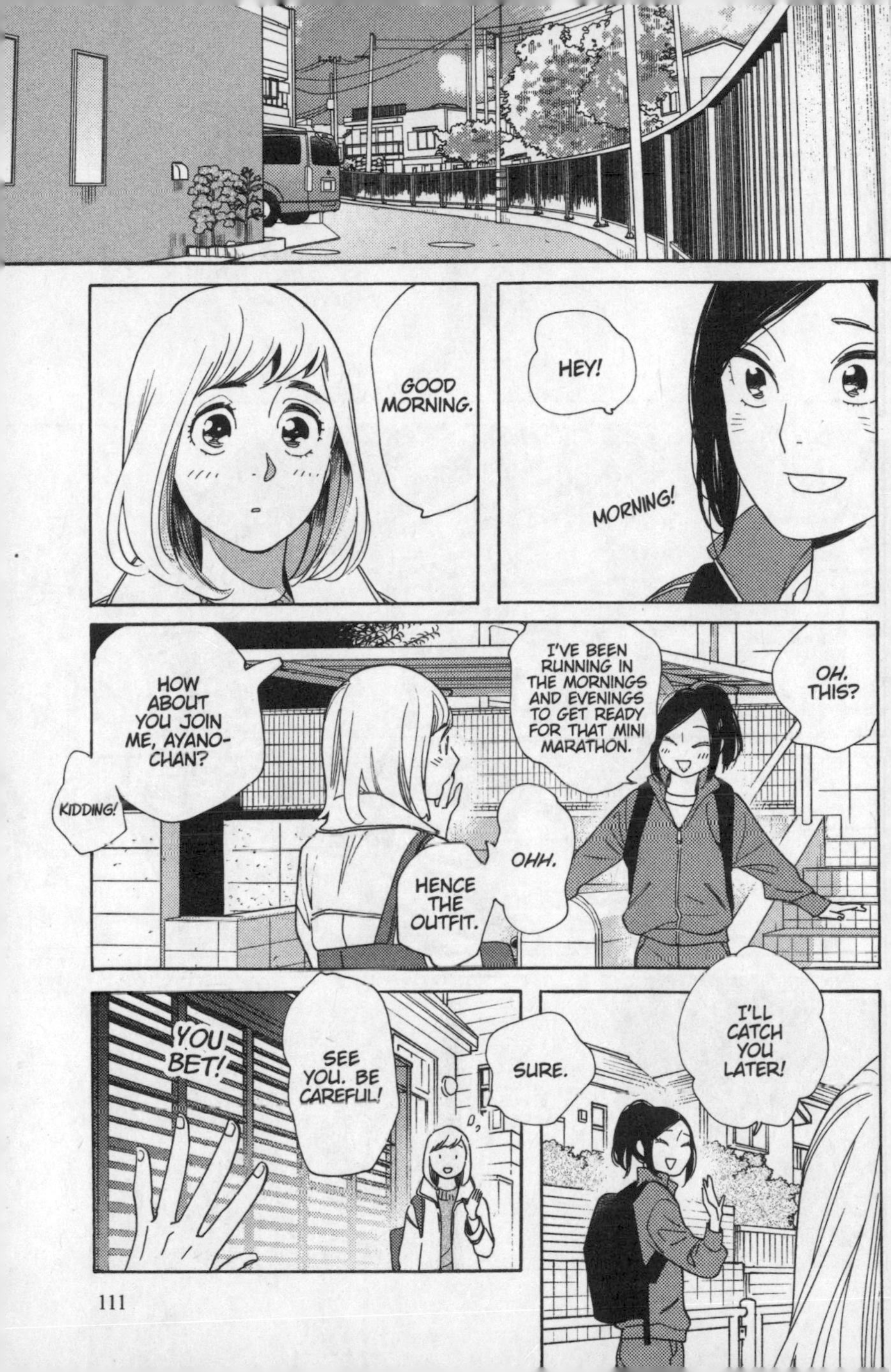
HEY!
MORNING!
GOOD MORNING.
OH. THIS?
I'VE BEEN RUNNING IN THE MORNINGS AND EVENINGS TO GET READY FOR THAT MINI MARATHON.
OHH.
HENCE THE OUTFIT.
HOW ABOUT YOU JOIN ME, AYANO-CHAN?
KIDDING!
I'LL CATCH YOU LATER!
SURE.
SEE YOU. BE CAREFUL!
YOU BET!

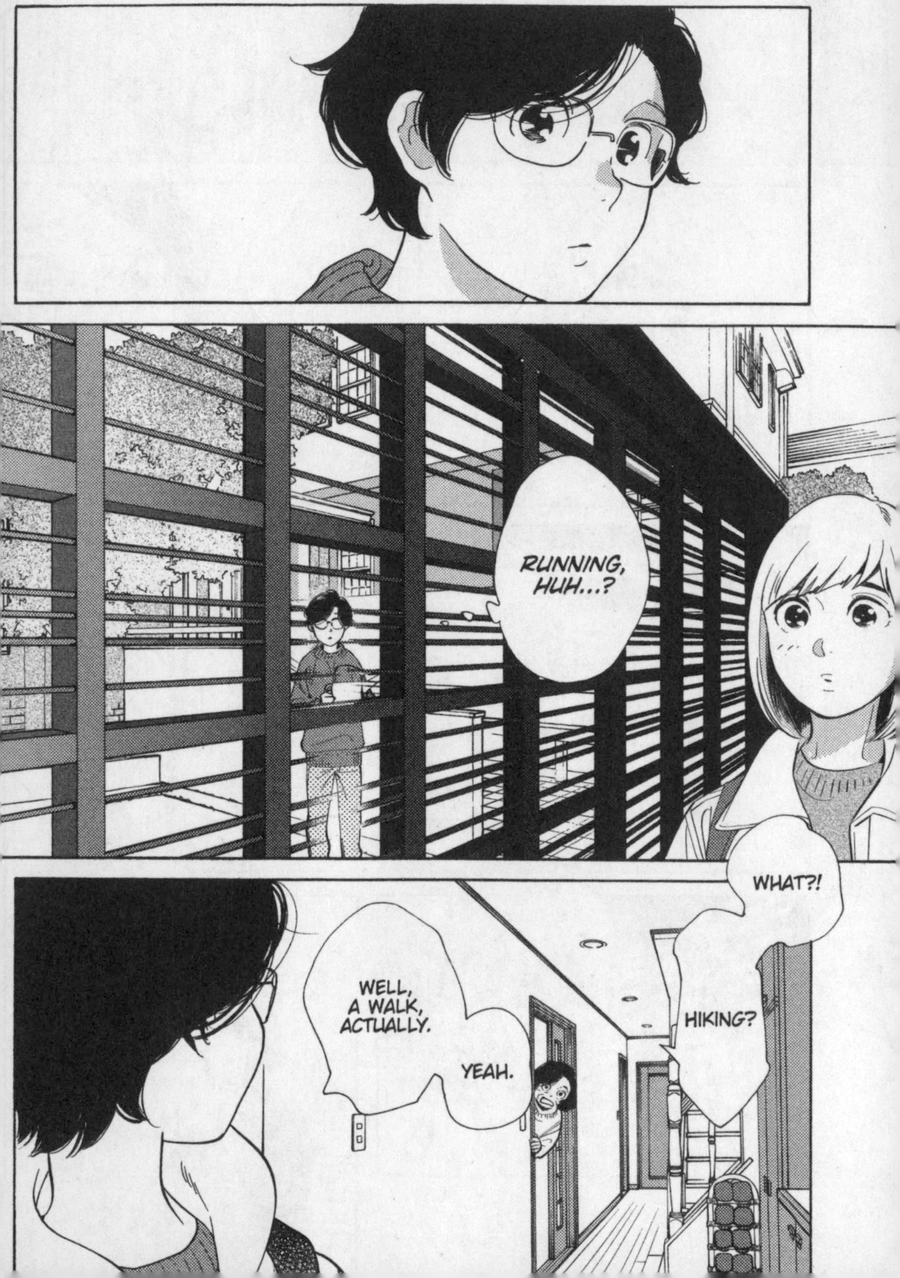
RUNNING, HUH...?
WHAT?!
HIKING?
WELL, A WALK, ACTUALLY.
YEAH.

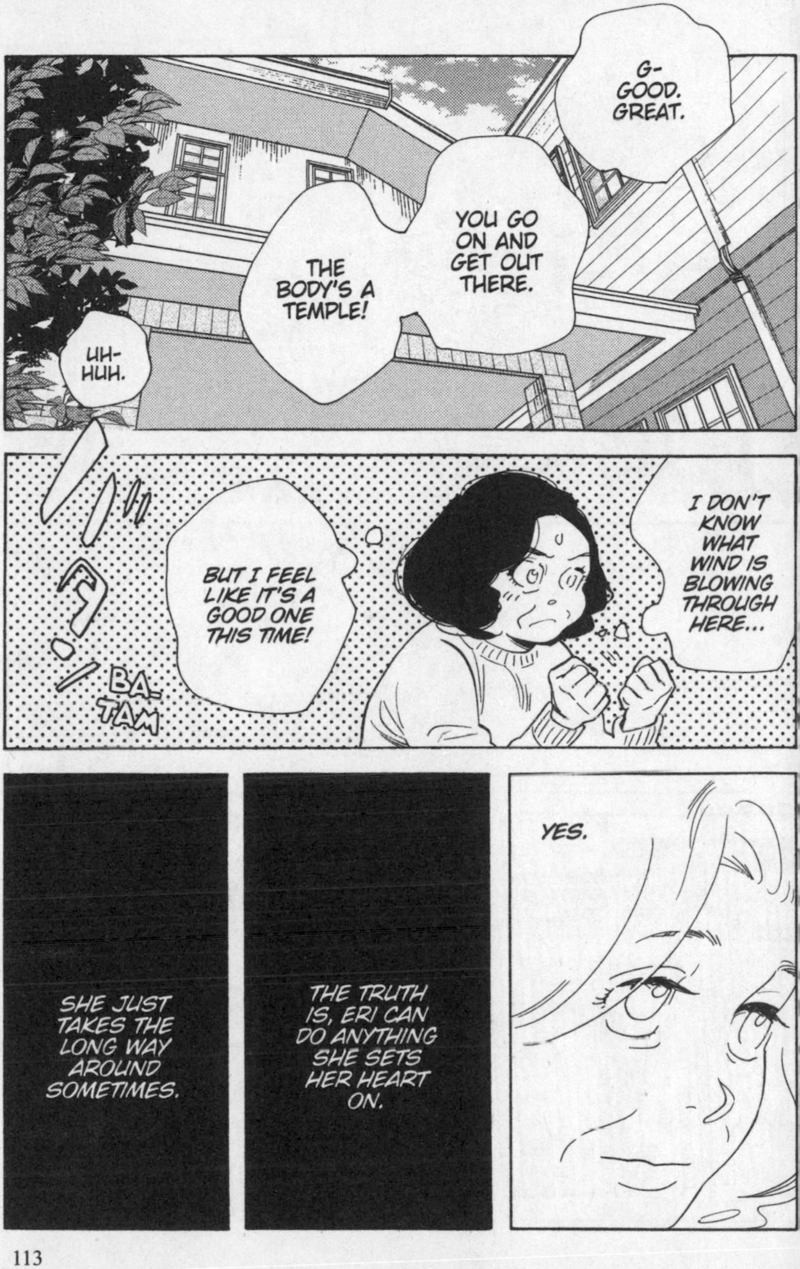
G- GOOD. GREAT.
YOU GO ON AND GET OUT THERE.
THE BODY'S A TEMPLE!
UH-HUH.
I DON'T KNOW WHAT WIND IS BLOWING THROUGH HERE...
BUT I FEEL LIKE IT'S A GOOD ONE THIS TIME!
BA-TAM
YES.
THE TRUTH IS, ERI CAN DO ANYTHING SHE SETS HER HEART ON.
SHE JUST TAKES THE LONG WAY AROUND SOMETIMES.

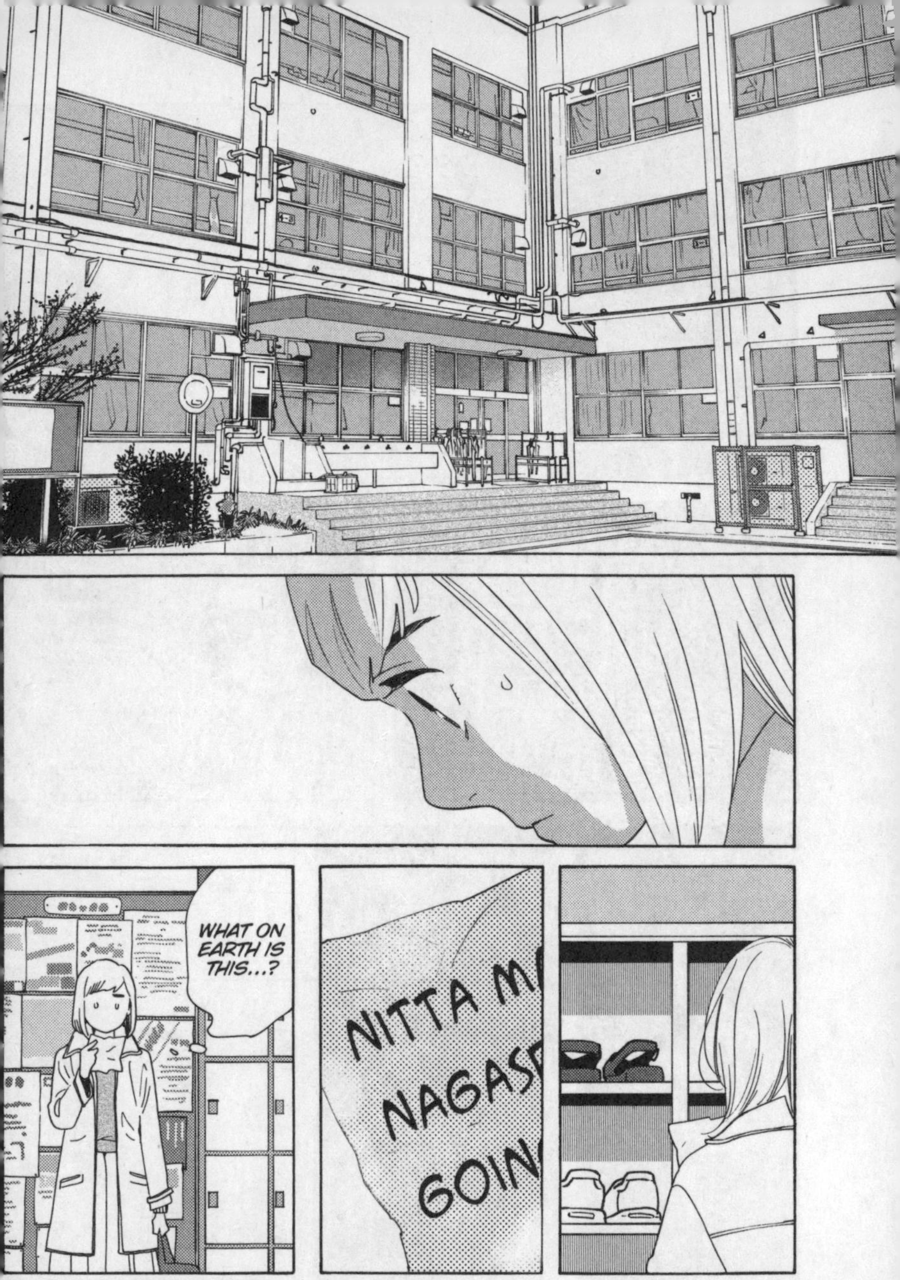
NITTA M
NAGAS
GOIN
WHAT ON EARTH IS THIS...?

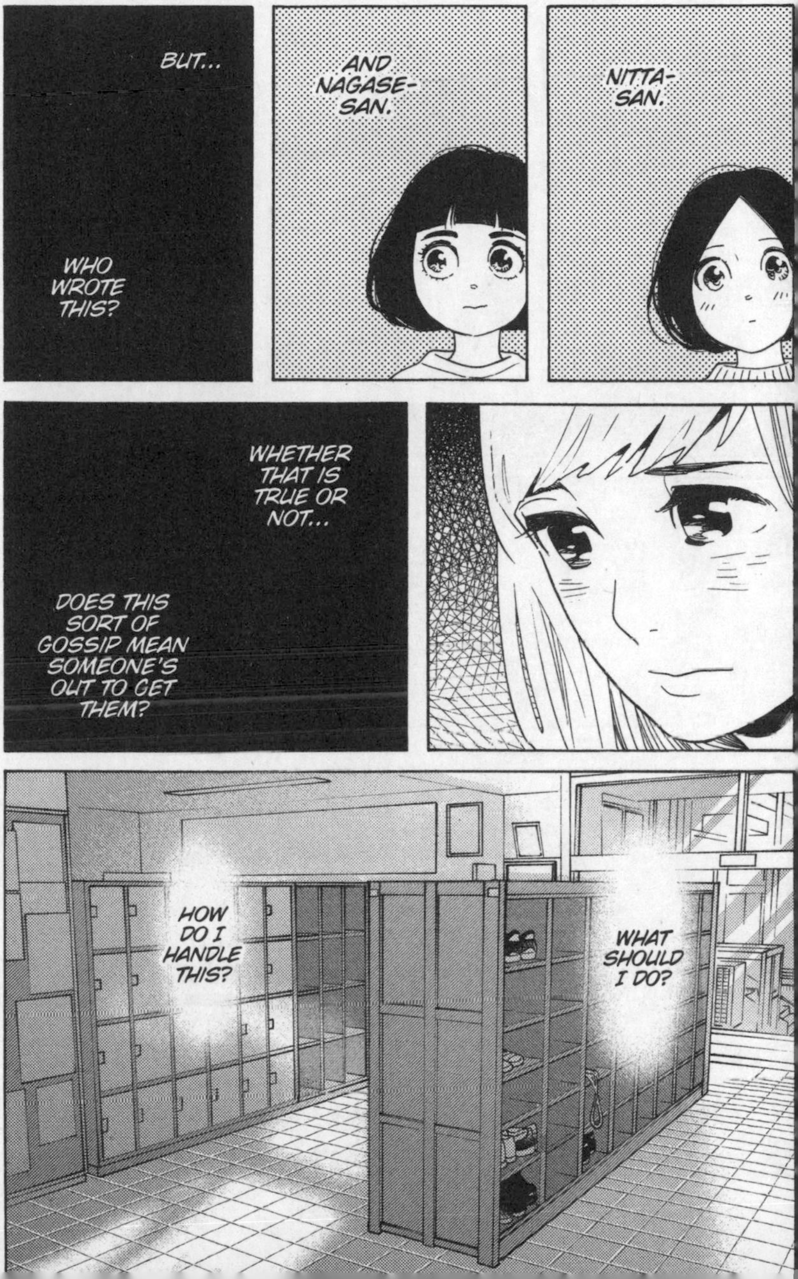
NITTA-SAN.
AND NAGASE-SAN.
BUT...
WHO WROTE THIS?
WHETHER THAT IS TRUE OR NOT...
DOES THIS SORT OF GOSSIP MEAN SOMEONE'S OUT TO GET THEM?
WHAT SHOULD I DO?
HOW DO I HANDLE THIS?

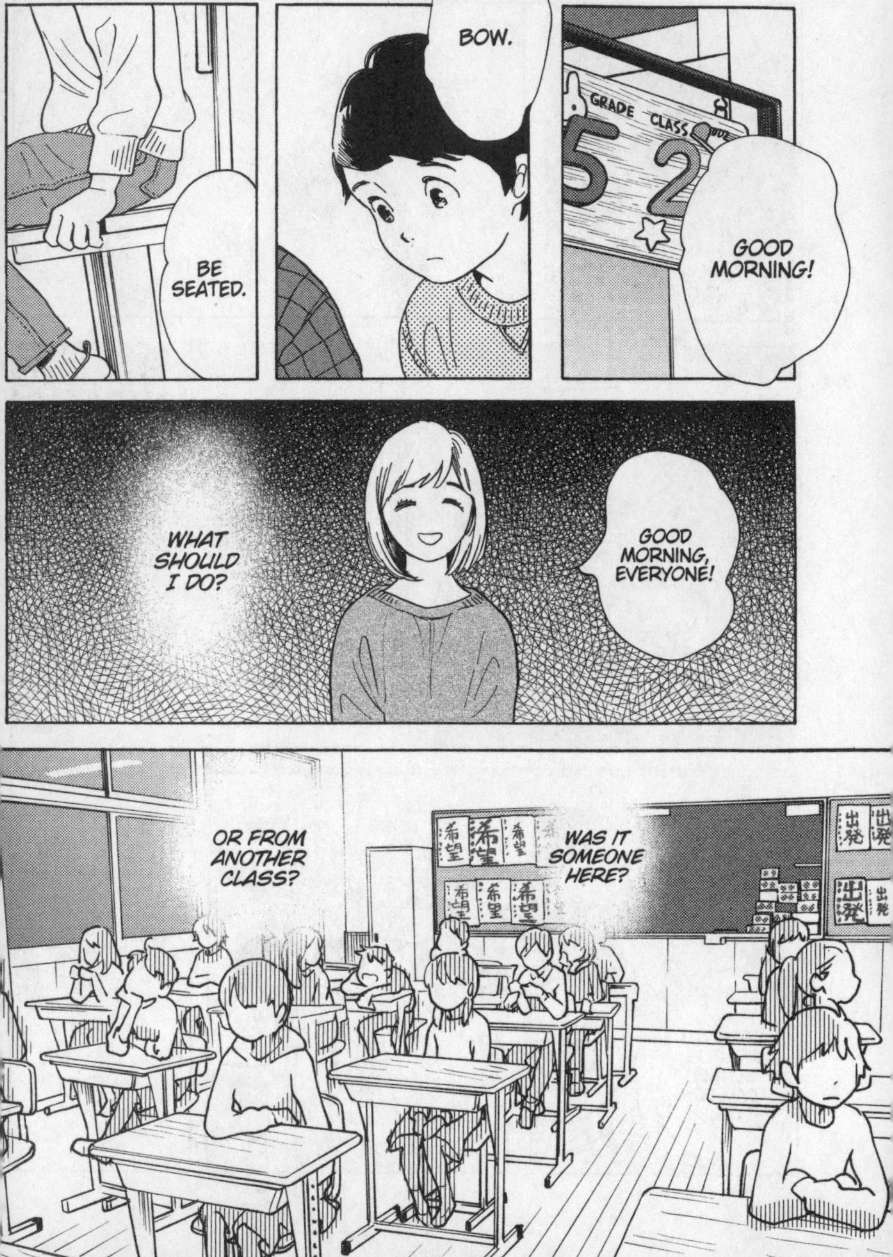
GRADE CLASS
5 2
GOOD MORNING!
BOW.
BE SEATED.
GOOD MORNING, EVERYONE!
WHAT SHOULD I DO?
出発
希望
WAS IT SOMEONE HERE?
OR FROM ANOTHER CLASS?

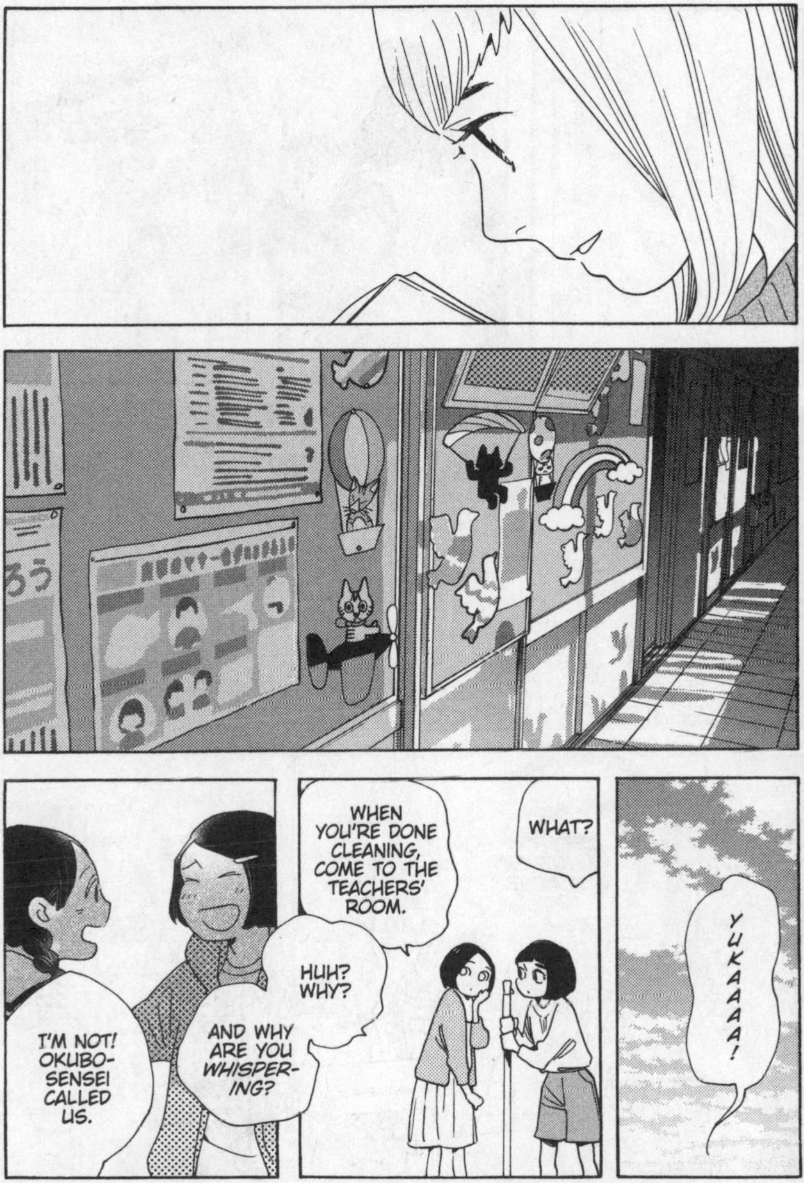
YUKAAAA!
WHAT?
WHEN YOU'RE DONE CLEANING, COME TO THE TEACHERS' ROOM.
HUH? WHY?
AND WHY ARE YOU WHISPERING?
I'M NOT! OKUBO-SENSEI CALLED US.

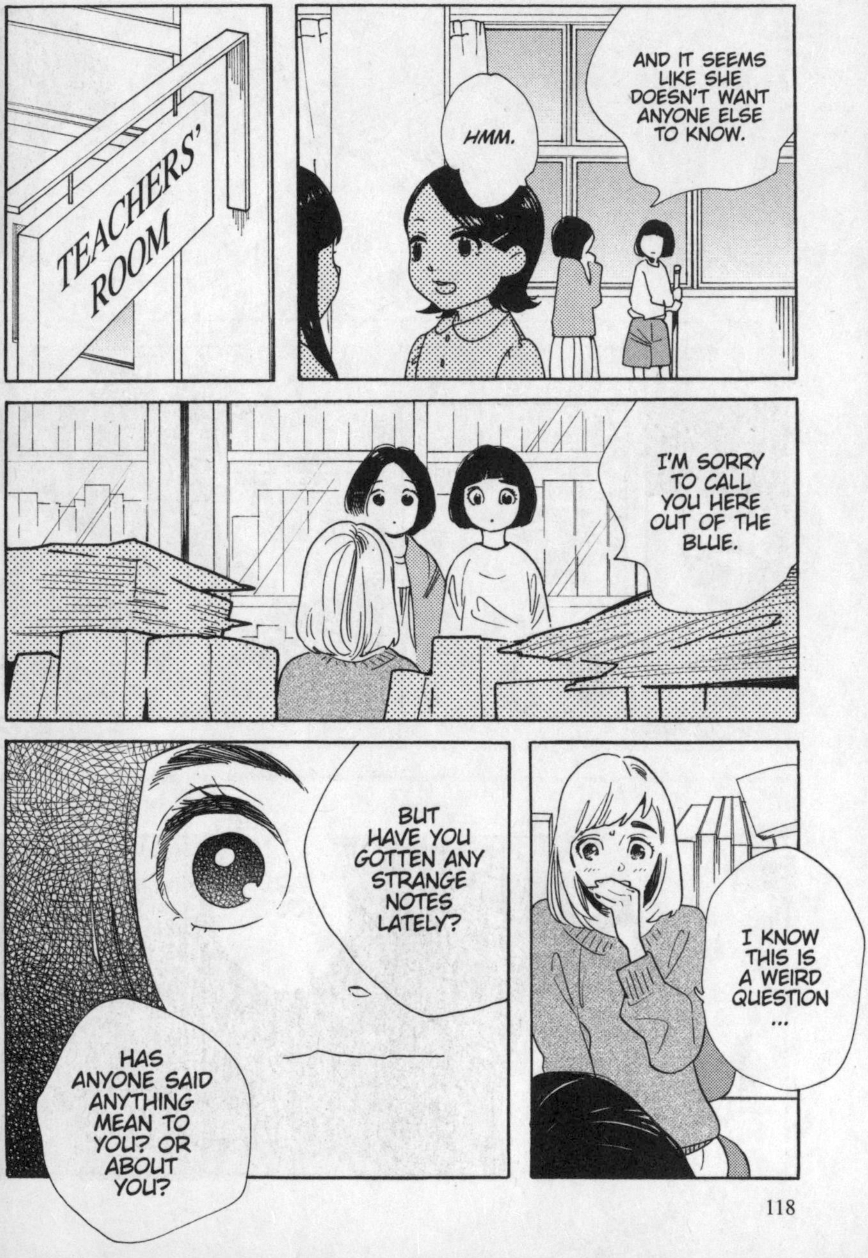
AND IT SEEMS LIKE SHE DOESN'T WANT ANYONE ELSE TO KNOW.
HMM.
TEACHERS' ROOM
I'M SORRY TO CALL YOU HERE OUT OF THE BLUE.
I KNOW THIS IS A WEIRD QUESTION ...
BUT HAVE YOU GOTTEN ANY STRANGE NOTES LATELY?
HAS ANYONE SAID ANYTHING MEAN TO YOU? OR ABOUT YOU?

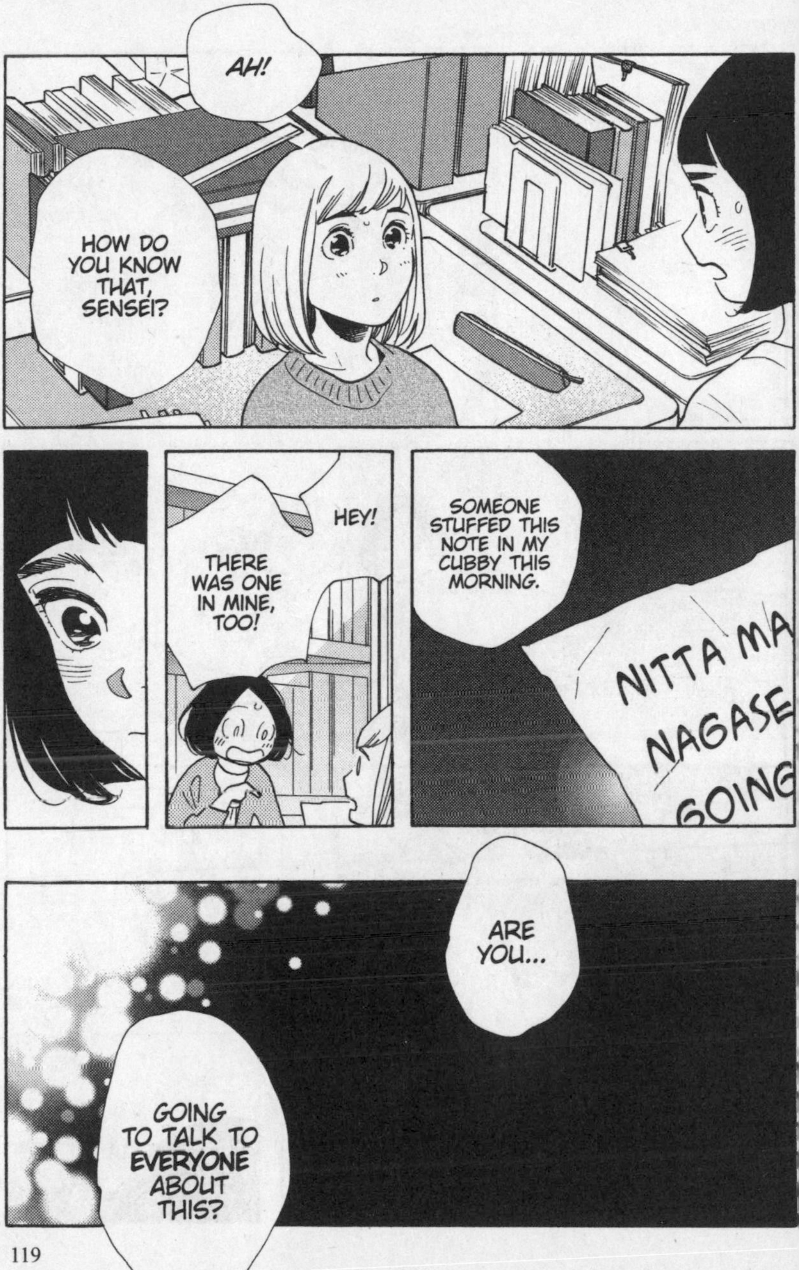
AH!
HOW DO YOU KNOW THAT, SENSEI?
SOMEONE STUFFED THIS NOTE IN MY CUBBY THIS MORNING.
NITTA MA
NAGASE
GOING
HEY!
THERE WAS ONE IN MINE, TOO!
ARE YOU...
GOING TO TALK TO EVERYONE ABOUT THIS?

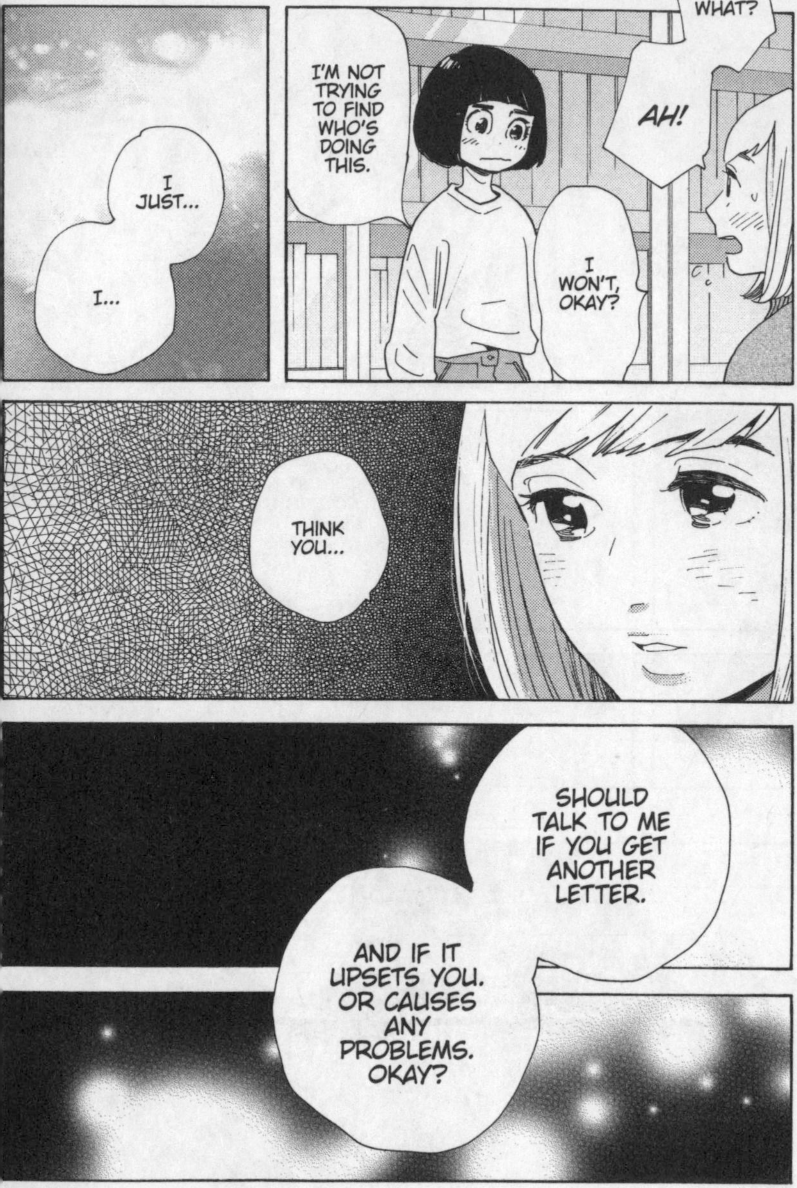
WHAT?
AH!
I'M NOT TRYING TO FIND WHO'S DOING THIS.
I WON'T, OKAY?
I JUST...
I...
THINK YOU...
SHOULD TALK TO ME IF YOU GET ANOTHER LETTER.
AND IF IT UPSETS YOU. OR CAUSES ANY PROBLEMS. OKAY?

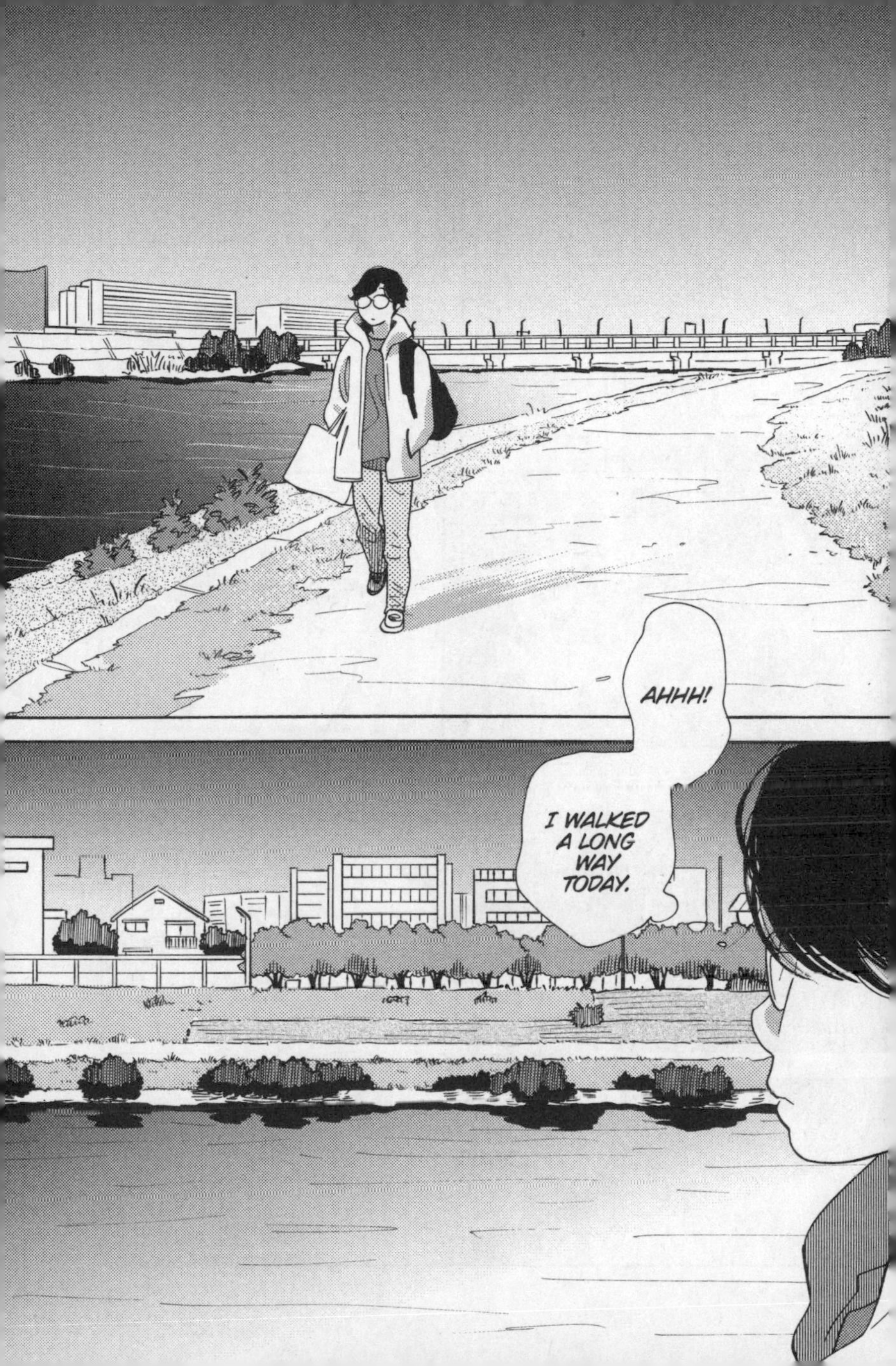
AHHH!
I WALKED A LONG WAY TODAY.

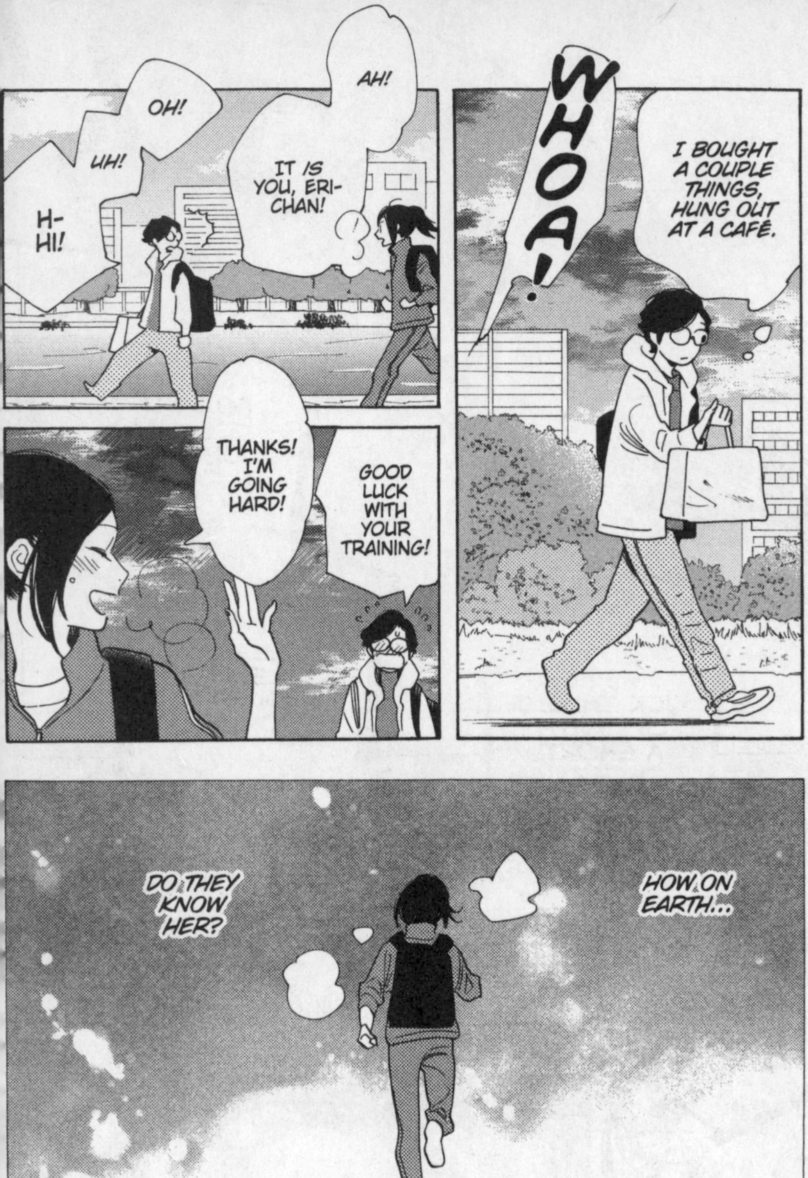
I BOUGHT A COUPLE THINGS, HUNG OUT AT A CAFÉ.
WHOA!
AH!
IT IS YOU, ERI-CHAN!
OH!
UH!
H-HI!
GOOD LUCK WITH YOUR TRAINING!
THANKS! I'M GOING HARD!
HOW ON EARTH...
DO THEY KNOW HER?

Chapter 15

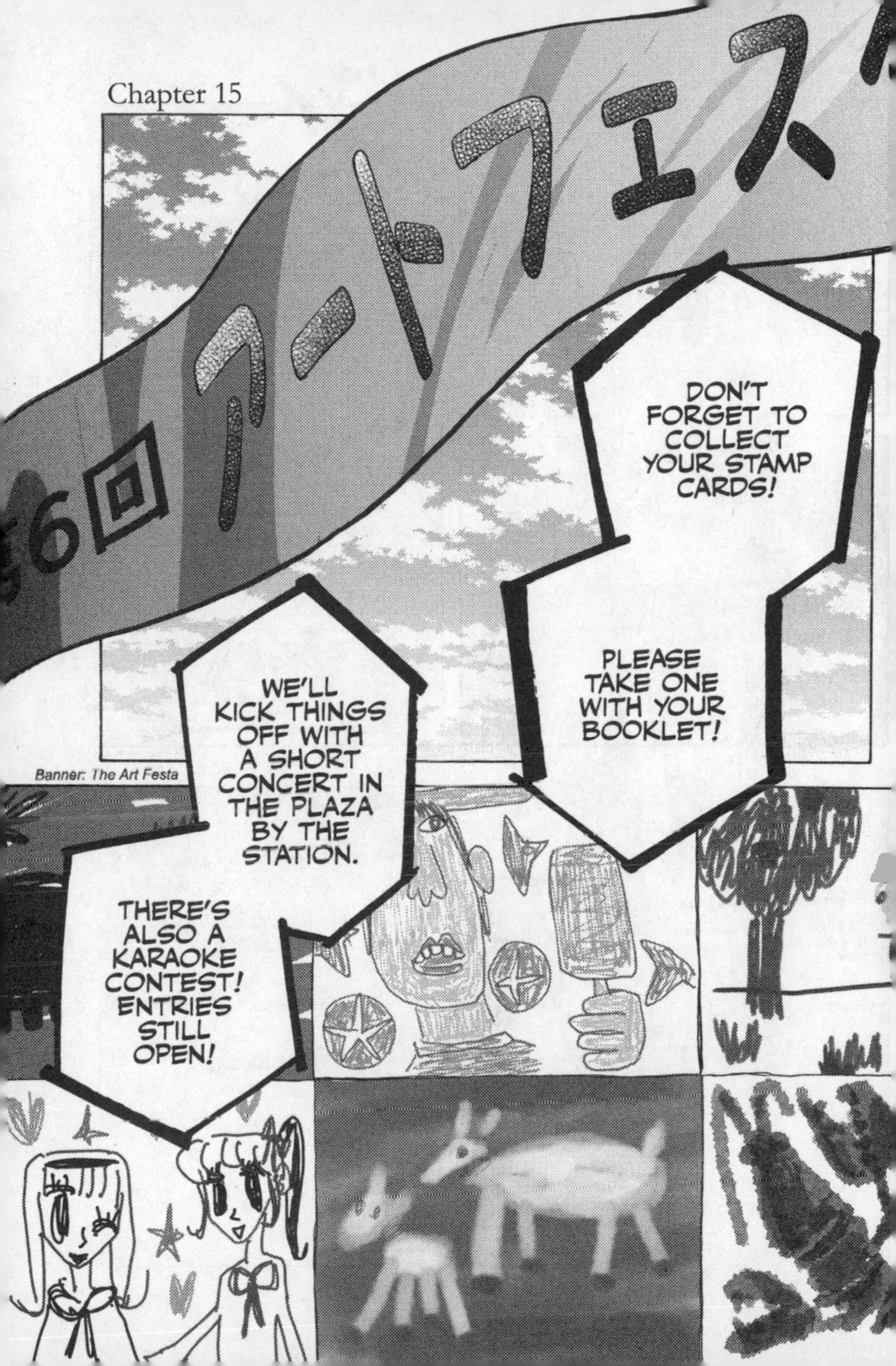

DON'T FORGET TO COLLECT YOUR STAMP CARDS!
PLEASE TAKE ONE WITH YOUR BOOKLET!
WE'LL KICK THINGS OFF WITH A SHORT CONCERT IN THE PLAZA BY THE STATION.
THERE'S ALSO A KARAOKE CONTEST! ENTRIES STILL OPEN!
Banner: The Art Festa

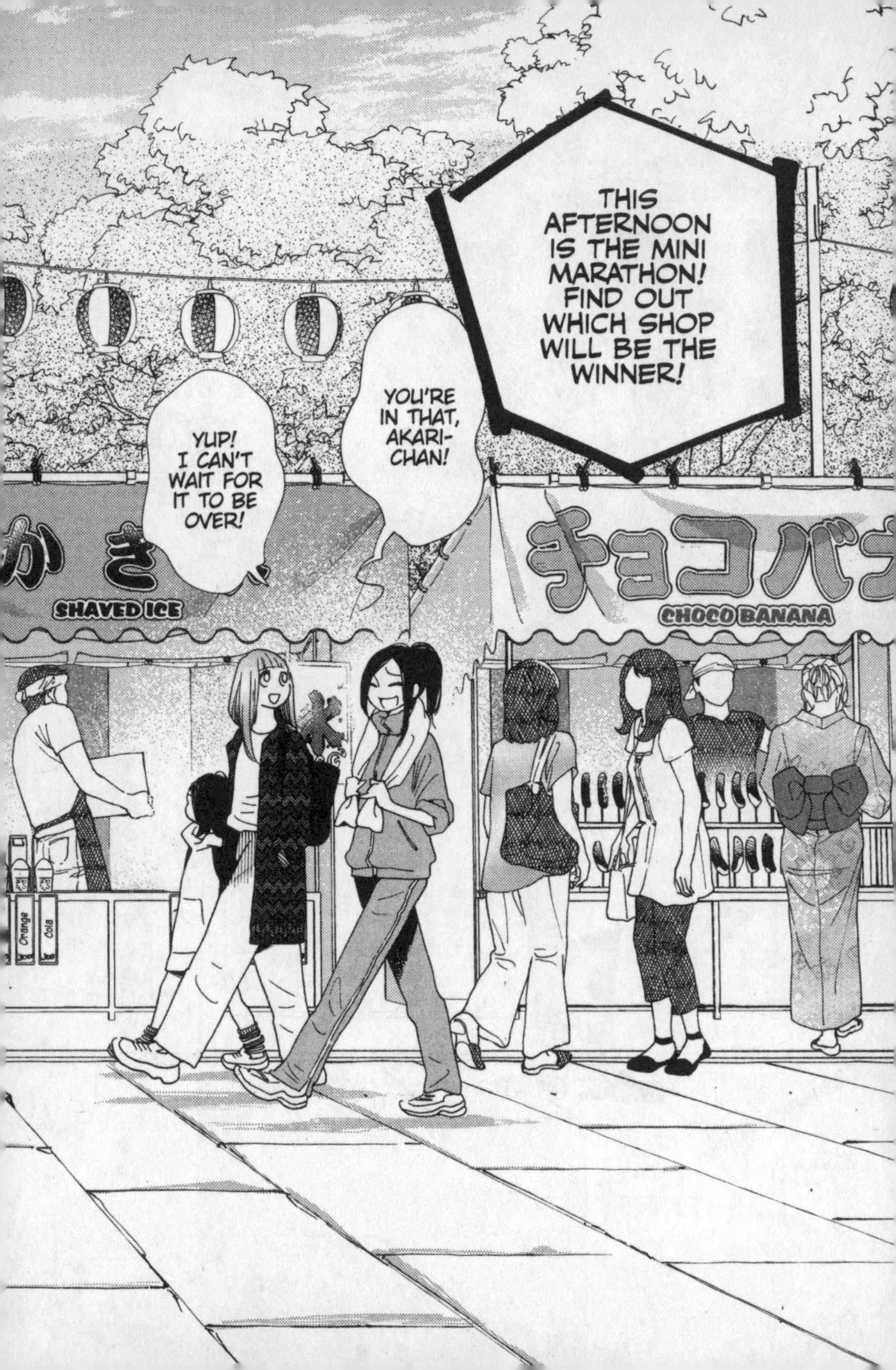
THIS AFTERNOON IS THE MINI MARATHON! FIND OUT WHICH SHOP WILL BE THE WINNER!
YOU'RE IN THAT, AKARI-CHAN!
YUP! I CAN'T WAIT FOR IT TO BE OVER!
チョコバナ
CHOCO BANANA
かき
SHAVED ICE
Orange
Cola

Chapter 15
Dial 6700 for Love

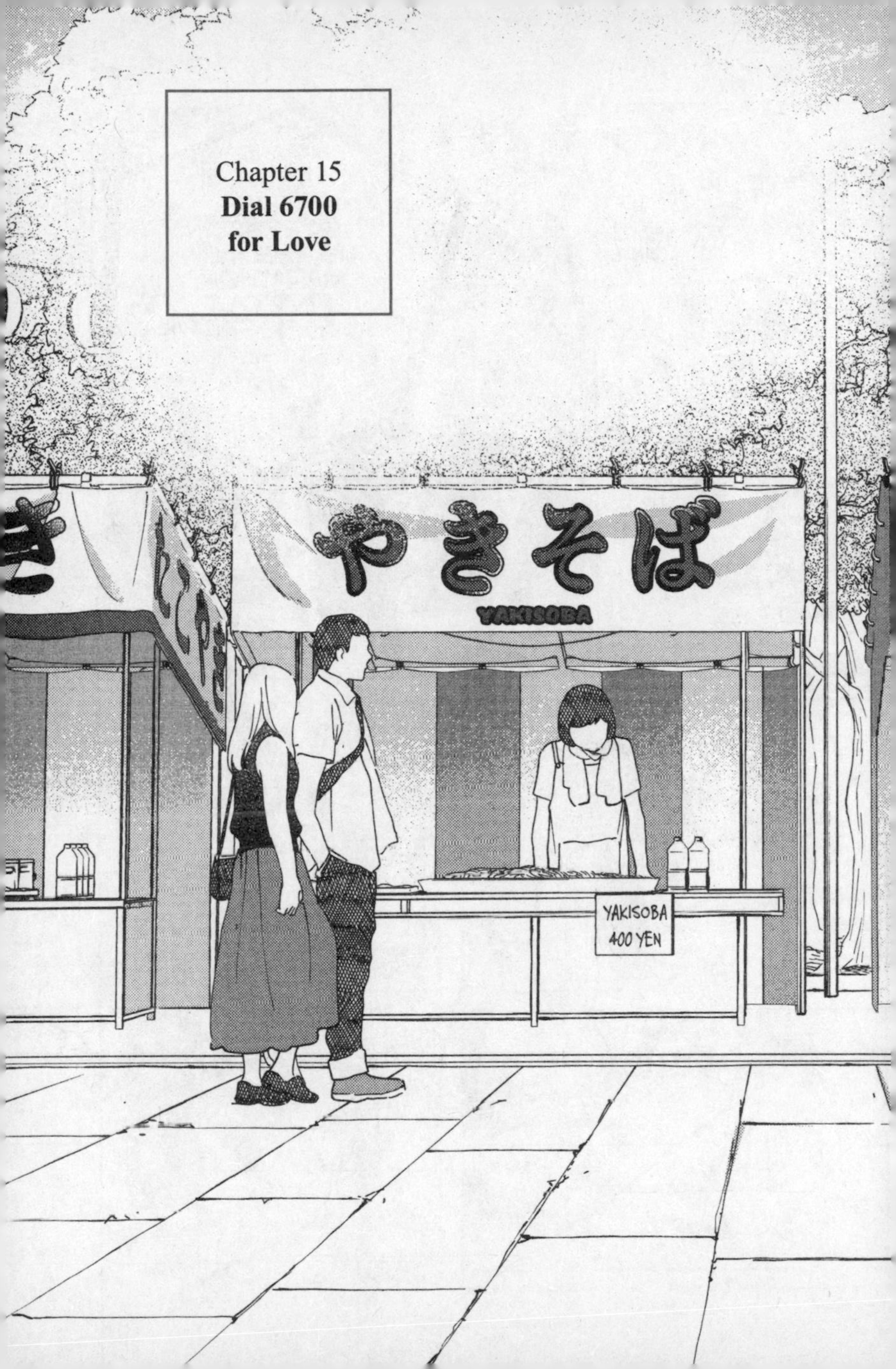
やきそば
YAKISOBA
YAKISOBA
400 YEN

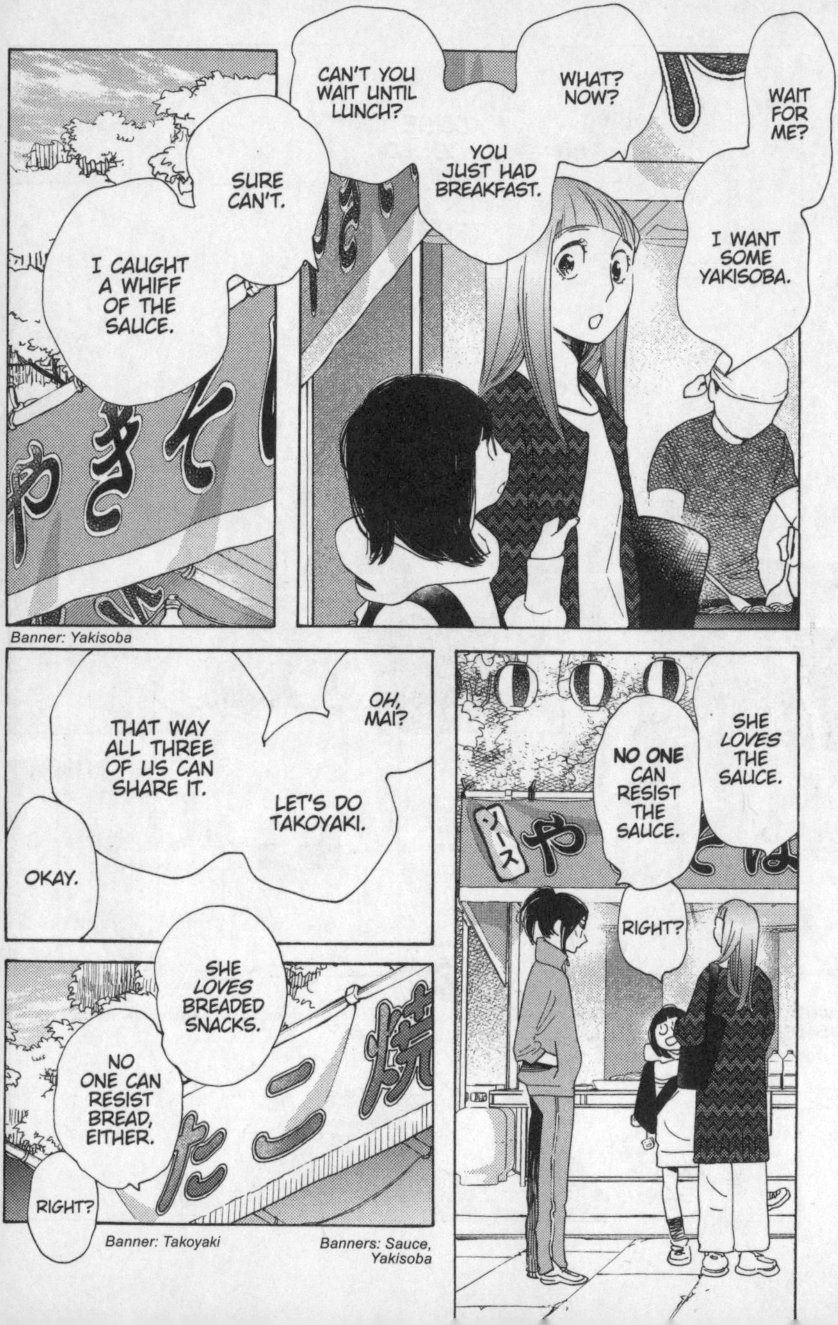
WAIT FOR ME?
I WANT SOME YAKISOBA.
WHAT? NOW?
YOU JUST HAD BREAKFAST.
CAN'T YOU WAIT UNTIL LUNCH?
SURE CAN'T.
I CAUGHT A WHIFF OF THE SAUCE.
SHE *LOVES* THE SAUCE.
NO ONE CAN RESIST THE SAUCE.
RIGHT?
OH, MAI?
LET'S DO TAKOYAKI.
THAT WAY ALL THREE OF US CAN SHARE IT.
OKAY.
SHE *LOVES* BREADED SNACKS.
NO ONE CAN RESIST BREAD, EITHER.
RIGHT?

Banner: Yakisoba

Banners: Sauce, Yakisoba

Banner: Takoyaki

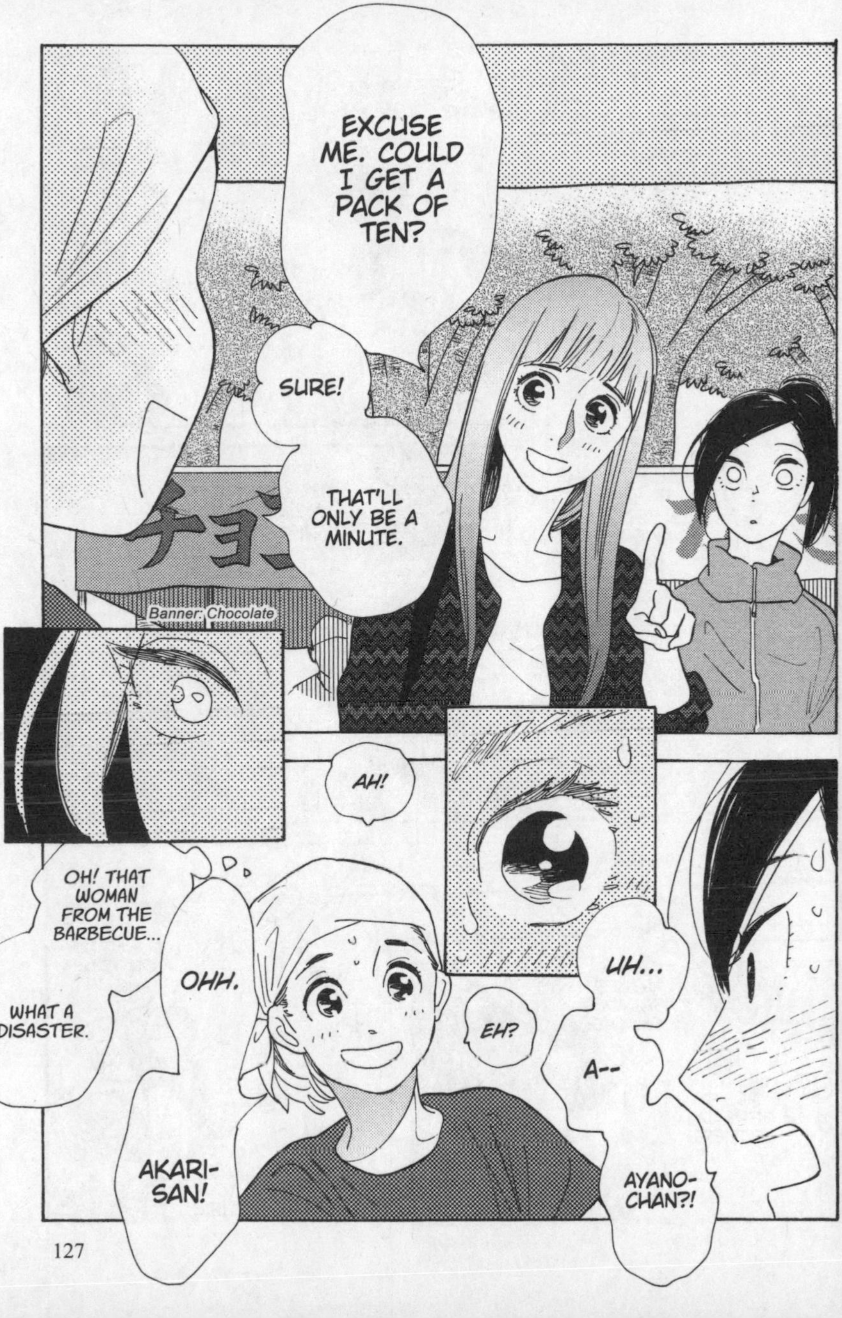
EXCUSE ME. COULD I GET A PACK OF TEN?
SURE!
THAT'LL ONLY BE A MINUTE.
Banner: Chocolate
AH!
UH...
A--
AYANO-CHAN?!
EH?
OHH.
AKARI-SAN!
OH! THAT WOMAN FROM THE BARBECUE...
WHAT A DISASTER.

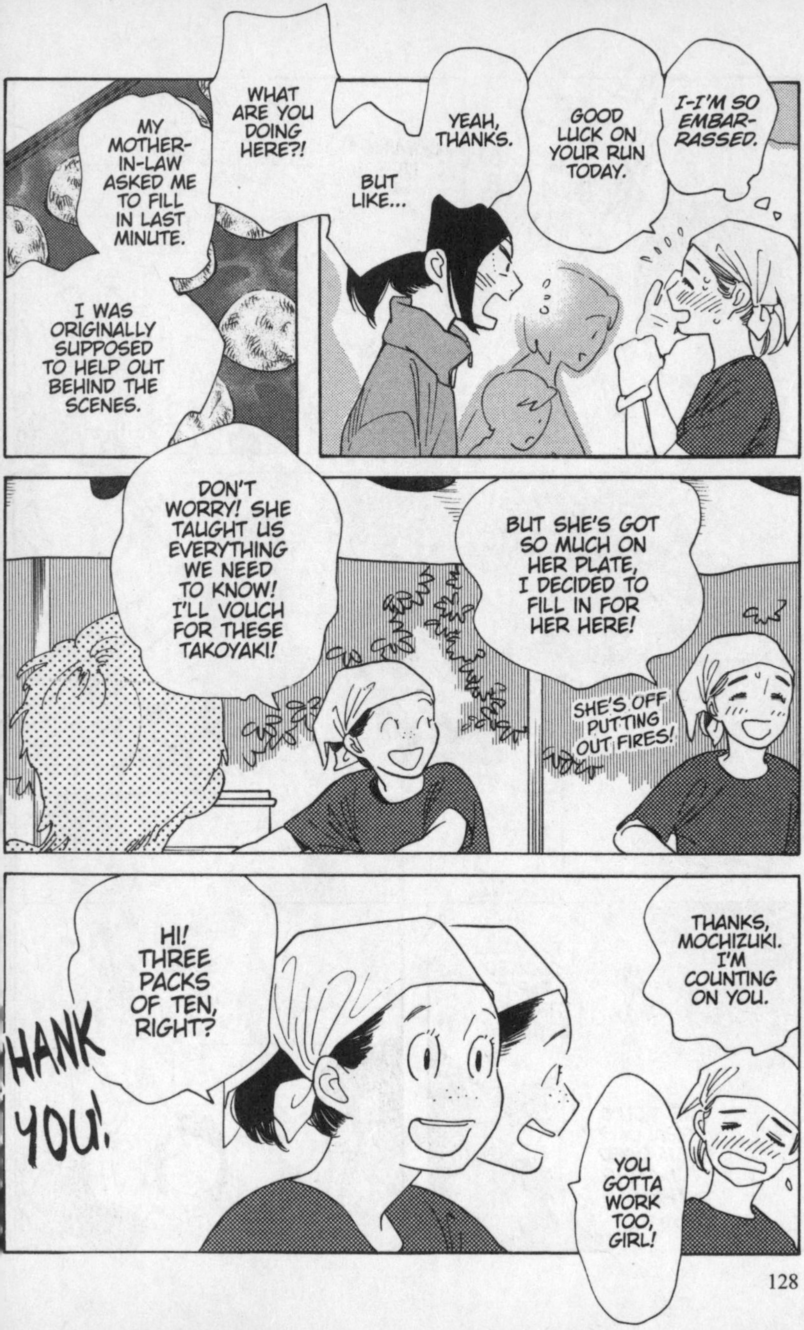
I-I'M SO EMBARRASSED.
GOOD LUCK ON YOUR RUN TODAY.
YEAH, THANKS.
BUT LIKE...
WHAT ARE YOU DOING HERE?!
MY MOTHER-IN-LAW ASKED ME TO FILL IN LAST MINUTE.
I WAS ORIGINALLY SUPPOSED TO HELP OUT BEHIND THE SCENES.
BUT SHE'S GOT SO MUCH ON HER PLATE, I DECIDED TO FILL IN FOR HER HERE!
SHE'S OFF PUTTING OUT FIRES!
DON'T WORRY! SHE TAUGHT US EVERYTHING WE NEED TO KNOW! I'LL VOUCH FOR THESE TAKOYAKI!
THANKS, MOCHIZUKI. I'M COUNTING ON YOU.
YOU GOTTA WORK TOO, GIRL!
HI! THREE PACKS OF TEN, RIGHT?
HANK YOU!

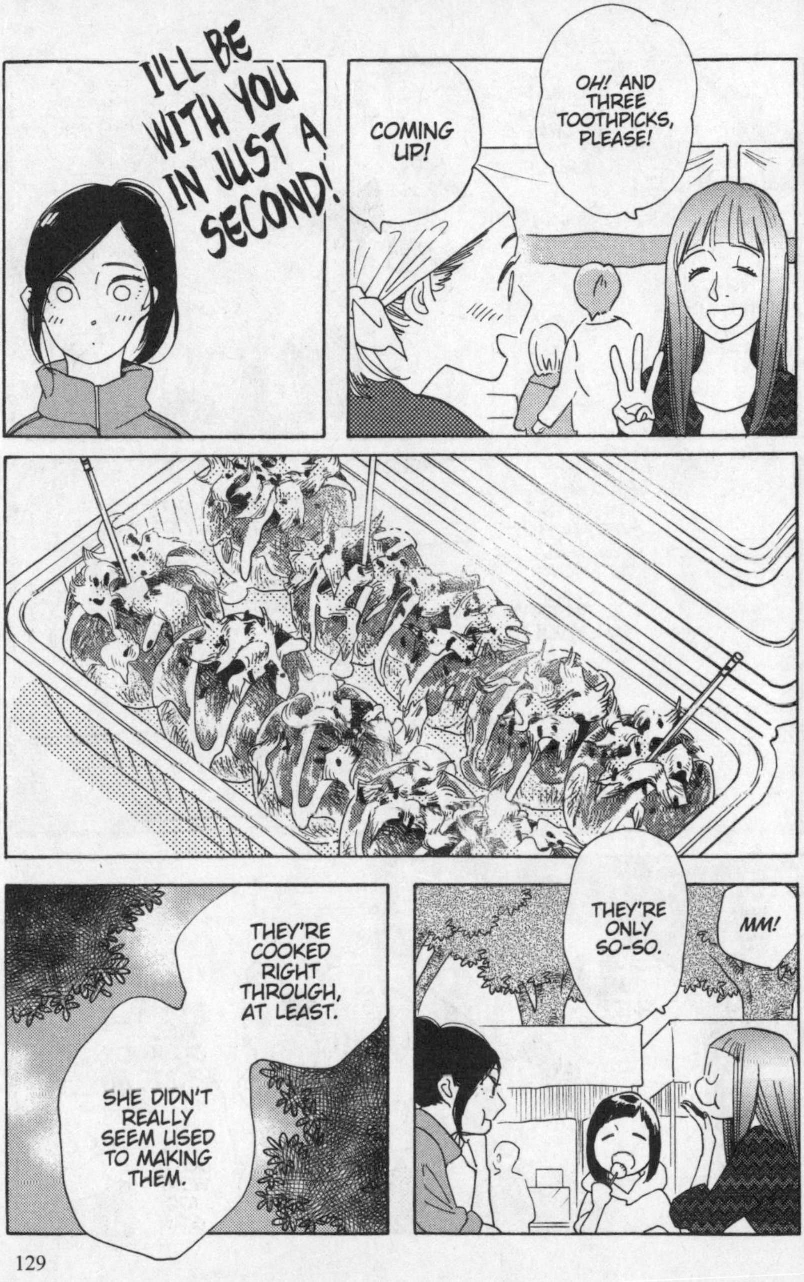
OH! AND THREE TOOTHPICKS, PLEASE!
COMING UP!
I'LL BE WITH YOU IN JUST A SECOND!
MM!
THEY'RE ONLY SO-SO.
THEY'RE COOKED RIGHT THROUGH, AT LEAST.
SHE DIDN'T REALLY SEEM USED TO MAKING THEM.

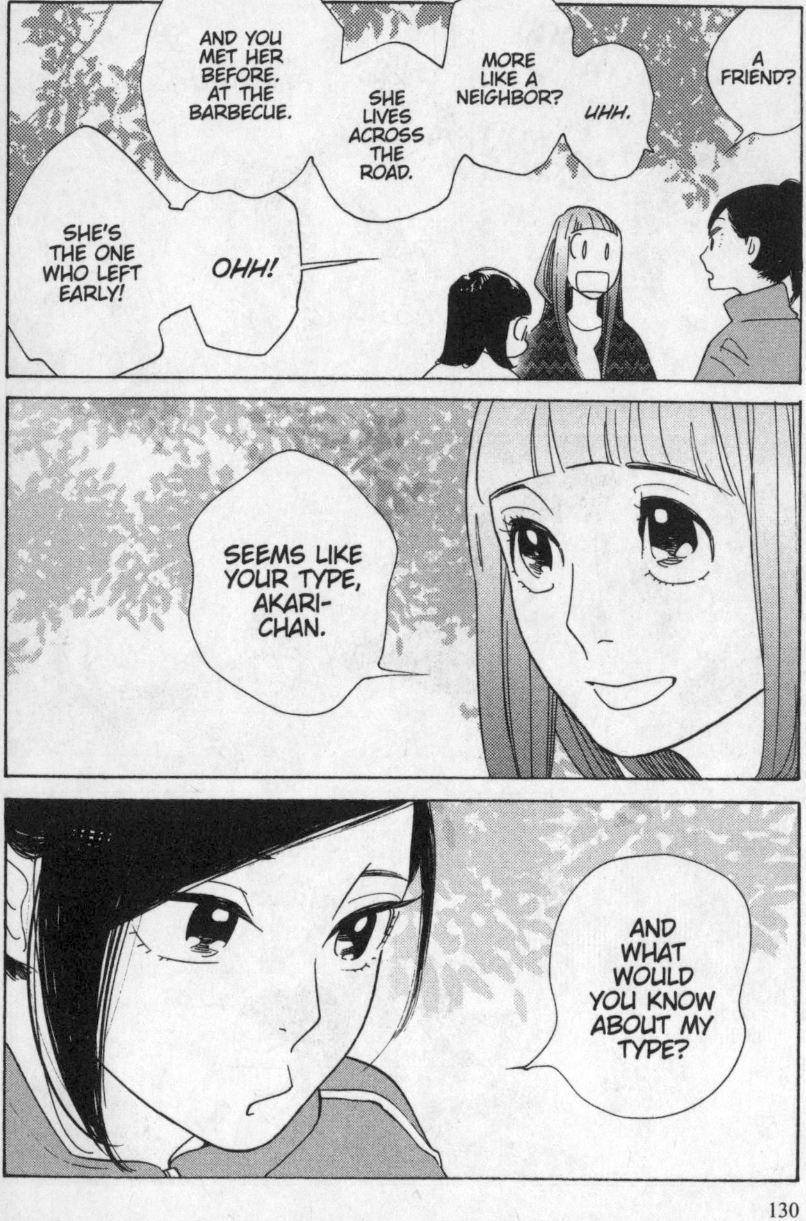
A FRIEND?
UHH.
MORE LIKE A NEIGHBOR?
SHE LIVES ACROSS THE ROAD.
AND YOU MET HER BEFORE. AT THE BARBECUE.
OHH!
SHE'S THE ONE WHO LEFT EARLY!
SEEMS LIKE YOUR TYPE, AKARI-CHAN.
AND WHAT WOULD YOU KNOW ABOUT MY TYPE?

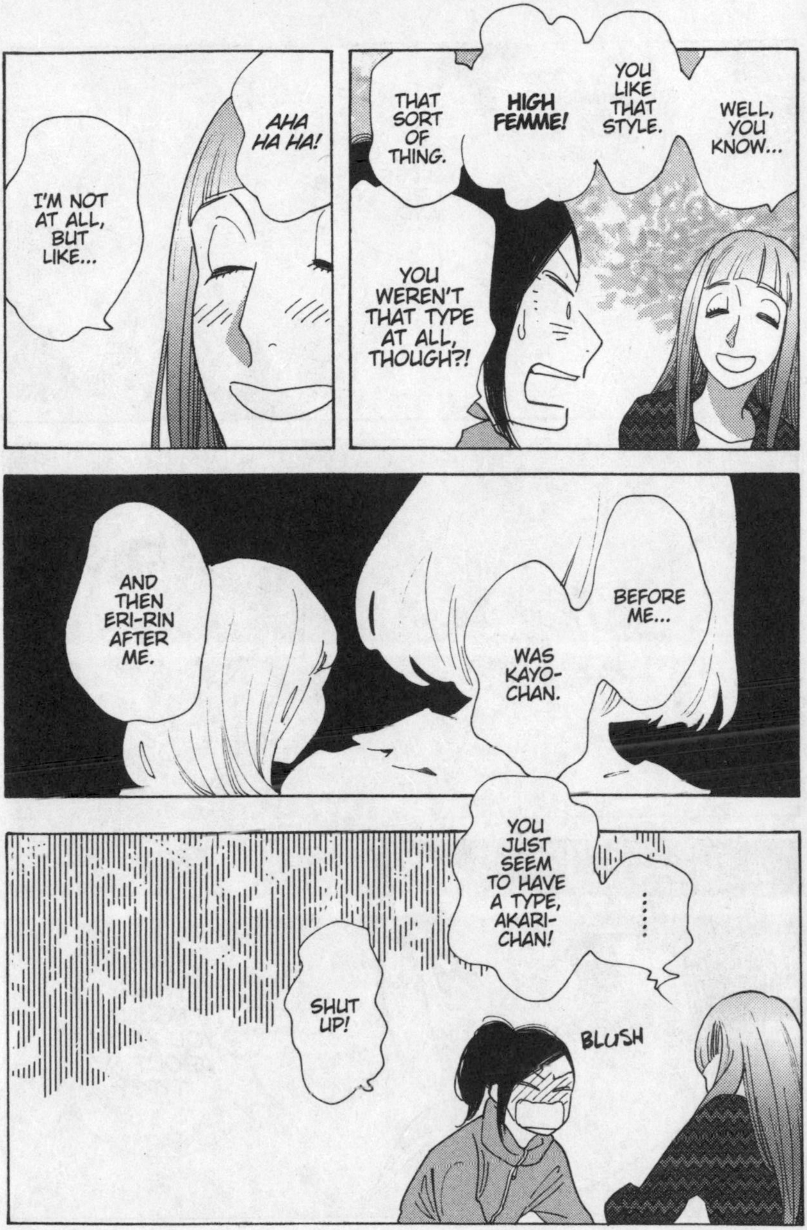
WELL, YOU KNOW...
YOU LIKE THAT STYLE.
HIGH FEMME!
THAT SORT OF THING.
YOU WEREN'T THAT TYPE AT ALL, THOUGH?!
AHA HA HA!
I'M NOT AT ALL, BUT LIKE...
BEFORE ME...
WAS KAYO-CHAN.
AND THEN ERI-RIN AFTER ME.
YOU JUST SEEM TO HAVE A TYPE, AKARI-CHAN!
......
BLUSH
SHUT UP!

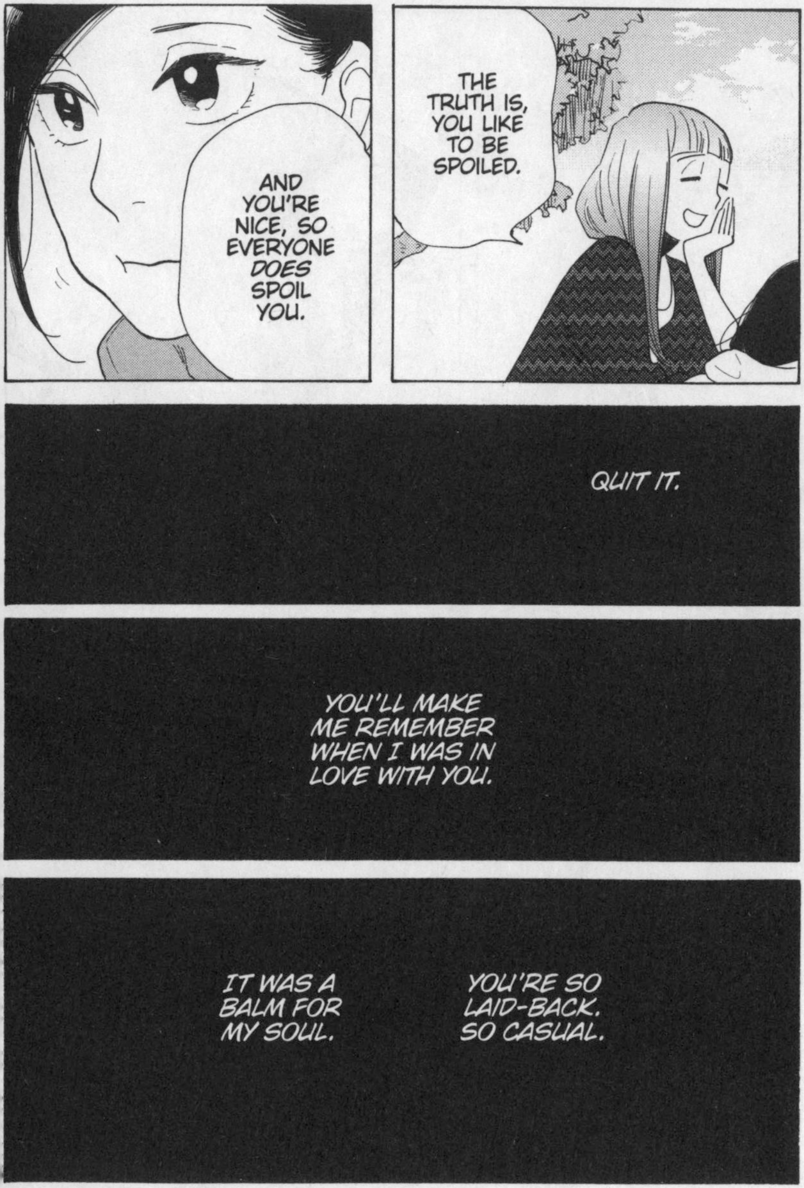
THE TRUTH IS, YOU LIKE TO BE SPOILED.
AND YOU'RE NICE, SO EVERYONE *DOES* SPOIL YOU.
QUIT IT.
YOU'LL MAKE ME REMEMBER WHEN I WAS IN LOVE WITH YOU.
YOU'RE SO LAID-BACK. SO CASUAL.
IT WAS A BALM FOR MY SOUL.

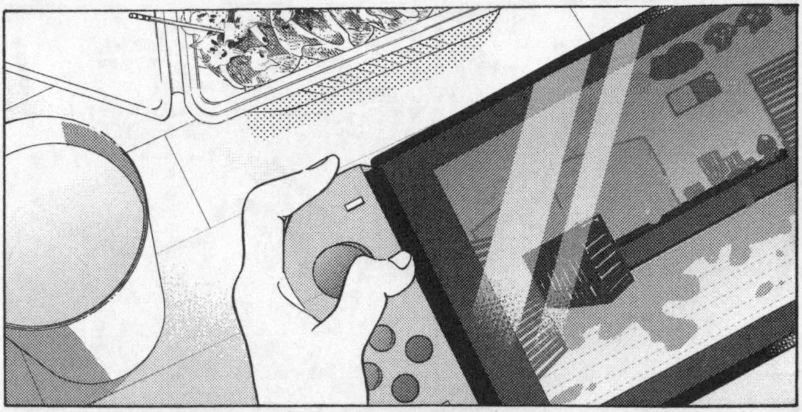
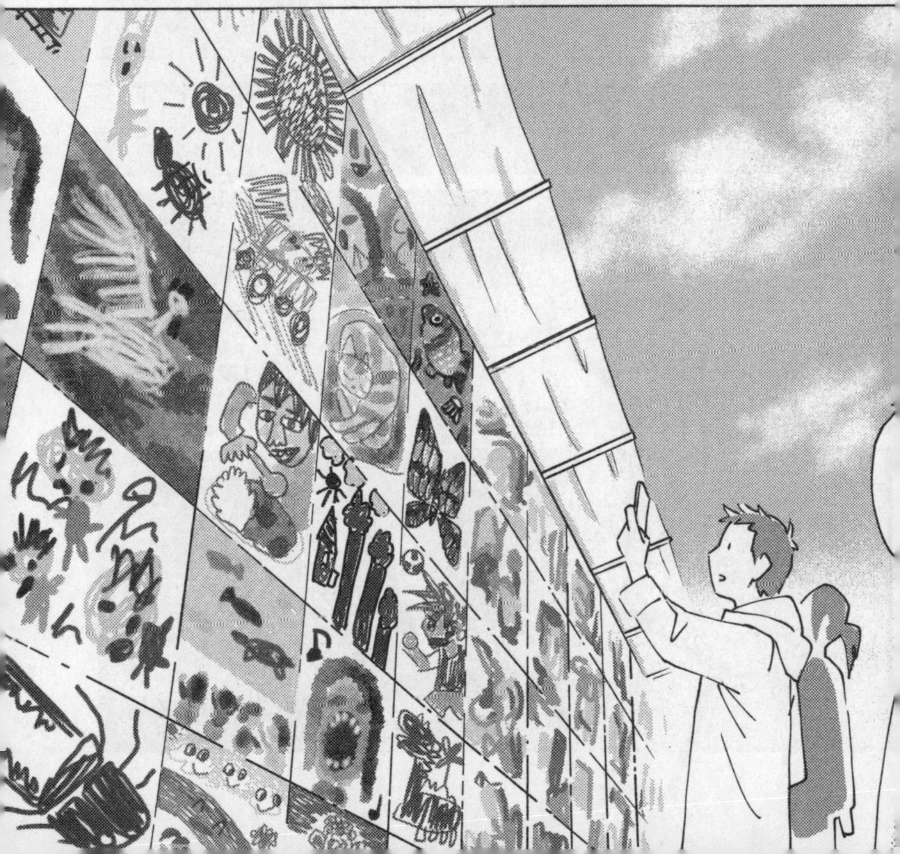

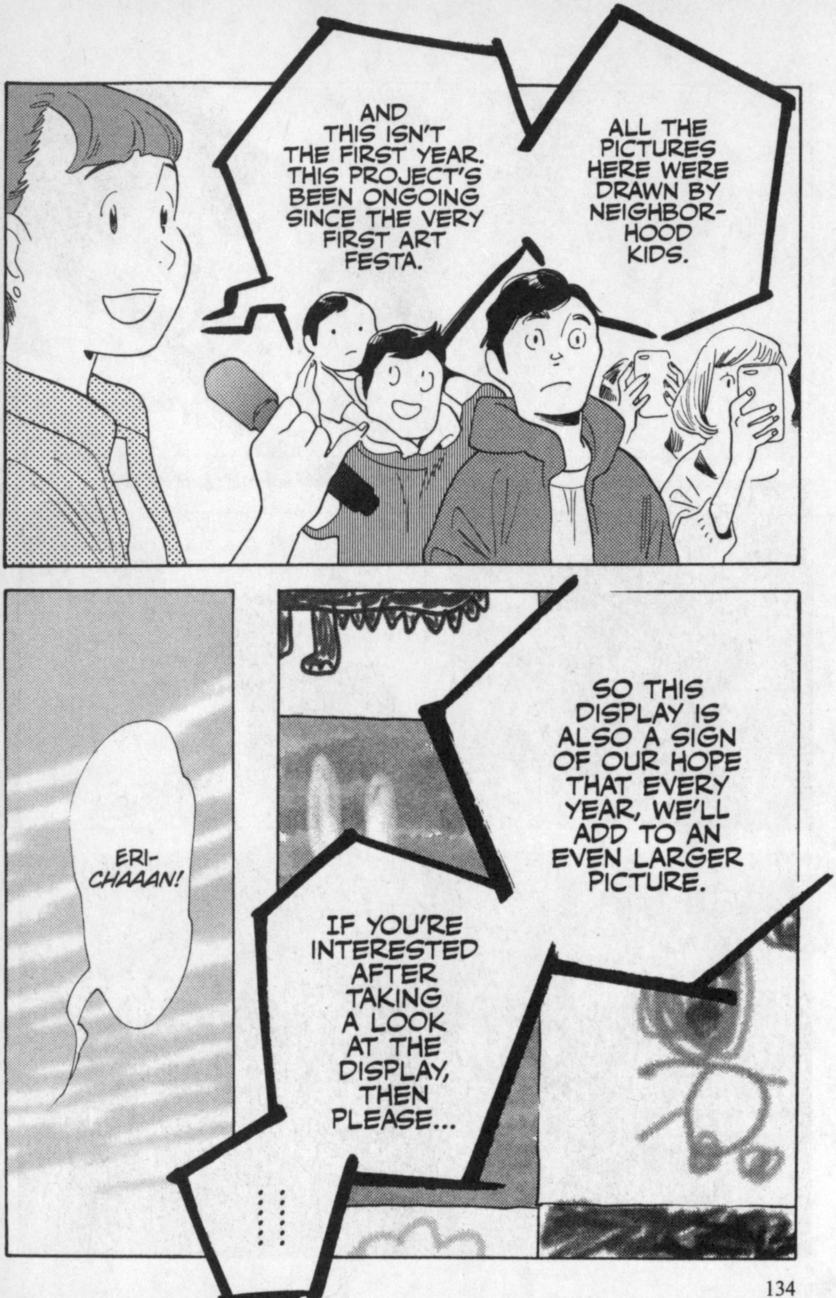
ALL THE PICTURES HERE WERE DRAWN BY NEIGHBOR-HOOD KIDS.
AND THIS ISN'T THE FIRST YEAR. THIS PROJECT'S BEEN ONGOING SINCE THE VERY FIRST ART FESTA.
SO THIS DISPLAY IS ALSO A SIGN OF OUR HOPE THAT EVERY YEAR, WE'LL ADD TO AN EVEN LARGER PICTURE.
IF YOU'RE INTERESTED AFTER TAKING A LOOK AT THE DISPLAY, THEN PLEASE...
ERI-CHAAAN!

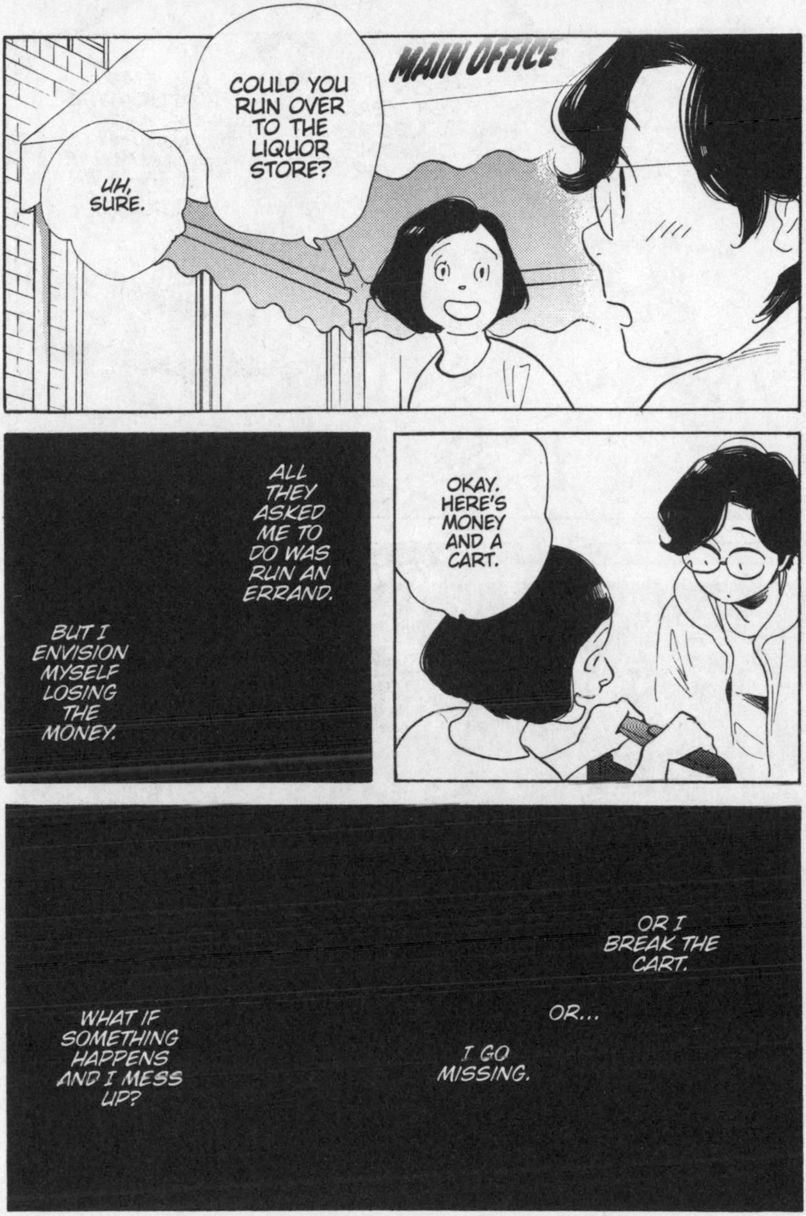
MAIN OFFICE
COULD YOU RUN OVER TO THE LIQUOR STORE?
UH, SURE.
OKAY. HERE'S MONEY AND A CART.
ALL THEY ASKED ME TO DO WAS RUN AN ERRAND.
BUT I ENVISION MYSELF LOSING THE MONEY.
OR I BREAK THE CART.
OR...
I GO MISSING.
WHAT IF SOMETHING HAPPENS AND I MESS UP?

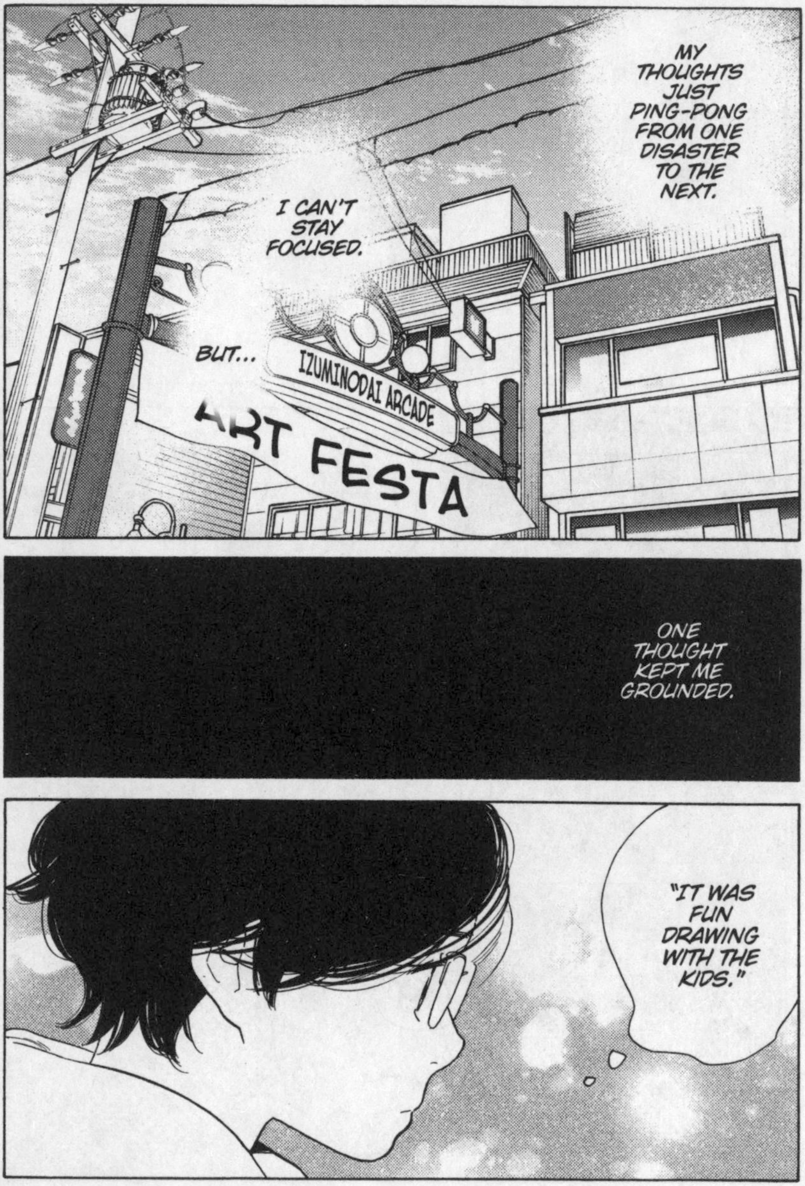
MY THOUGHTS JUST PING-PONG FROM ONE DISASTER TO THE NEXT.
I CAN'T STAY FOCUSED.
BUT...
IZUMINODAI ARCADE
ART FESTA
ONE THOUGHT KEPT ME GROUNDED.
"IT WAS FUN DRAWING WITH THE KIDS."

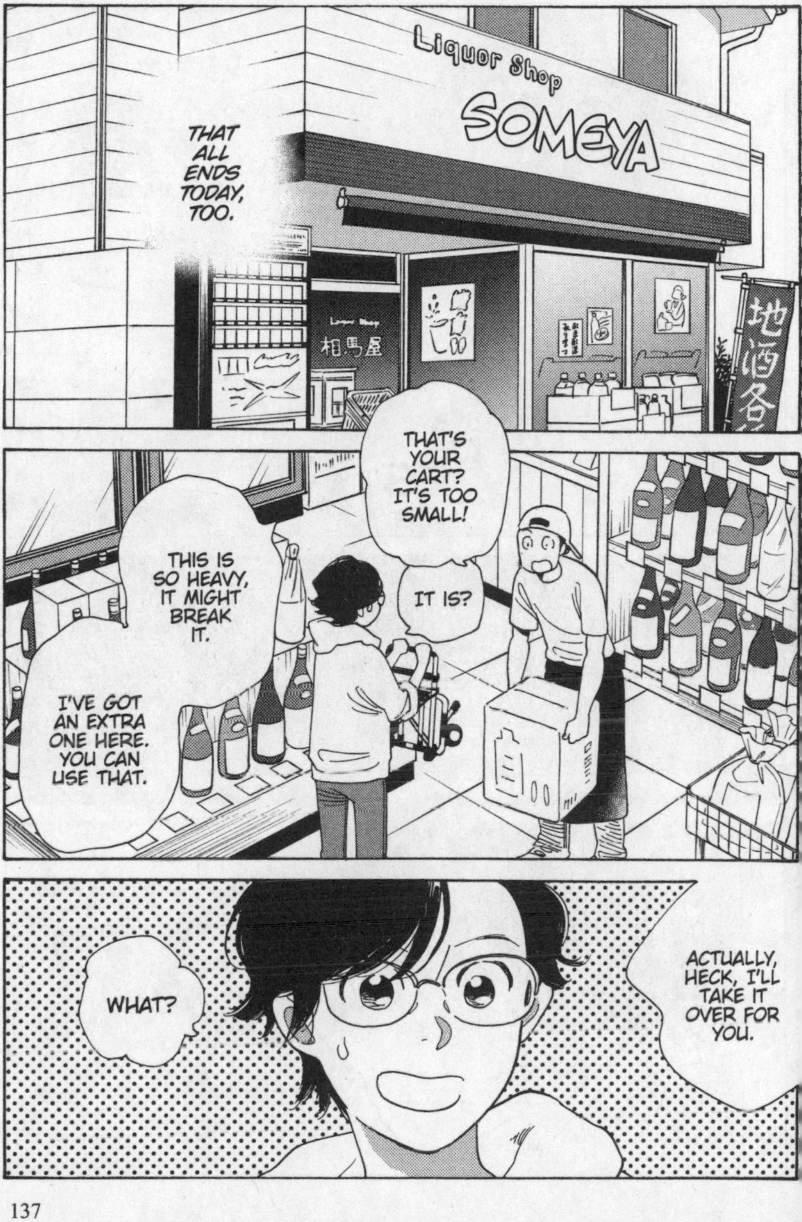
Liquor Shop
SOMEYA
THAT ALL ENDS TODAY, TOO.
相馬屋
THAT'S YOUR CART? IT'S TOO SMALL!
IT IS?
THIS IS SO HEAVY, IT MIGHT BREAK IT.
I'VE GOT AN EXTRA ONE HERE. YOU CAN USE THAT.
ACTUALLY, HECK, I'LL TAKE IT OVER FOR YOU.
WHAT?

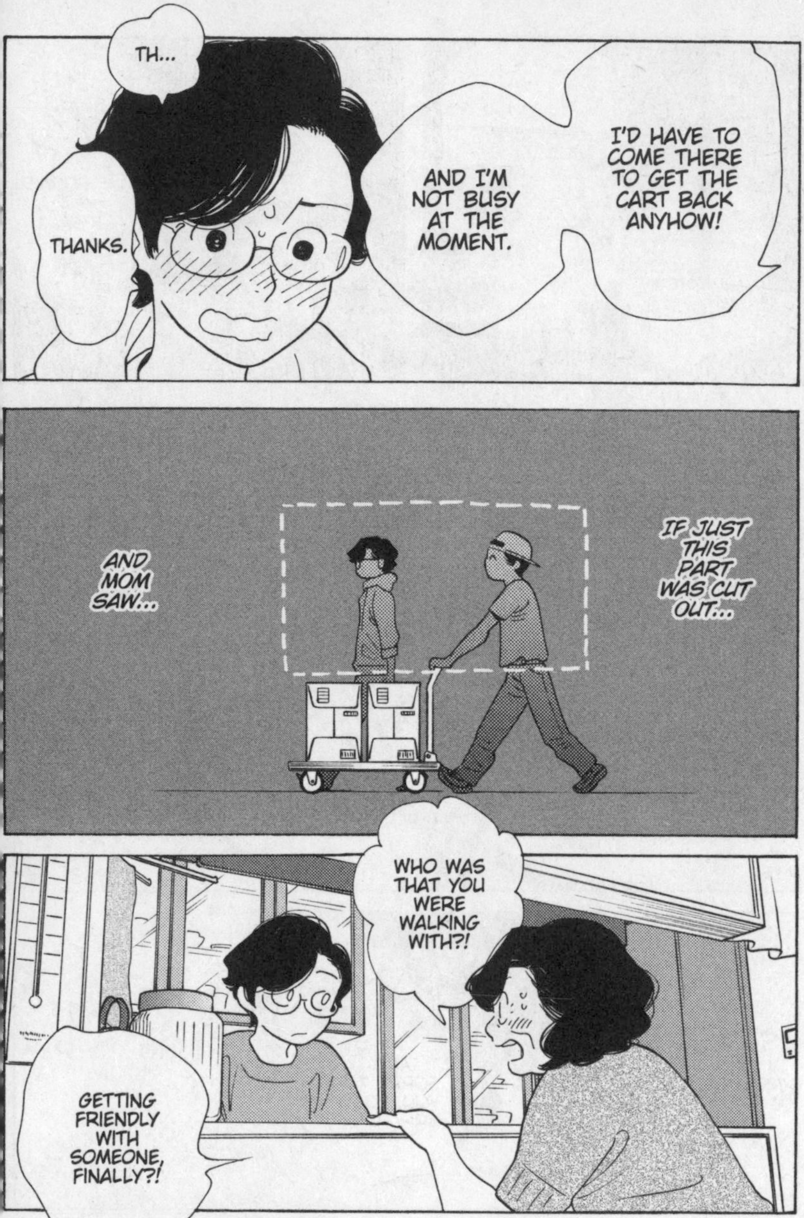

I'D HAVE TO COME THERE TO GET THE CART BACK ANYHOW!
AND I'M NOT BUSY AT THE MOMENT.
TH...
THANKS.
IF JUST THIS PART WAS CUT OUT...
AND MOM SAW...
WHO WAS THAT YOU WERE WALKING WITH?!
GETTING FRIENDLY WITH SOMEONE, FINALLY?!

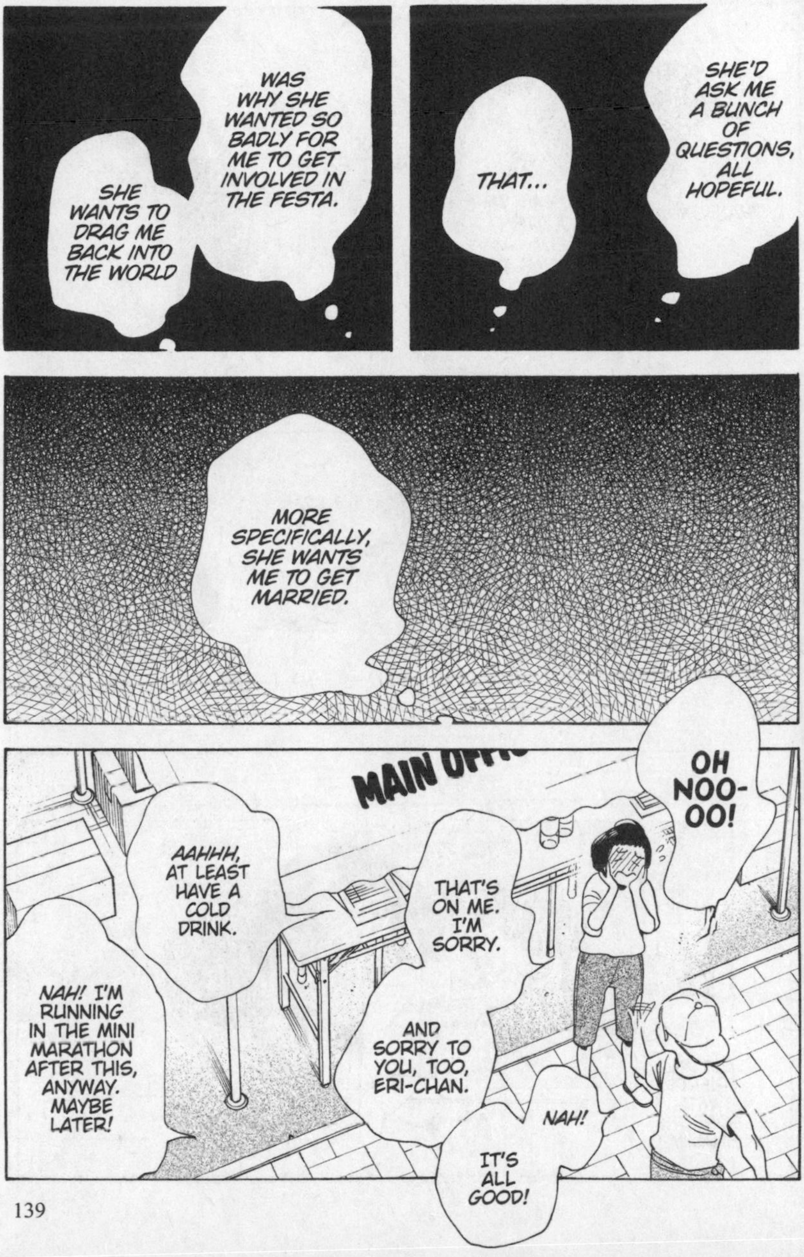
SHE'D ASK ME A BUNCH OF QUESTIONS, ALL HOPEFUL.
THAT...
WAS WHY SHE WANTED SO BADLY FOR ME TO GET INVOLVED IN THE FESTA.
SHE WANTS TO DRAG ME BACK INTO THE WORLD
MORE SPECIFICALLY, SHE WANTS ME TO GET MARRIED.
OH NOOO-OO!
THAT'S ON ME. I'M SORRY.
AND SORRY TO YOU, TOO, ERI-CHAN.
NAH!
IT'S ALL GOOD!
AAHHH, AT LEAST HAVE A COLD DRINK.
NAH! I'M RUNNING IN THE MINI MARATHON AFTER THIS, ANYWAY. MAYBE LATER!

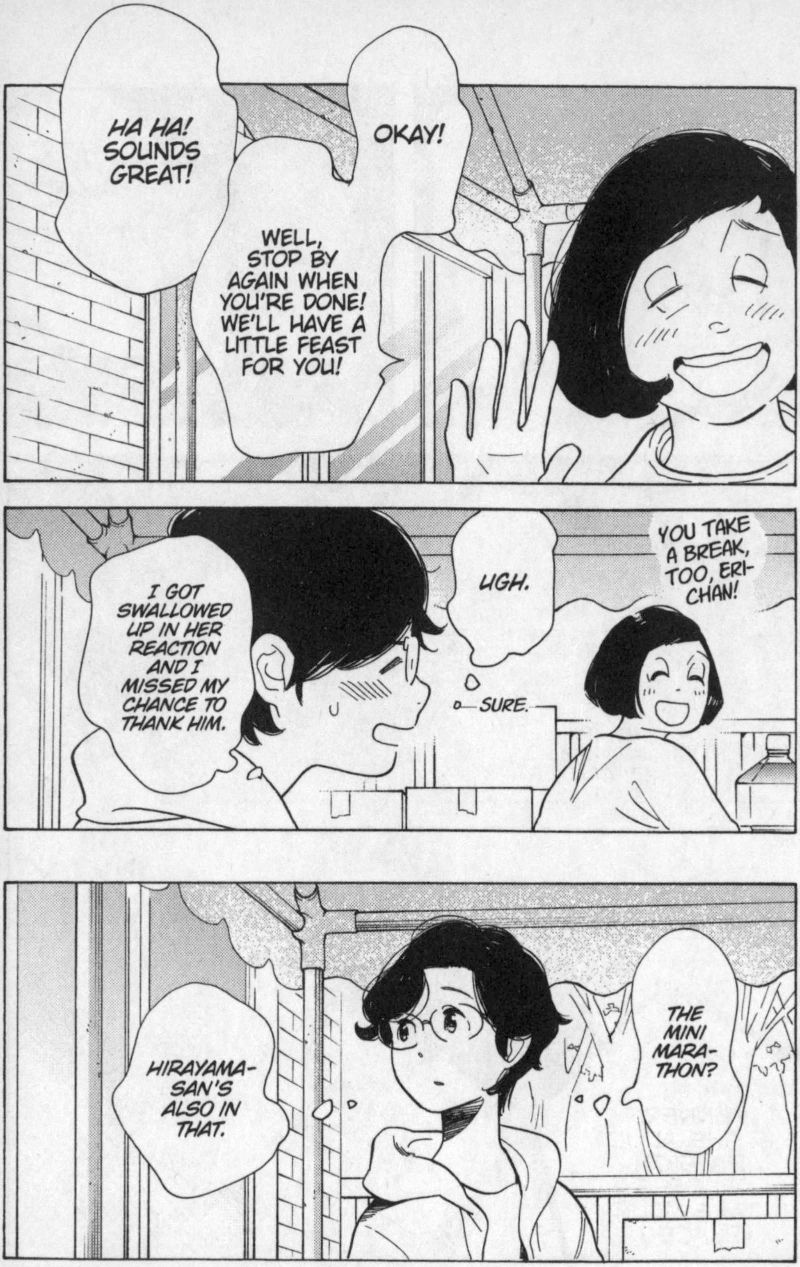
OKAY!
WELL, STOP BY AGAIN WHEN YOU'RE DONE! WE'LL HAVE A LITTLE FEAST FOR YOU!
HA HA! SOUNDS GREAT!
YOU TAKE A BREAK, TOO, ERI-CHAN!
UGH.
SURE.
I GOT SWALLOWED UP IN HER REACTION AND I MISSED MY CHANCE TO THANK HIM.
THE MINI MARA-THON?
HIRAYAMA-SAN'S ALSO IN THAT.

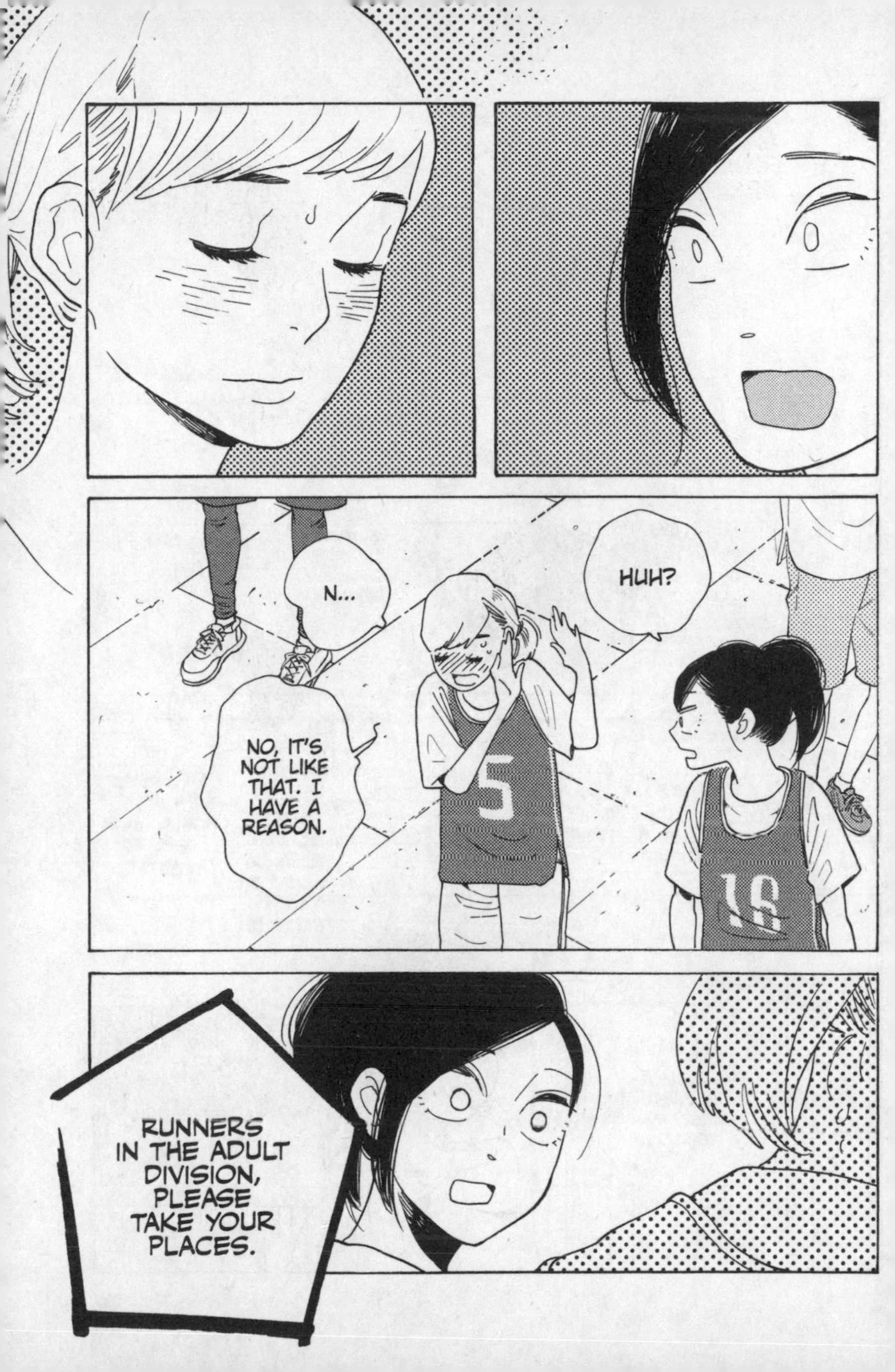
HUH?
N...
NO, IT'S NOT LIKE THAT. I HAVE A REASON.
RUNNERS IN THE ADULT DIVISION, PLEASE TAKE YOUR PLACES.

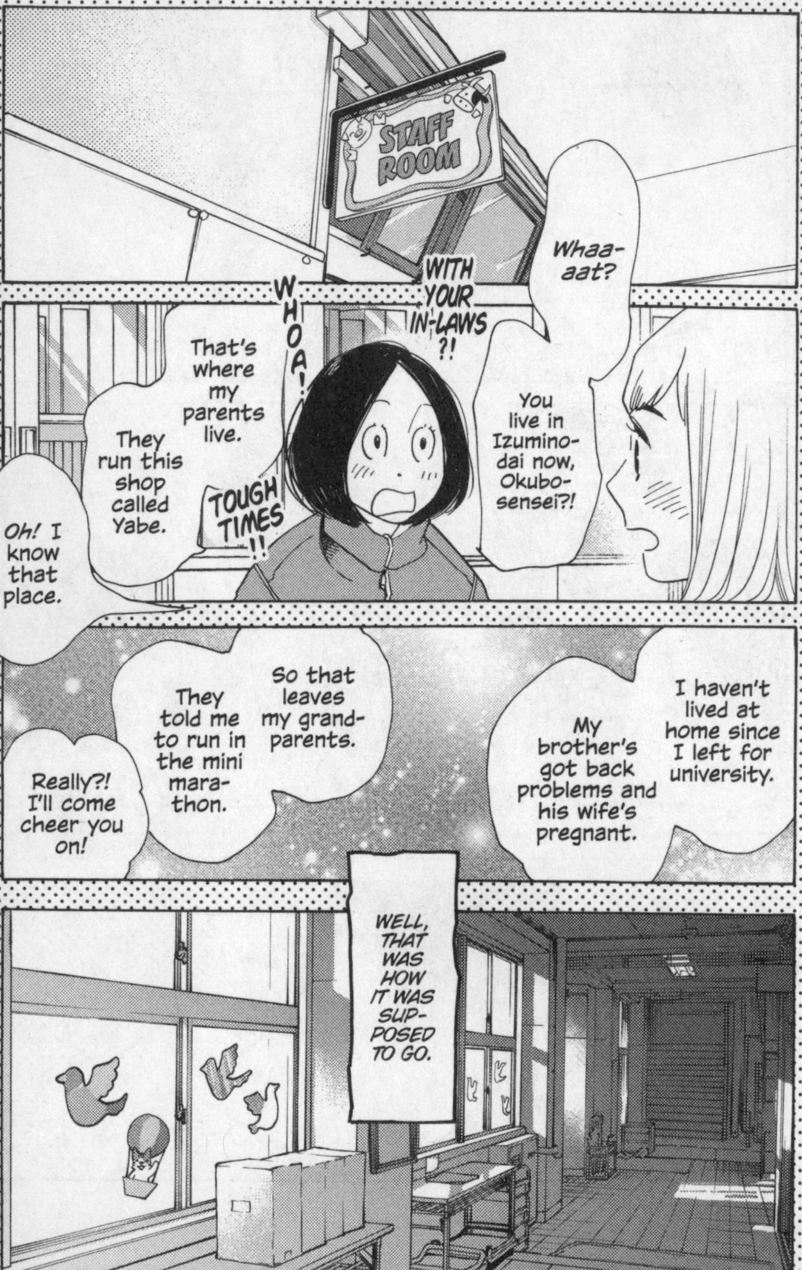
STAFF ROOM
Whaaa-aat?
You live in Izumino-dai now, Okubo-sensei?!
WITH YOUR IN-LAWS?!
WHOA!
That's where my parents live.
They run this shop called Yabe.
TOUGH TIMES!!
Oh! I know that place.
I haven't lived at home since I left for university.
My brother's got back problems and his wife's pregnant.
So that leaves my grand-parents.
They told me to run in the mini mara-thon.
Really?! I'll come cheer you on!
WELL, THAT WAS HOW IT WAS SUP-POSED TO GO.

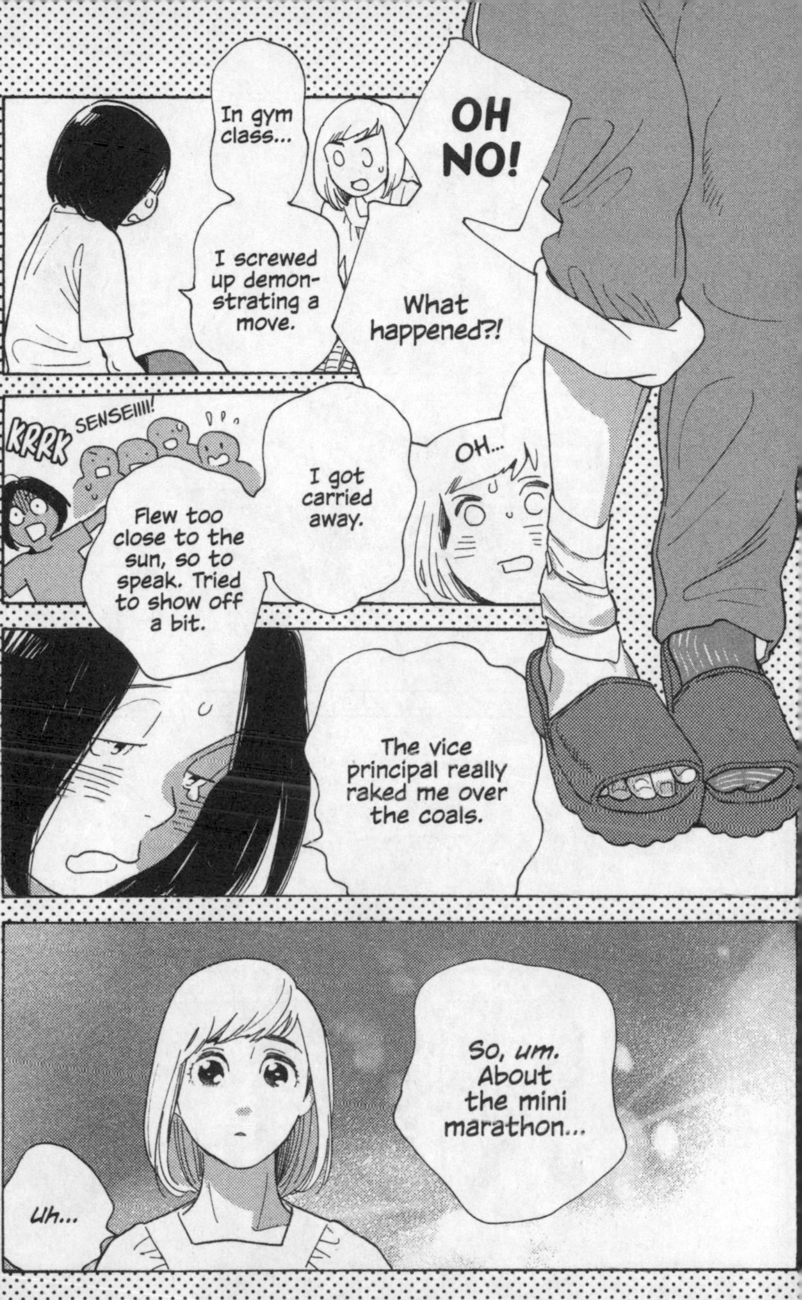
OH NO!
What happened?!
In gym class...
I screwed up demon-strating a move.
OH...
I got carried away.
Flew too close to the sun, so to speak. Tried to show off a bit.
SENSEIIII!
KRRK
The vice principal really raked me over the coals.
So, um. About the mini marathon...
Uh...

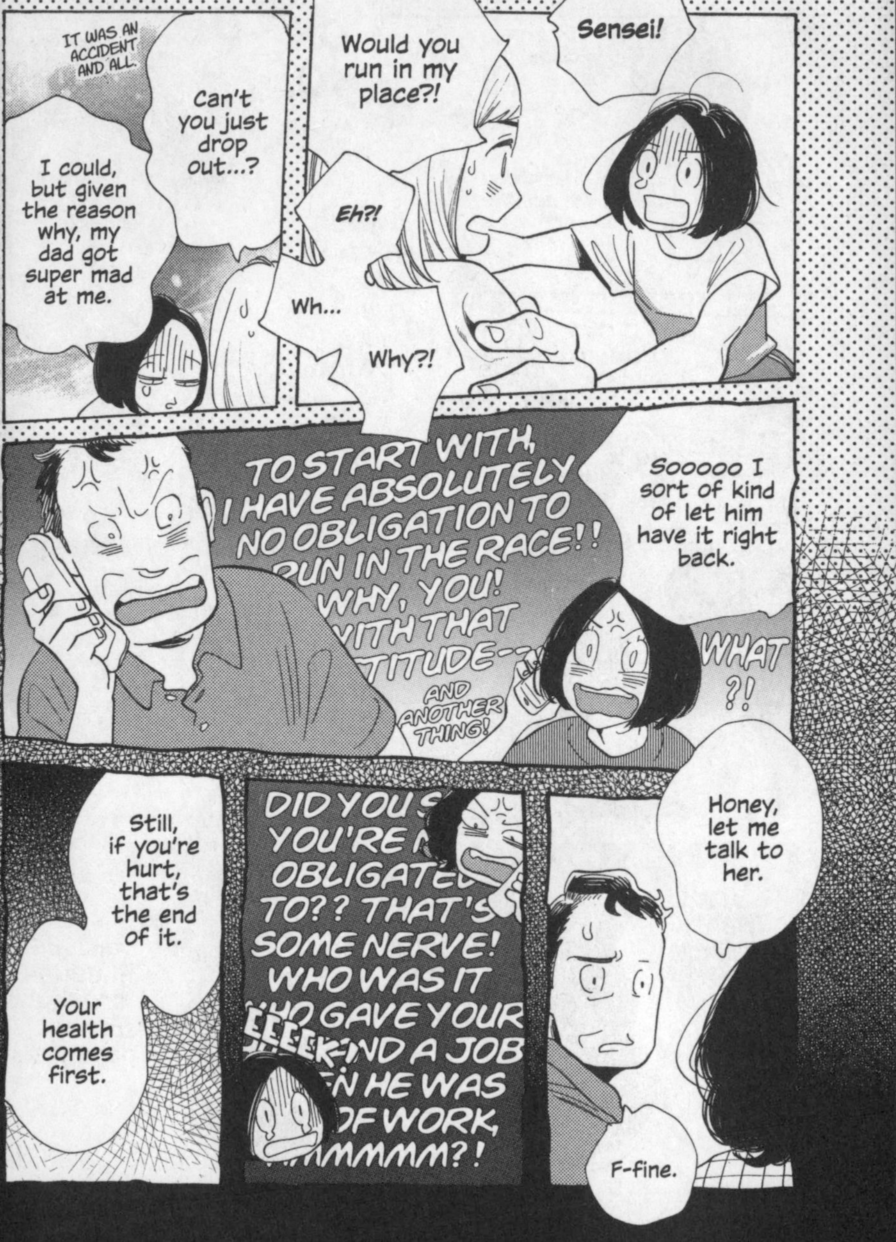
Sensei!
Would you run in my place?!
Eh?!
Wh...
Why?!
Can't you just drop out...?
IT WAS AN ACCIDENT AND ALL.
I could, but given the reason why, my dad got super mad at me.
Sooooo I sort of kind of let him have it right back.
WHAT ?!
TO START WITH, I HAVE ABSOLUTELY NO OBLIGATION TO RUN IN THE RACE!! WHY, YOU! WITH THAT TITUDE--
AND ANOTHER THING!
Honey, let me talk to her.
F-fine.
DID YOU S YOU'RE N OBLIGATE TO?? THAT'S SOME NERVE! WHO WAS IT HO GAVE YOUR IND A JOB EN HE WAS OF WORK, MMMMM?!
EEEEK
Still, if you're hurt, that's the end of it.
Your health comes first.

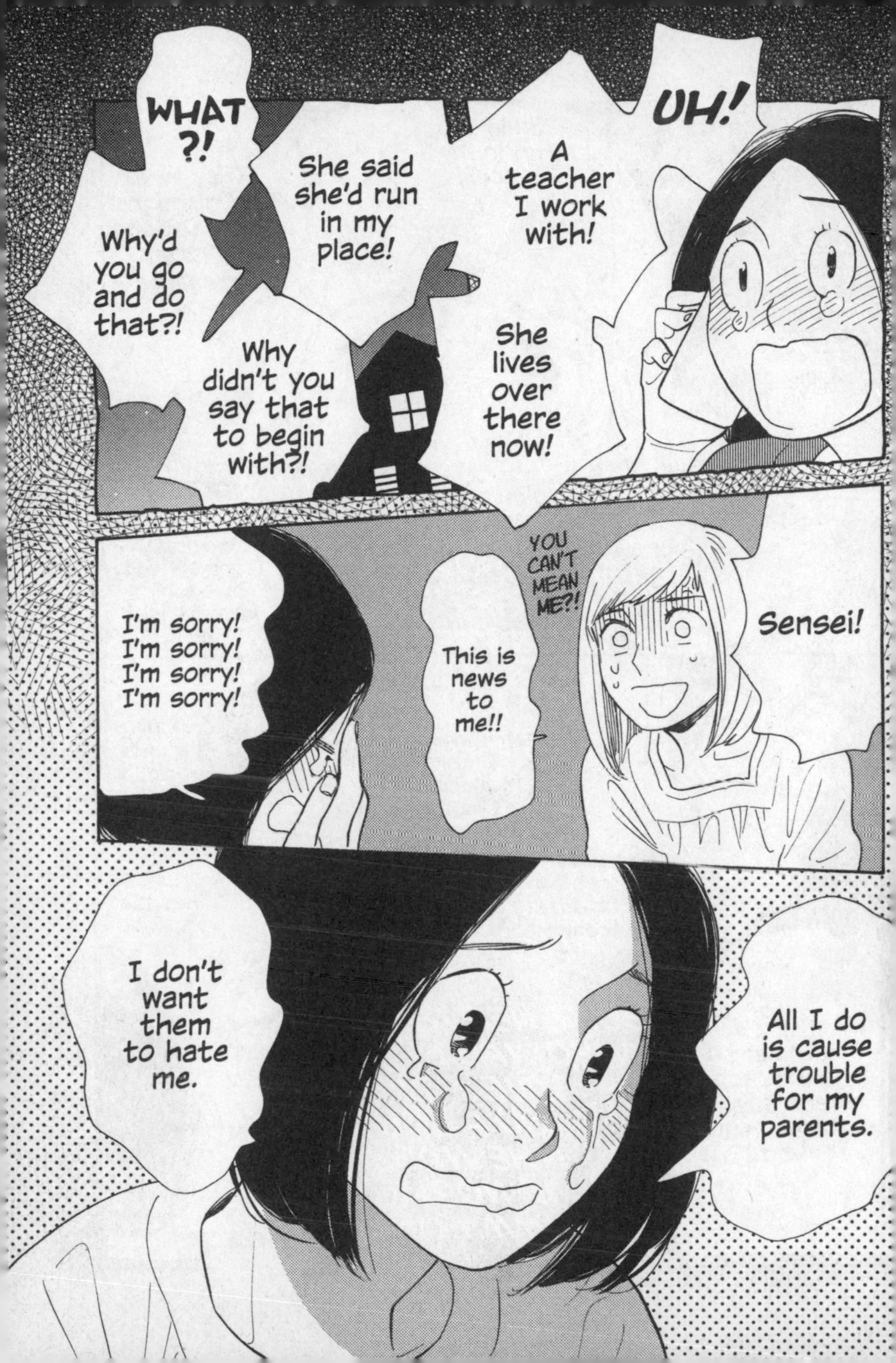
UH!
A teacher I work with!
She lives over there now!
She said she'd run in my place!
WHAT?!
Why'd you go and do that?!
Why didn't you say that to begin with?!
Sensei!
YOU CAN'T MEAN ME?!
This is news to me!!
I'm sorry! I'm sorry! I'm sorry! I'm sorry!
All I do is cause trouble for my parents.
I don't want them to hate me.

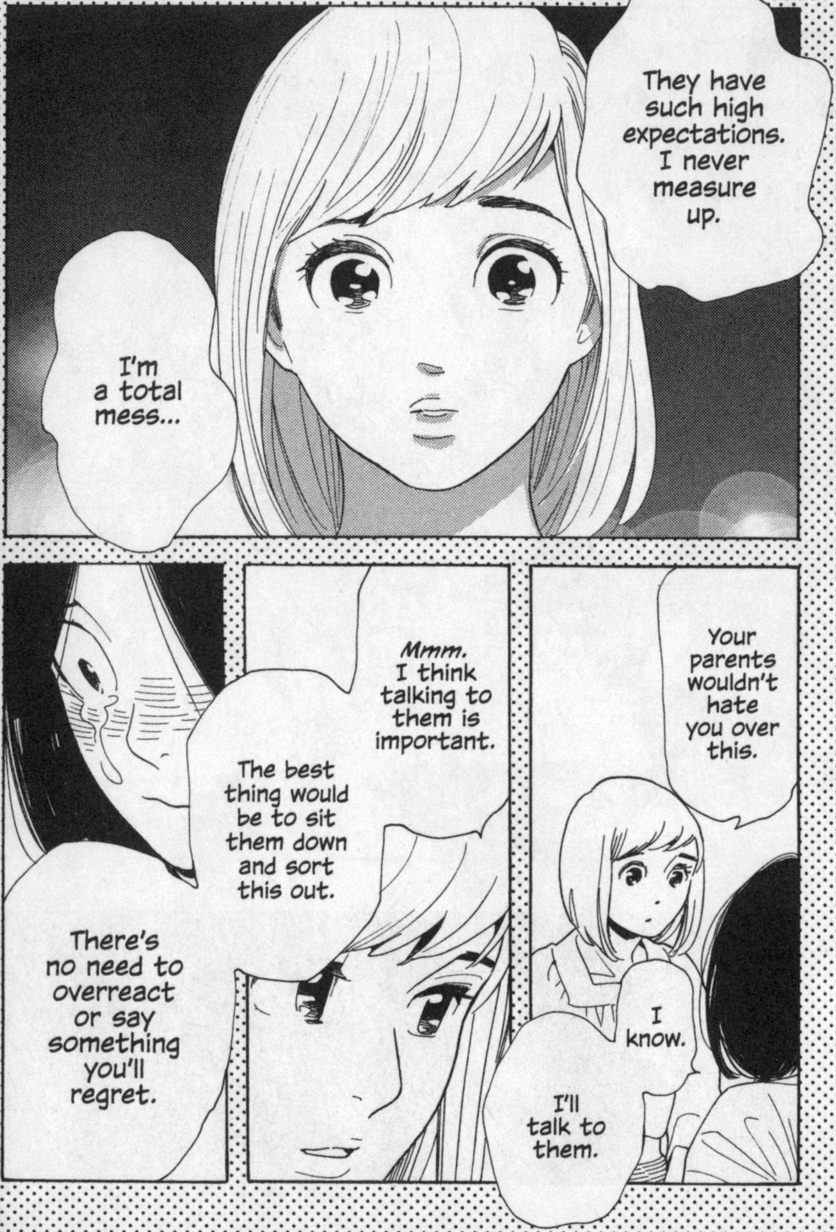
They have such high expectations. I never measure up.
I'm a total mess...
Your parents wouldn't hate you over this.
I know.
I'll talk to them.
Mmm. I think talking to them is important.
The best thing would be to sit them down and sort this out.
There's no need to overreact or say something you'll regret.

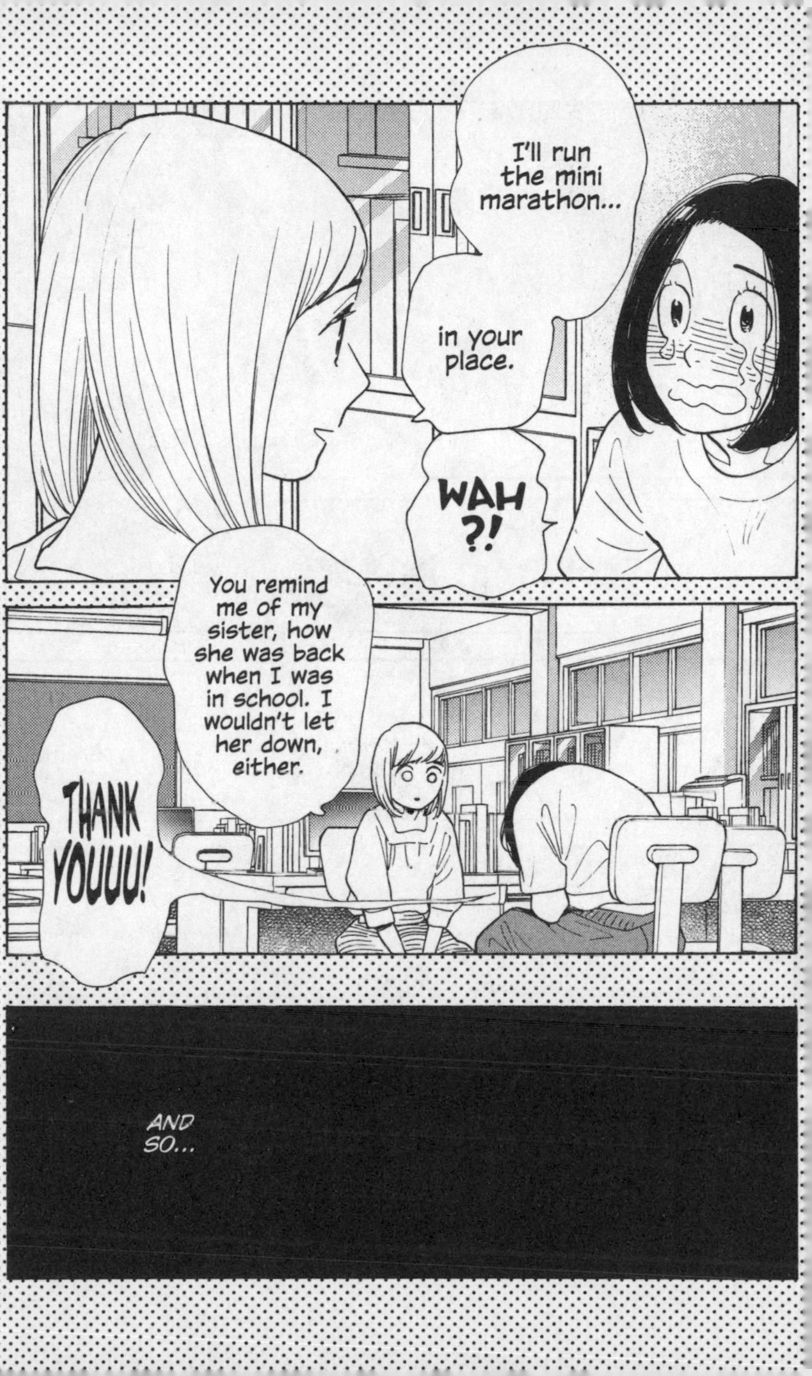
I'll run the mini marathon...
in your place.
WAH ?!
You remind me of my sister, how she was back when I was in school. I wouldn't let her down, either.
THANK YOUUU!
AND SO...

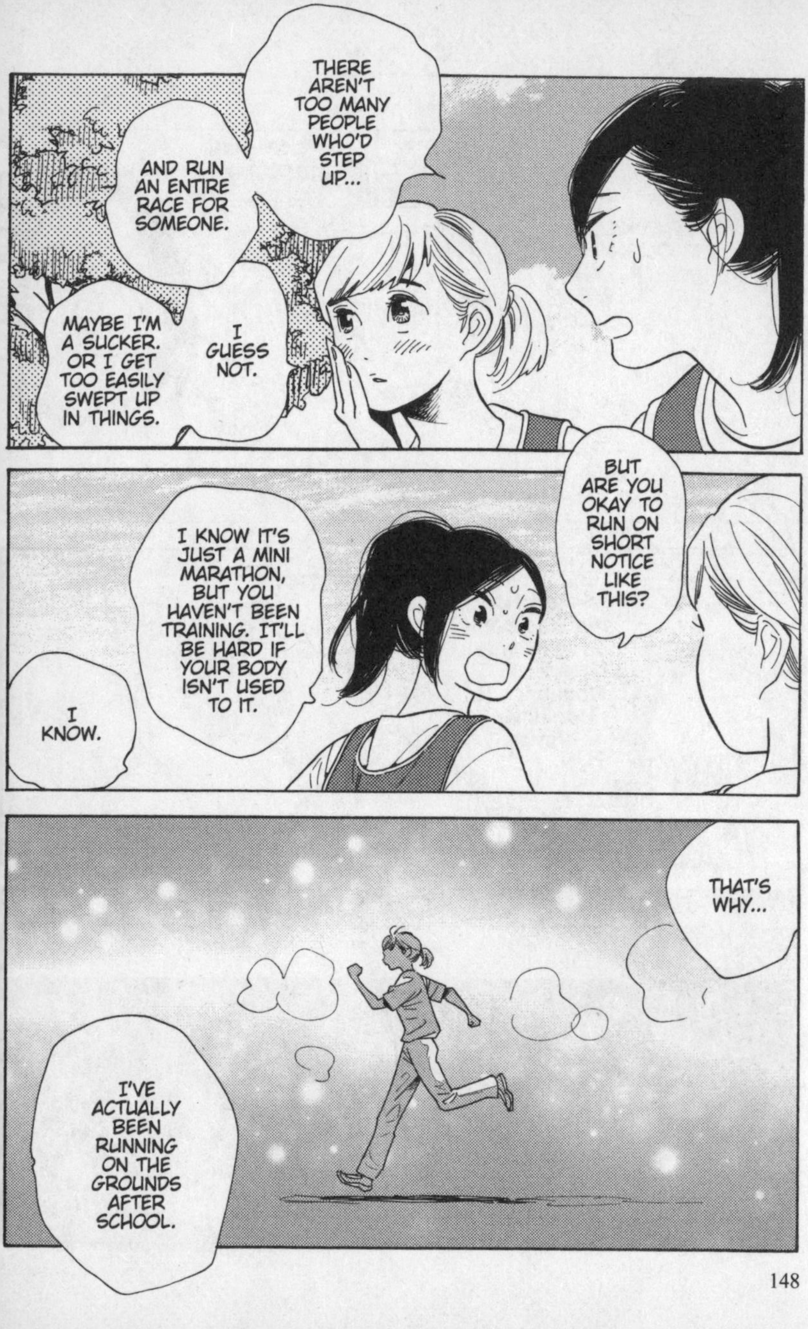
THERE AREN'T TOO MANY PEOPLE WHO'D STEP UP...
AND RUN AN ENTIRE RACE FOR SOMEONE.
I GUESS NOT.
MAYBE I'M A SUCKER. OR I GET TOO EASILY SWEPT UP IN THINGS.
BUT ARE YOU OKAY TO RUN ON SHORT NOTICE LIKE THIS?
I KNOW IT'S JUST A MINI MARATHON, BUT YOU HAVEN'T BEEN TRAINING. IT'LL BE HARD IF YOUR BODY ISN'T USED TO IT.
I KNOW.
THAT'S WHY...
I'VE ACTUALLY BEEN RUNNING ON THE GROUNDS AFTER SCHOOL.

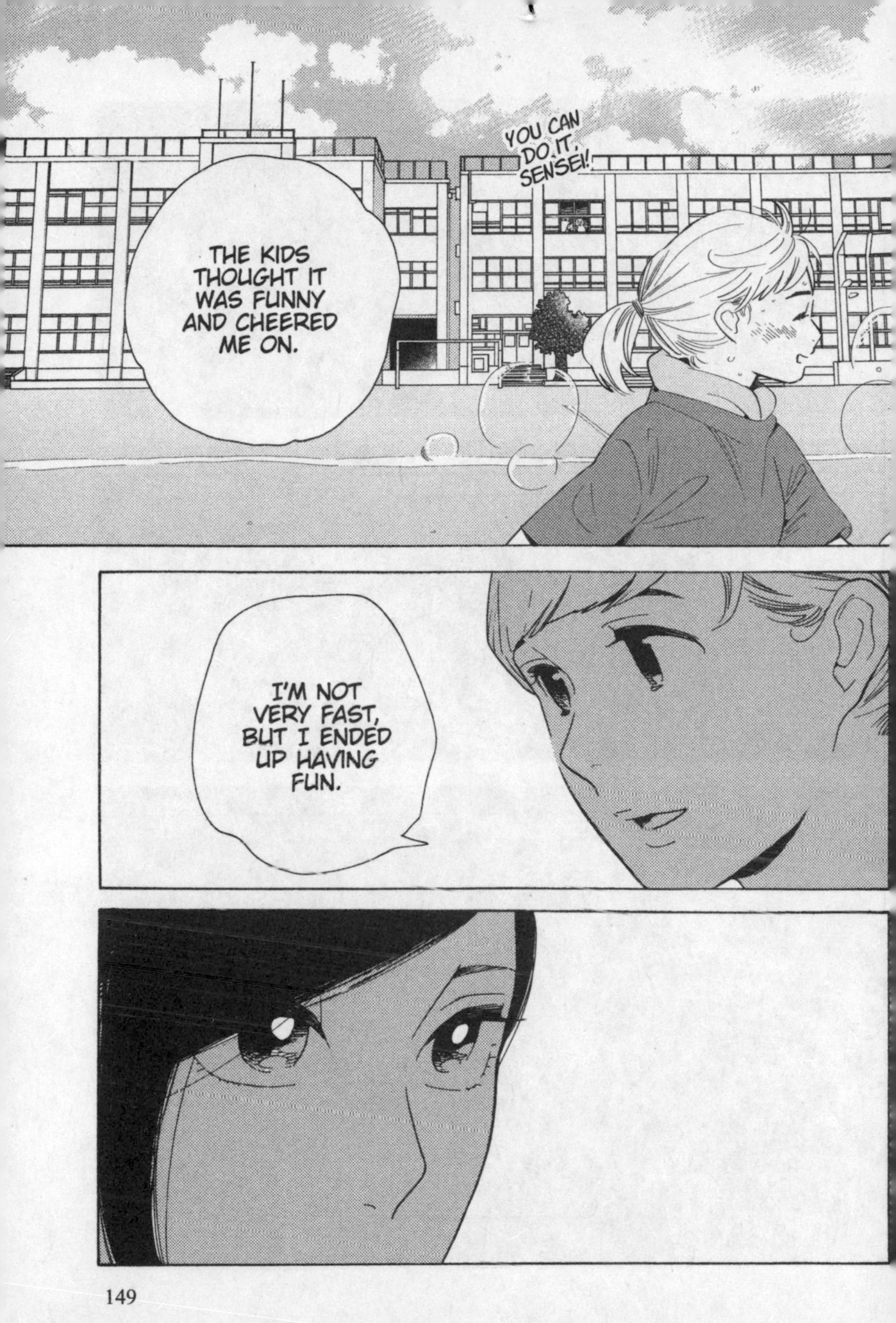
YOU CAN DO IT, SENSEI!
THE KIDS THOUGHT IT WAS FUNNY AND CHEERED ME ON.
I'M NOT VERY FAST, BUT I ENDED UP HAVING FUN.

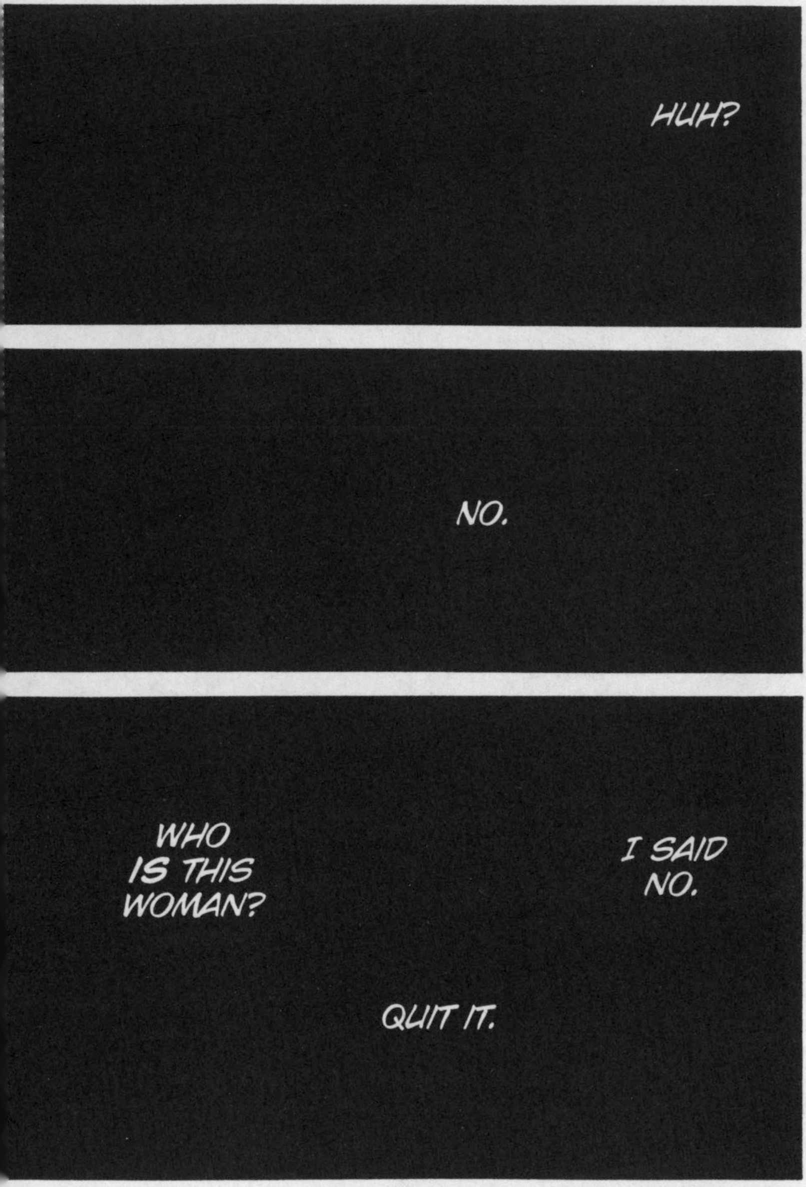
HUH?
NO.
I SAID NO.
WHO IS THIS WOMAN?
QUIT IT.

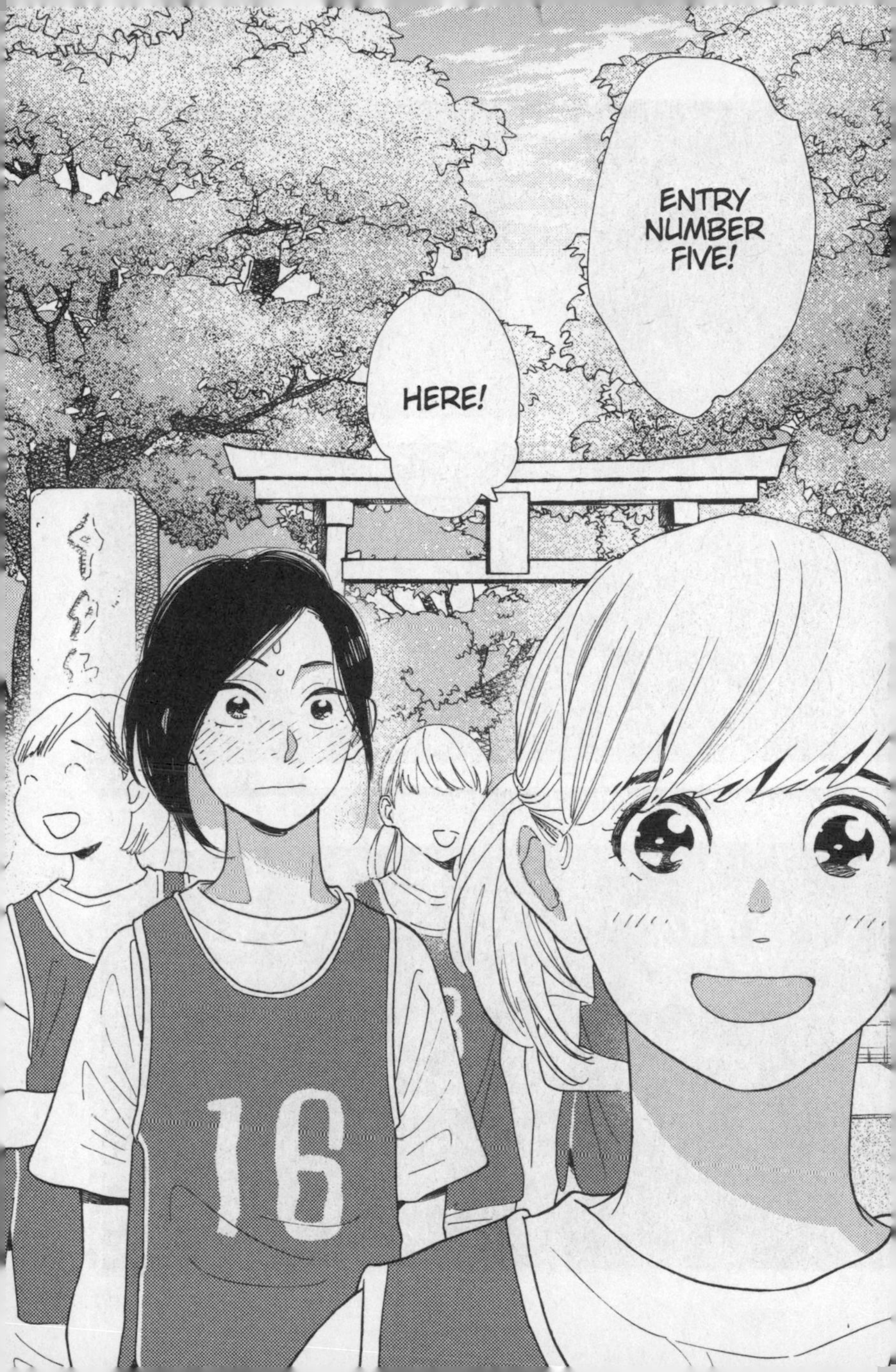
ENTRY NUMBER FIVE!
HERE!

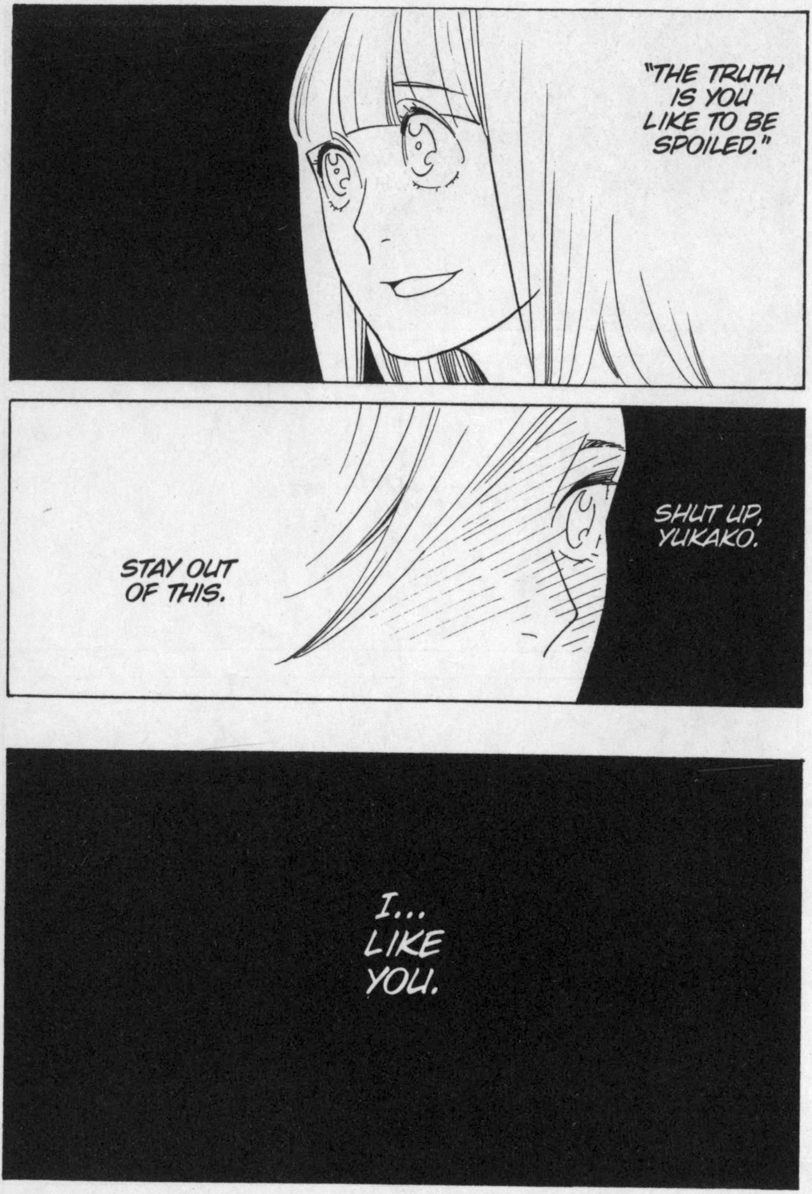
"THE TRUTH IS YOU LIKE TO BE SPOILED."
SHUT UP, YUKAKO.
STAY OUT OF THIS.
I... LIKE YOU.

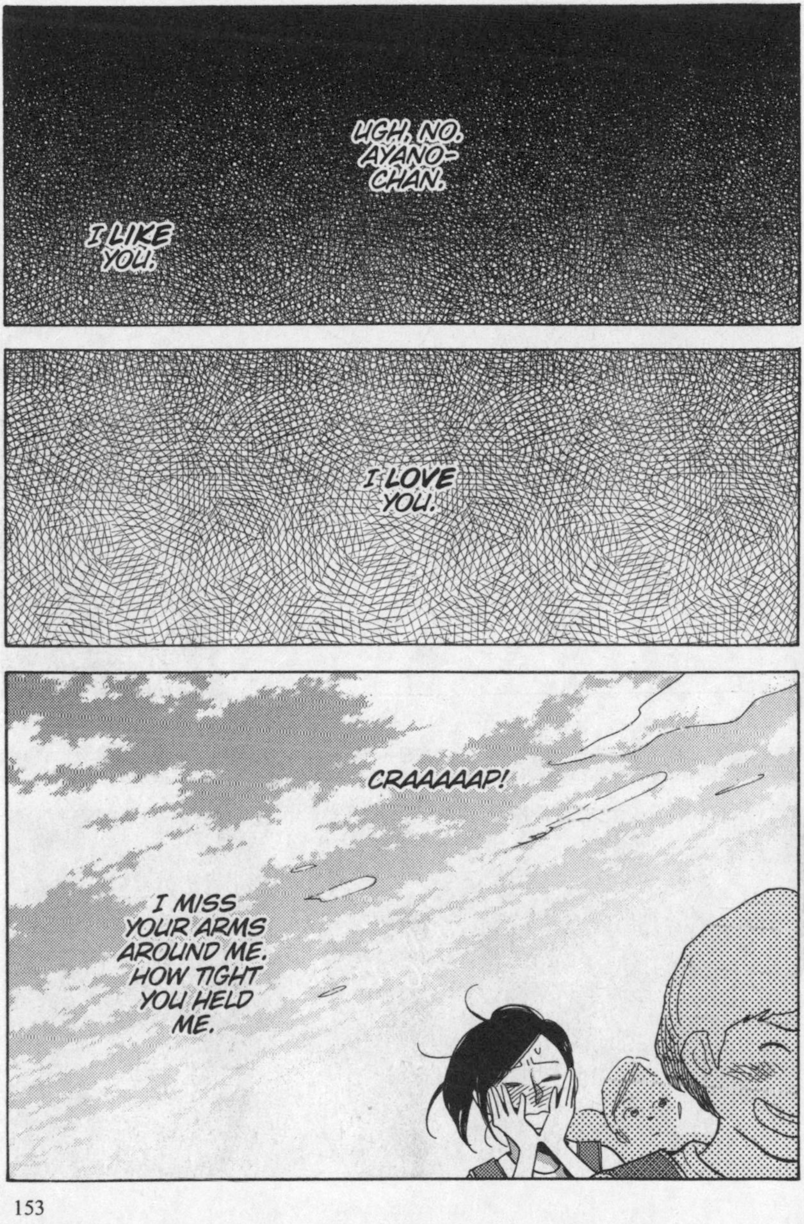
UGH, NO. AYANO-CHAN.
I LIKE YOU.
I LOVE YOU.
CRAAAAAP!
I MISS YOUR ARMS AROUND ME. HOW TIGHT YOU HELD ME.

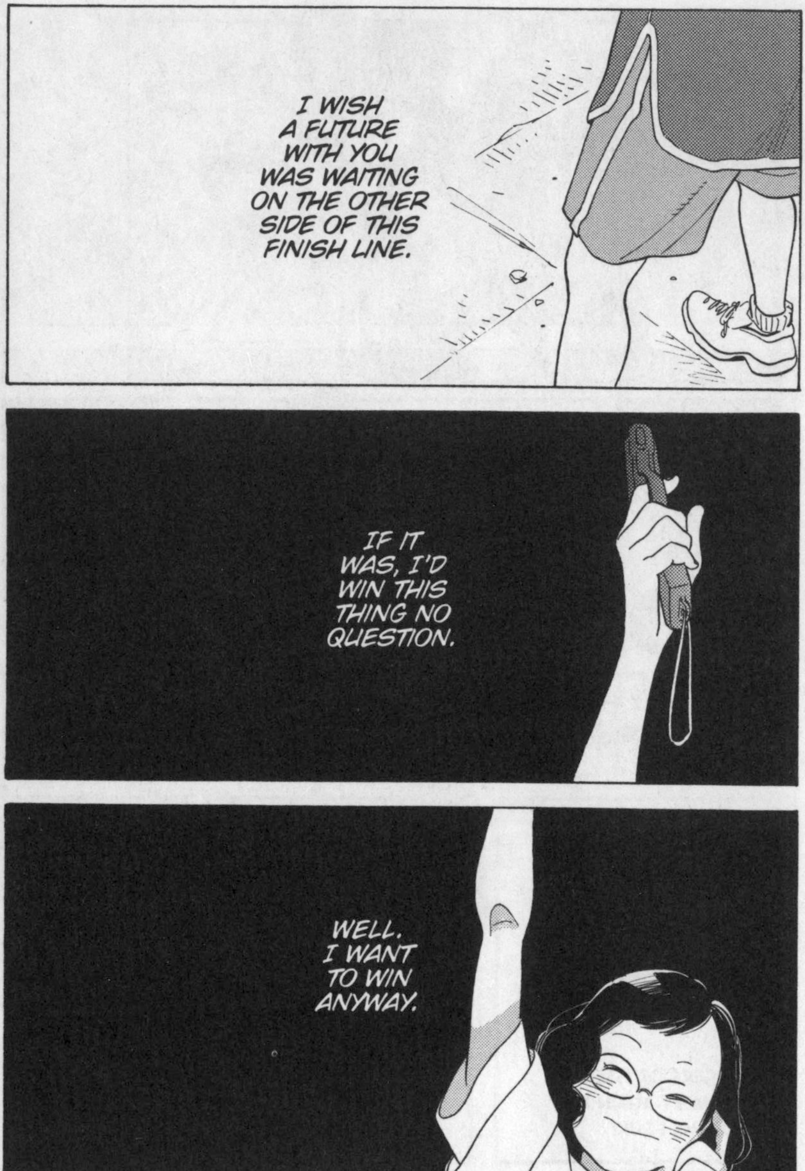
I WISH A FUTURE WITH YOU WAS WAITING ON THE OTHER SIDE OF THIS FINISH LINE.
IF IT WAS, I'D WIN THIS THING NO QUESTION.
WELL. I WANT TO WIN ANYWAY.

Even Though We're Adults 3 / END

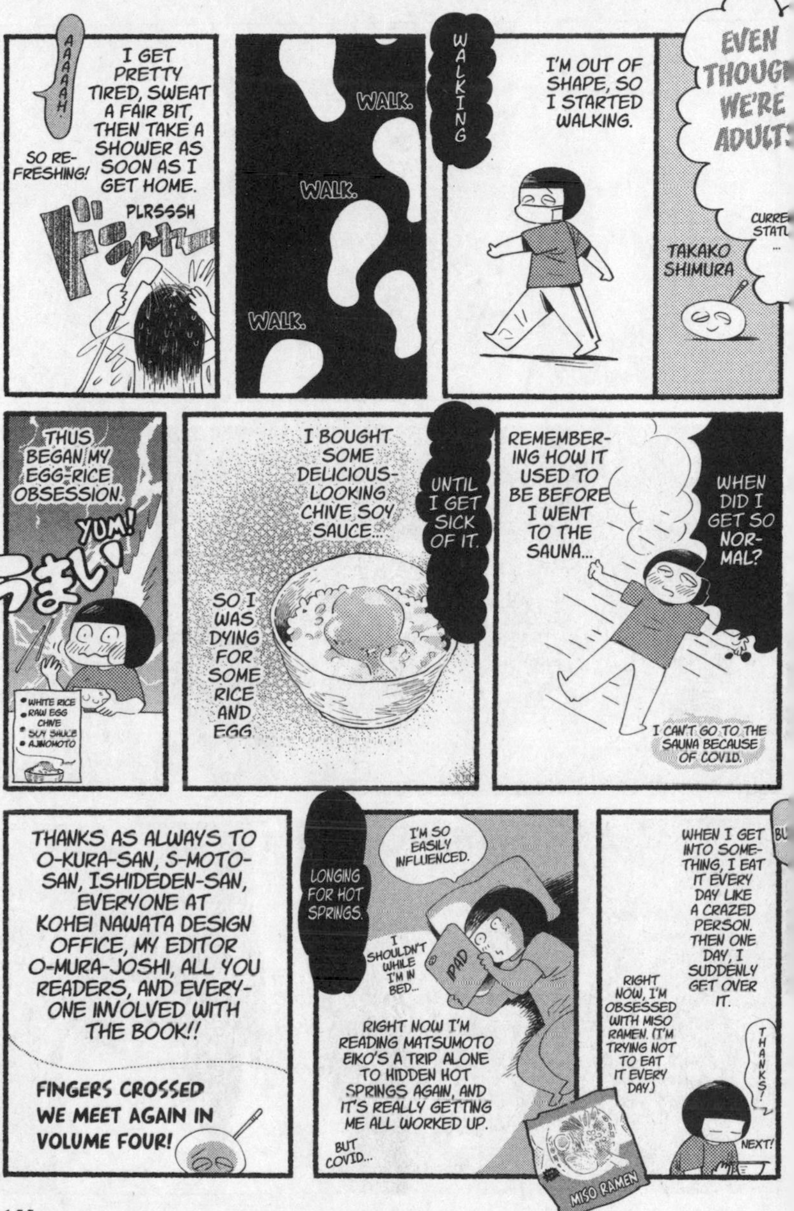
EVEN THOUG WE'RE ADULT
CURRE STATU ...
TAKAKO SHIMURA
WALKING
I'M OUT OF SHAPE, SO I STARTED WALKING.
WALK.
WALK.
WALK.
AAAAAH!
I GET PRETTY TIRED, SWEAT A FAIR BIT, THEN TAKE A SHOWER AS SOON AS I GET HOME.
SO RE-FRESHING!
PLRSSSH
WHEN DID I GET SO NOR-MAL?
REMEMBER-ING HOW IT USED TO BE BEFORE I WENT TO THE SAUNA...
I CAN'T GO TO THE SAUNA BECAUSE OF COVID.
UNTIL I GET SICK OF IT.
I BOUGHT SOME DELICIOUS-LOOKING CHIVE SOY SAUCE...
SO I WAS DYING FOR SOME RICE AND EGG
THUS BEGAN MY EGG-RICE OBSESSION.
YUM!
うまい
WHITE RICE
RAW EGG
CHIVE
SOY SAUCE
AJINOMOTO
WHEN I GET INTO SOME-THING, I EAT IT EVERY DAY LIKE A CRAZED PERSON. THEN ONE DAY, I SUDDENLY GET OVER IT.
RIGHT NOW, I'M OBSESSED WITH MISO RAMEN. (I'M TRYING NOT TO EAT IT EVERY DAY.)
THANKS!
NEXT!
LONGING FOR HOT SPRINGS.
I'M SO EASILY INFLUENCED.
I SHOULDN'T WHILE I'M IN BED...
PAD
RIGHT NOW I'M READING MATSUMOTO EIKO'S A TRIP ALONE TO HIDDEN HOT SPRINGS AGAIN, AND IT'S REALLY GETTING ME ALL WORKED UP.
BUT COVID...
MISO RAMEN
THANKS AS ALWAYS TO O-KURA-SAN, S-MOTO-SAN, ISHIDEDEN-SAN, EVERYONE AT KOHEI NAWATA DESIGN OFFICE, MY EDITOR O-MURA-JOSHI, ALL YOU READERS, AND EVERY-ONE INVOLVED WITH THE BOOK!!
FINGERS CROSSED WE MEET AGAIN IN VOLUME FOUR!

Next issue...

I wish I had...

> I KNOW I SHOULDN'T SAY THIS...

> BUT I THINK I REALLY DO LIKE YOU, AYANO-CHAN.

a future with you.

Now that Akari's moved into Ayano's neighborhood, she's getting friendly with her husband's family. She realizes she can't just forget her feelings for Ayano, so she decides she has to put some distance between them...

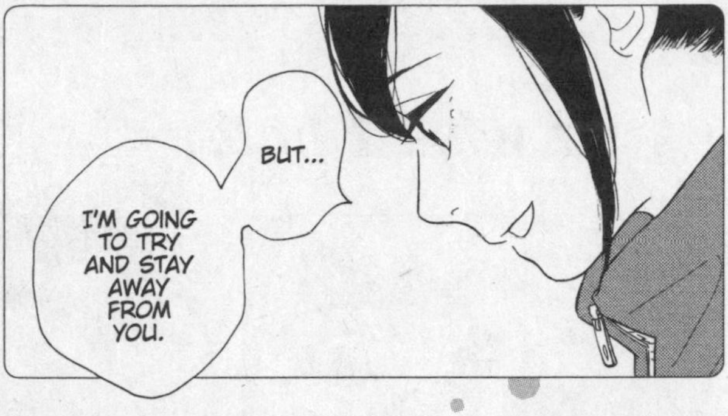
BUT...
I'M GOING TO TRY AND STAY AWAY FROM YOU.

The two of them, tangled up in a secret love.

The husband that refuses to divorce her... even though he knows how she feels.

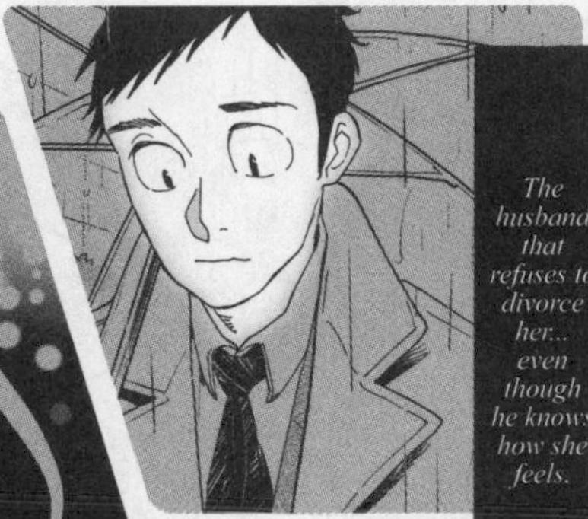

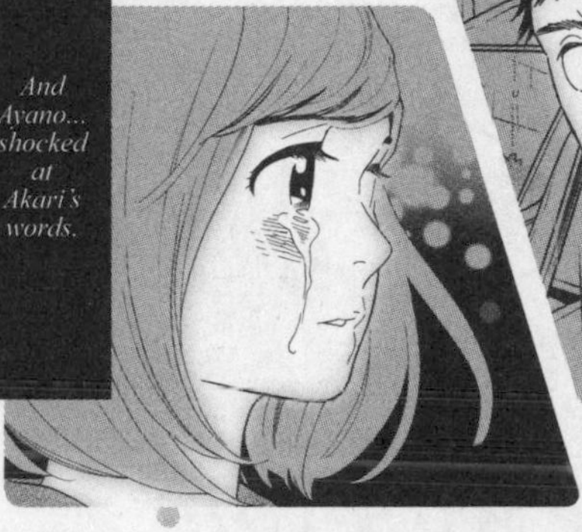

And Ayano... shocked at Akari's words.

Where will it go?

Even Though We're Adults 4

A HEART-POUNDING YURI TALE!

On sale soon!

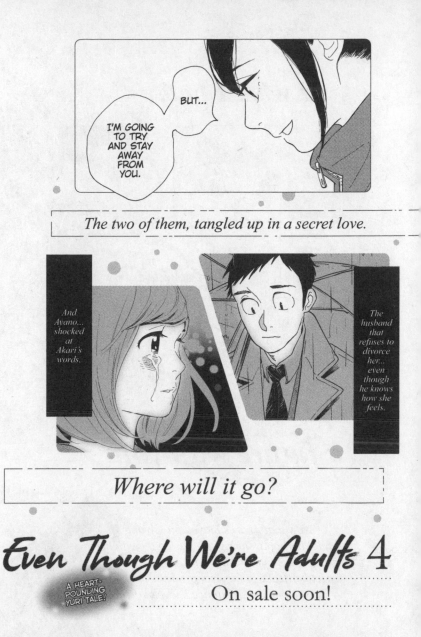

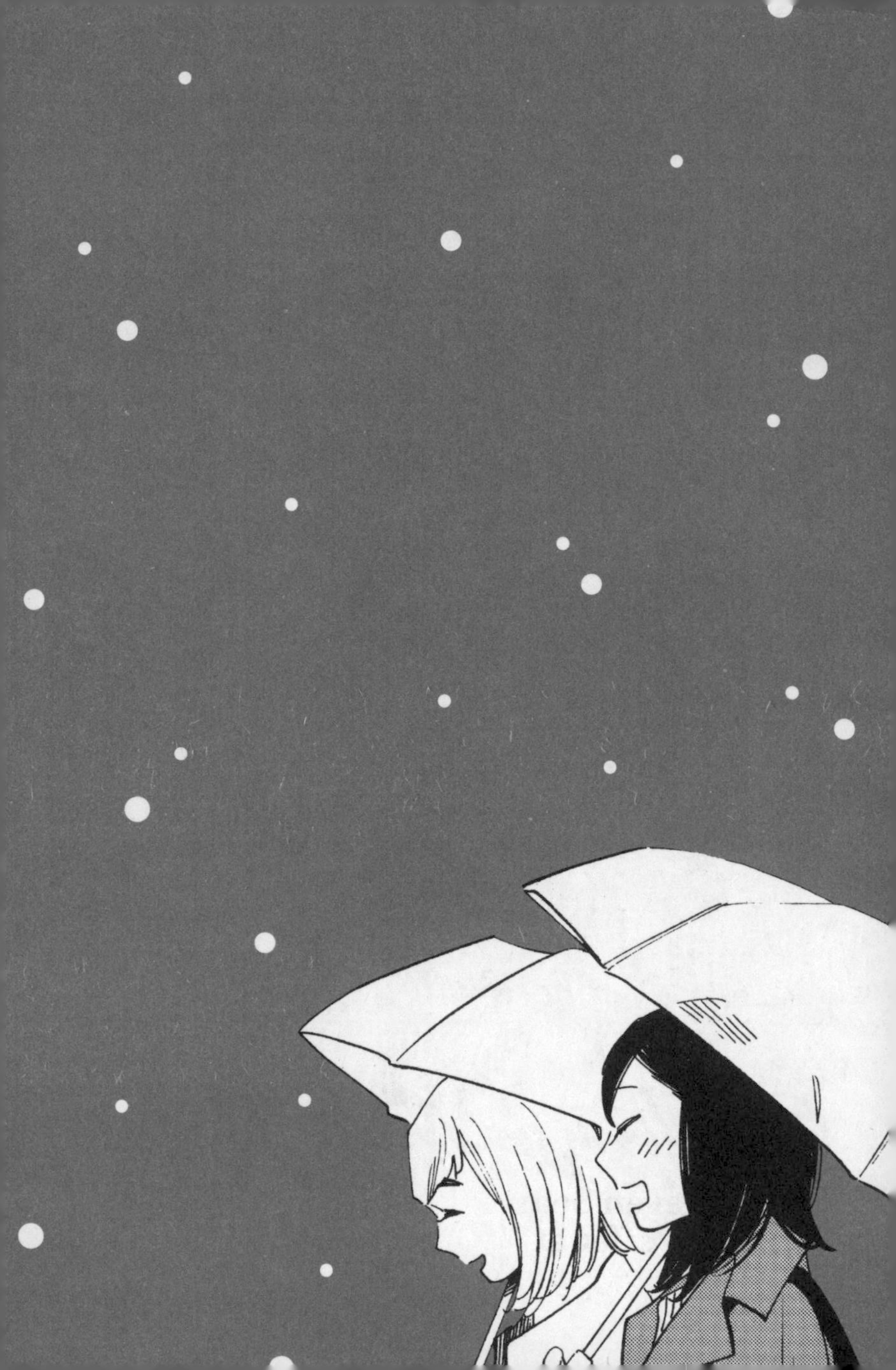

SEVEN SEAS ENTERTAINMENT PRESENTS

Even Though We're Adults

story and art by TAKAKO SHIMURA

VOLUME 3

TRANSLATION
Jocelyne Allen

ADAPTATION
Casey Lucas

LETTERING AND RETOUCH
Rina Mapa

COVER DESIGN
Hanase Qi

COPY EDITOR
Dawn Davis

EDITOR
Shannon Fay

PREPRESS TECHNICIAN
Rhiannon Rasmussen-Silverstein

PRODUCTION MANAGER
Lissa Pattillo

MANAGING EDITOR
Julie Davis

ASSOCIATE PUBLISHER
Adam Arnold

PUBLISHER
Jason DeAngelis

Seven Seas press and purchase enquiries can be sent to Marketing Manager
Lianne Sentar at press@gomanga.com. Information regarding the distribution
and purchase of digital editions is available from Digital Manager CK Russell
at digital@gomanga.com.

Seven Seas and the Seven Seas logo are trademarks of
Seven Seas Entertainment. All rights reserved.

ISBN: 978-1-64827-344-5

Printed in Canada

First Printing: October 2021

10 9 8 7 6 5 4 3 2 1

FOLLOW US ONLINE: www.sevenseasentertainment.com

READING DIRECTIONS

This book reads from ***right to left***, Japanese style.
If this is your first time reading manga, you start
reading from the top right panel on each page and
take it from there. If you get lost, just follow the
numbered diagram here. It may seem backwards at
first, but you'll get the hang of it! Have fun!!

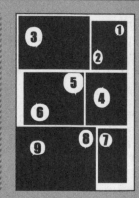